After Perfect

-A DAUGHTER'S MEMOIR-

CHRISTINA McDOWELL

G

Gallery Books

New York London Toronto Sydney New Delhi

G

Gallery Books
A Division of Simon & Schuster, Inc.
1230 Avenue of the Americas
New York, NY 10020

Certain names and identifying characteristics have been changed, whether or not so noted in the text. The timeline for certain events has been reordered or compressed.

First Gallery Books hardcover edition June 2015

GALLERY BOOKS and colophon are registered trademarks of Simon & Schuster, Inc.

For information about special discounts for bulk purchases, please contact Simon & Schuster Special Sales at 1-866-506-1949 or business@simonandschuster.com.

The Simon & Schuster Speakers Bureau can bring authors to your live event. For more information or to book an event, contact the Simon & Schuster Speakers Bureau at 1-866-248-3049 or visit our website at www.simonspeakers.com.

Interior design by Jaime Putorti

Manufactured in the United States of America

10 9 8 7 6 5 4 3 2 1

Library of Congress Cataloging-in-Publication Data
McDowell, Christina.
After perfect : a memoir / by Christina McDowell.
   pages cm
   1. McDowell, Christina.   2. McDowell, Christina—Childhood and youth.   3. Prousalis, Tom.   4. Fathers and daughters—Biography.   5. Securities fraud—United States.   6. Securities industry—United States.   I. Title.
CT275.M465358A3 2015
306.874'2—dc23
                 2014039144

ISBN 978 1 4767 8532 5
ISBN 978-1-4767-8542-4 (ebook)

This book is dedicated to the children of the incarcerated
and to the children who are incarcerated.

Spit out the venom from their bite. Calmly
and confidently know you can have the only thing that
matters in this illusory world. They will always struggle,
but the open heart needs nothing. Build a private
mansion with your own hands out of what others ignore.
That is the unassailable castle.

—Anonymous

Memorial Day Flyby

MEMORIAL DAY, 1993
McLEAN, VIRGINIA

I took a bucket of chalk and told my little sister Chloe to lie down.

"Lie down."

"Why?" Chloe asked, cautiously for a five-year-old.

"I'm a detective, and I'm going to sketch your body. Pretend like you're dead."

"Okay, but Mom's going to be mad." We were in our matching Laura Ashley party dresses.

Mara, my older sister, rode her banana-seat bike in circles on the stone walkway, ignoring us as usual.

As I began smearing yellow chalk along the side of Chloe's dress, we heard the sound of rumbling and buzzing coming toward us from a distance, louder with each passing second. I looked over at Mara, who had dragged her bike onto the grass. Her head was tilted toward the sky, watching birds fly out of the trees. Then Chloe jumped up and placed both hands over her ears to block the deafening sound. Seconds later, my mother flew out the front door, barefoot in her pink Chanel suit. Her red hair was pulled back with a pearl headband, and she was fumbling with the family video camera.

"Girls!" she cried. "There's Daddy! Wave!"

Chloe and I darted toward our mother, who had run into the middle of the street, spinning around with the camera. We looked up into the sky, and there was dad circling the rooftop of our Georgian estate in his red and yellow single-engine prop Porsche Mooney airplane. He flew so low to the ground that we could see him laughing and waving to us in his aviator sunglasses.

"Daddy!" we screamed, his engine drowning our voices. We danced and twirled and threw our arms up into the air, waving to him as we watched. The red wings of his plane swayed from side to side with each passing turn before coming back around again to surprise us even closer to the rooftop of our house. Our American flag whipped in the wind when he came back around once more before disappearing into the distant sky.

He was my superhero.

Chloe and I spun around and around, falling dizzily into the grass, and Mara, who seemed concerned, ran over to our mother.

"Mom?" She tugged on her arm.

"Yeah, sweetheart?" The video camera was still recording.

"Is Dad going to get in trouble?"

My mother laughed at the thought. "I hope not."

Ten Years Later

The Phone Call

The roads were quiet, and white frost covered the otherwise green hills of Virginia. No one could hear the engines of several government-marked SUVs traveling one before the other, like soldiers down Dolley Madison Boulevard.

Like every other typical morning in our house, my father was the first awake. He was leaning over the marble sink in the master bathroom in his boxer shorts shaving the outer edges of his Clark Gable mustache with an electric razor. His collection of Hermès ties hung on a rack alongside the open closet door opposite his collection of Brooks Brothers suits. In the background, CNN reported on the television screen behind him: "Jury selection began Tuesday in the Martha Stewart criminal trial, where the self-made lifestyle maven will try to defend herself against charges of obstruction of justice, making false statements, and securities fraud." The NASDAQ and Dow Jones numbers crawled along the bottom. I asked my father once what the numbers meant. He replied, "Don't worry about it, that's your dad's job."

My mother was sitting in front of the gold-framed mirror at her vanity table just down the corridor. Her hair pulled back with a navy scrunchy, she was examining her wrinkles and moving her skin with her hands to see how she would look with a face-lift.

Sometimes she forgot how beautiful she was. As a little girl, strangers would pull me aside at the market and ask, "Hey, kid, is your mom a movie star?"

She wrapped her silk bathrobe around her nightgown and headed to the kitchen to put on the morning coffee.

Chloe was upstairs grabbing her gym bag and lacrosse stick. Her boyfriend kept honking the horn of his Jeep Grand Cherokee out front.

"Coming!" she yelled as if he could hear her.

The SUVs continued on, passing an unmarked security house where, next to it in the gravel path, a sign had been planted: George Bush Center for Intelligence CIA Next Right. Hardly noticeable for the average tourist passing by on the way to Dulles International Airport, intentionally inconspicuous as all of the secret intelligence of the world lies just a mile down what looks to be a harmless suburban road. It was the winter of 1993 when I found out what it was, in the car with my mother on the way to school, and a secret agent stopped us at the red light. He questioned her. I remember asking what for, and she explained to me what was hidden down the street. A gunman had opened fire on several cars entering the CIA headquarters, wounding three and killing two employees. I understood then, despite the quiet feeling in our neighborhood, that things happened all around us every day that we weren't privy to.

The SUVs turned onto Georgetown Pike, gaining speed, passing the Kennedys' Hickory Hill estate to the left down Chain Bridge Road, and the little yellow schoolhouse on the hill to the right, a place my sisters and I used to march to with our Fisher-Price sleds each winter. But when the vehicles approached the corner to our street, Kedleston Court, a quiet cul-de-sac of mansions, Chloe flew out the front door, struggling to whip her backpack over her shoulder and lugging her lacrosse stick and gym bag in her other hand. She hopped into the passenger's side of her boyfriend's Jeep, and they took off, passing the SUVs without a second thought. It had been three years since 9/11; since US Air

Force F-16 fighter jets flew so low to the ground they shook our beds at night. The days of my father flying his airplane above our home were long gone. We had become accustomed to this quiet feeling. We trusted that we were safe.

The SUVs came to a screeching halt, blocking our driveway and forty-foot stone walkway. The slamming of car doors and the heavy clicking of loaded guns disturbed our quiet morning routine when a dozen men covered in black bulletproof vests with yellow emblazoned letters on the back fanned out across the lawn, toward the front door of our estate, framed by Corinthian columns that beckoned the movers and shakers of Washington, DC—the entire property engulfed by green ivy and willow trees.

My mother was leaning against the kitchen island, sipping her coffee as she watched the morning banter of the *Today* show's Matt Lauer and Katie Couric. If only she had turned around, had the TV not been so loud, she would have seen through the open shutters the infamous emblazoned letters—

"FBI!"

If she didn't look the other way, maybe she would have known. It was too late.

"Get on the ground! *Get on the ground! Now! Now!*"

She dropped her mug, shattering it to pieces at her feet, spilling coffee all over the marble floor, running for the front door to find it wide open. My father was being handcuffed, his face smashed against the pink Persian rug in the foyer.

"You have the right to remain silent. Anything you do or say can be used against you in a court of law . . ."

My mother shook, begging my father for an explanation as she asked a series of cluttered and hysterical questions. He pleaded with her while the FBI lifted him to his feet. He told her he was innocent. He told her not to worry. He told her to call Bernie Carl. Had his hands not been handcuffed behind his back, he would have been pointing his finger at her.

My mother, watching from the foyer as my father was thrown into the back of a black Suburban, crumbled to the floor, barely breathing, heaving from shock.

She didn't know.

The year was 2004, and America was unaware that it was about to fall into its worst economic recession since the Great Depression. George W. Bush was president, the "War on Terror" had begun, Lehman Brothers still existed, the real estate industry was skyrocketing, and everyone was happy stretching the limits of his or her livelihood on multiple credit cards and second mortgages. The rich grew richer. The poor grew poorer. And I—well, I had been lucky. Most who knew me then would have said that I was from the 1 percent. Although I never knew how much money my family was worth, how much liquid cash we had, or how much was sitting in crooked stocks. I have since discovered that one's financial security is often an illusion, although I didn't always feel that way. At eighteen years old, I had never paid much attention to the feeling of safety—of security. It was never discussed. It didn't have to be. I grew up a few blocks west of Ethel and Bobby Kennedy's Hickory Hill estate, and a few blocks south of the CIA in McLean, Virginia—the affluent suburb of Washington, DC, filled with politicians, spies, and newscasters. "Security" was just a privileged afterthought lingering in my subconscious somewhere as I floated through my seemingly fairy-tale life without a care in the world.

I was the girl who had everything: The mansion, the private plane, the Range Rover, summers on Nantucket Island. I was popular, had loving sisters who were my best friends, happily married parents, and dreams of being a movie star. Raised among the American elite, my father had created the epitome of an American Dream.

We looked perfect.

My father didn't come from money. He built our life for us from the ground up. The grandson of Greek immigrants, the eldest of seven children, born and raised a sweet, southern boy from Richmond, Virginia, who spent his summers watching ball games at Fenway Park in Boston with his grandparents. "I ate all the cherries on the cherry tree and broke windows playing baseball in the backyard. I remember seeing the last baseball game in 1960 between the Boston Red Sox and the New York Yankees at Fenway Park when Ted Williams and Mickey Mantle played against each other. The Red Sox won." He loved to tell that story.

Being the grandson of immigrants, he was proud of the life he worked so hard to build. He was the first of his family to graduate from college, the College of William & Mary in the historic town of Williamsburg, Virginia. The alma mater to the founding fathers James Monroe and Thomas Jefferson, the blue blood that shaped the principles on which this nation was built. Once, my father took me to a tavern for lunch in Colonial Williamsburg where all of the employees dressed up as pilgrims. He wanted me to engage in its history. I remember our server reminded me of Mammy the housemaid from *Gone with the Wind*, my favorite film growing up. She was a round African American woman dressed in a white bonnet and blue smock. As she set my plate of meat loaf and grits on the table, I looked at her, and instead of feeling like beautiful Scarlett O'Hara, I felt racist. I swore to myself I'd never go back there. I'd never, ever be seen with all those pilgrims wearing buckled shoes.

But my father looked back on his college days with great nostalgia. He was young and broke, and told us stories like the time he broke into the school cafeteria and ate all the Jell-O because he didn't have any money for dinner. Or how he charmed all of the wealthy New England girls into cooking for him. After graduation, he was drafted during the Vietnam War and served his time dutifully in the air force, where he learned how to fly fighter jets. He went on to attend Howard University Law School, the prestigious all-black university in Washington,

DC, where he wrote for the law journal and became a clerk at the White House in the still rippling years and aftermath of Dr. Martin Luther King Jr. and the civil rights movement. It was less expensive than a place like Harvard. When someone would ask me, as a kid, where my father went to law school, and I replied, "Howard," they would respond as if they hadn't heard correctly. "Harvard?" "No," I'd say, "*How*ard." Without fail, there was a moment of confusion for the other person. With all of the wealth we accumulated, people found it hard to believe he was a die-hard liberal. When I was older, my father would explain to me the importance of equal rights, affirmative action, gun control, and health care. Always rooting for the underdog in the quest to achieve the American Dream.

It would be years before I put together the pieces, the truth about my father, and the truth about myself. I had no idea the day the FBI came that I was being propelled into a reality that would strip me of everything I ever knew to be true, where all my life the lie was the truth and the truth was the lie, how the silver spoon would be ripped from my mouth, and how, in the end, denial would fail to save me.

I wasn't there the day the FBI arrested my father. It was the narrative I created and replayed over and over in my head when my mother called me two hours later, as I had been fast asleep in my boyfriend's bed in sunny California.

Blake placed his hand on my bare back as I glanced up at the blurry numbers of his alarm clock. I let out a groggy groan, still hungover from the night before, and switched sides of my pillow to face him; his sweet brown eyes looked at me. It was one of our last mornings to sleep in together before I headed back across town to finish my second semester of freshman year at Loyola Marymount University in Los Angeles. We were nestled in the northeast corner of his father's mansion in Hancock Park, a high-profile neighborhood where rows of giant palm trees line the sidewalks of English Tudors and Mediterranean mansions. Home to consulates, studio executives, and movie stars—where old money lives.

Blake pulled down the covers as he kissed me and then pushed my left shoulder, turning me over on my back, exposing my naked body to the morning air, and I shivered as he kissed farther down my torso. My phone started ringing. It was the original Nokia ringtone, the one everyone hated—"do-do do do, do-do do do, do-do do do do"—it wouldn't stop. I would have ignored it, but my heart was pounding, and I had this feeling: *someone's died.* It was too early for a phone call. I put my fingers through Blake's wavy hair and whispered, "Sorry," as I scooted up toward the headboard and grabbed my phone off the nightstand.

"Are you serious?" Blake quipped, stranded at the foot of the bed.

"Home calling."

I answered. "Hello?"

"Honey?" It was my mother. Her voice was trembling.

"Hi, Mom," I replied, my heart thumping out of my chest. I yanked the comforter off the bed, wrapped it around my body, and turned away from Blake, who made his way over to his turntables and put on his headphones, annoyed by my rejection.

"I have some bad news," she said, her voice moving into a higher register, the way she sounds when she's trying not to cry.

"What's going on, Mom?" I just wanted her to get it out and over with.

"The FBI came to the house this morning. They arrested your dad on fraud charges."

"What?" I wasn't sure I had heard correctly. "What do you mean, 'fraud charges'?"

"You know Martha Stewart? It's—it's sort of like that."

I knew by the way she hesitated that she was unsure of how to explain it. "You need to get a job as soon as possible," she continued. "There's no money left. The bank is going to take our home."

As my mother's words pierced through my conscience, I began stuttering from shock. Then I asked a series of my own hysterical questions: "Is he guilty?" "Is he going to be in the news?" "Is he going to prison?" "What do you mean, the bank is taking our home?" Each new question charged with escalating tears, and my mother didn't have an answer to any of them. She claimed to know nothing but that it would only be a matter of days before we would lose everything. She couldn't have known in that moment to what extent *everything* meant. Her intention of the word *everything* was used to imply material possessions. Houses, planes, cars, jewelry, clothing—the things that defined us, the things that made us worthy, the things we thought we needed— somehow, in the end, destroyed us. Neither of us knowing how lost we'd be without them, floundering in a world where love was no longer the answer. She couldn't have known what would painstakingly prove to be the greatest loss of all. All of those things we could never ever get back: ourselves, each other. Family.

I hung up the phone and wiped my tears. Blake took off his head-phones and looked at me. "Divorce?" he said, buttoning his pants, an unlit cigarette dangling from his lips. His tone wasn't a question, more like he knew why I was crying and didn't need to ask because he'd been entangled in his parents' bitter divorce battle at the age of five, watching them rip each other's hearts to shreds; a childhood wound still raw and untouched given the way he would, or most of the time, wouldn't, talk about it.

"No," I replied, staring into a blurred distance. Blake lit his ciga-rette, waiting for an answer—any answer to explain my sudden fugue state.

"The FBI came to my house this morning. They arrested my dad on fraud charges," I said in a wave of eerie calm, as if the words had come from someone else, someone I didn't know yet.

Blake's eyes met mine. He inhaled his cigarette and then exhaled. He stared at me, thinking of what to say, the smoke lingering between us. Blake shook his head with confusion. "What?"

An instant sense of urgency kicked my system into overdrive. I leapt out of bed and kneeled down over my sprawled-out suitcase on the floor, searching for my favorite vintage 20th Century Fox T-shirt Blake had given me. I threw it over my head; the iconic gold block letters were faded from years of someone else's wear and tear. I jumped up, putting one foot and then the other inside a new pair of Seven jeans that Mom had allowed me to put on the credit card.

"I have to call my sister," I blurted out, turning around in circles, disoriented, trying to button my pants, not remembering where I put my cell phone. I searched for it, throwing pillows across the bed, lifting the top of my suitcase and throwing it over my pile of clothes spewing from all sides, shoving Blake's skateboard upside down next to the door so it banged against the wall, and finally pulling the entire comforter over the bed with both hands, as if I were a magician getting ready to whip a tablecloth out from under the china. "Where *is it*?" I screamed. The comforter went flailing behind me with the sound of a pathetic thud as my cell phone hit the dresser and, at last, fell to the ground.

"Hey, hey, hey." Blake rushed over, restraining me as I tried to get past him to pick up my phone. "Slow down. Breathe," he said. I glared at him as he held my upper arms in place just below my shoulders. "Why don't we go for a drive?" he suggested, knowing that nothing he could say would fix the overwhelming confusion that overtook any chance of my having a normal day.

"Okay," I said, and then took a deep breath, "but don't tell anyone about this. Not your dad—anyone."

"I won't," Blake promised.

I didn't know whom I could trust. I had known Blake for just over a year. We met at the Hollywood location of the New York Film Academy, a summer program that only the offspring of the affluent can afford, where students are given a vintage 33 millimeter film camera, all-access passes to the Universal Studios back lot, and a suite at the Oakwood Apartments, infamous for housing its rising Disney stars or the next Justin Biebers of the world. Blake was unfazed by it all. He broke all the rules, drove a fast car, smoked weed, had neon blue hair when I met him. He was the antithesis of Ralph Lauren, Ivy Leagues, and loafers—the guys I was surrounded by in Virginia. I was instantly drawn to him. He'd sneak me into forbidden places, like the haunted house from Alfred Hitchcock's *Psycho*, where we once found loose nails from a previous film set, then climbed to the rooftop and carved our names into the rotting wood. Blake's carefree attitude came from being raised in a family of Hollywood lineage tracing back to the golden age. His father grew up next to the likes of Judy Garland and silent film stars such as Harold Lloyd, and was friends with Hugh Hefner.

One time at a private party at the Playboy Mansion when I was seventeen, I was pulled from the kids' table (yes, there was a *kids' table*) by one of the Playmates, who said to me, "Oh boy, when Hugh gets his eyes on you . . ." I remember staring down at my double-A-size breasts. "Oh, don't worry about that, honey; he'd take care of it," she said, like it was no big deal, like just another trip to the grocery store. By the end of the night, I found myself being chased by wild peacocks in the back-yard amid naked, spray-painted Playboy bunnies while fireworks burst through the sky.

I was on the edge of adulthood in a city where your wildest fantasies become distorted realities; where boundaries become blurred lines. A far cry from the rigidity of a nine-to-five in public service in our nation's capital for which I might have been destined otherwise. I longed to be a part of it all: the sex, the drugs, the rock and roll. Fame. My father had always told me I was going to be a movie star: a frail brunette beauty like Audrey Hepburn, he said.

Blake and I climbed into my BMW—a gift my father had given me the day before my high school graduation. Covered in a red bow, and tucked in the windshield was a note that read "Dear Christina Bam-bina, you owe me an airplane, Love Dad." Later I found out my father had sold his airplane to buy the car. Money had been tight, but I never knew. My family, we never discussed that sort of thing. I never, ever had to think about money. In fact, I was told it was rude to discuss money.

Blake drove, and I sat in the passenger seat and called Mara, who was starting her junior year at Southern Methodist University in Dallas. Mara and I had always been close. Even after she left for boarding school when the the academic pressures at the National Cathedral School for girls became too intense and my parents decided it would be better if she finished high school in the Swiss Alps, where there were more snow days than school days. I never understood the choice to go from the culturally eclectic boarding school in Switzerland, with Saudi princes and princesses, and the future successors of oil tycoons, to the finest breeding ground for the next Mr. and Mrs. George Bush. I suppose there wasn't a difference. Either way, she was my cool big sister who taught me how to freak dance and who cried when Kurt Cobain died.

The phone rang, and I knew I would feel better once we talked.

"Hey," she said. Her voice was raspy, as though she had been crying.

"Hey."

"Did you talk to Mom?"

"Yeah, and I just talked to Dad."

"You did? How?"

"Mr. Carl bailed him out. He's going to call you when he can."

Bernie Carl was one of my father's wealthiest friends, a banker. He and his wife, Joan, a Washington socialite, and their three children were close family friends. We traveled together on each other's private planes, spent summers in Southampton, Nantucket, and St. Barths, and Thanksgivings in London and Scotland.

"What else did he say?" I wanted to know everything.

"He said it's all a misunderstanding and that the government is trying to make an example out of him."

I had no idea what she was talking about. "Okay," I said. "Have you talked to Chloe?"

"No, she's at school. I don't think she knows yet."

Chloe was a freshman in high school. She had become an avid
lacrosse player with more friends than anyone could keep track of and a
bit of a wild card, as no one ever knew whether she would bring home
an A on an exam or hijack the Range Rover when our parents left town.
Once, when she was five, she decided to swing from the gold chandelier
in the family room with her best friend. Like two monkeys swinging
from tree branches. The mischief ended in a near-fatal accident when
the chandelier came crashing to the floor, shattering lightbulbs across
the room. She and her friend were lucky they ran away unscathed.

I never spoke to Chloe that day, and it would be years before she
would ever talk about what it was like for her when she found out about
our father's arrest.

Mara was rambling on about possible job options already. "Strip-
ping?" she joked. Was it a joke, though? It was too overwhelming. I told
her I had to hang up. For once, I didn't want to keep talking.

Blake pulled the car over somewhere near the top of Laurel Canyon
and Mulholland Drive. We got out, and I hurdled the metal guard-
rail along the cliff and sat with my feet dangling over the edge. Blake
hopped over and took a seat next to me. He pulled out a joint from his
pocket and sparked the end.

"Here," he said, passing it to me. I took a long drag, hoping that in
minutes I would be numb to the world.

I squinted, looking out over the hazy Los Angeles skyline. The Hollywood sign was barely visible in the morning fog; its alluring presence
waiting for the sun to shine before it mocked the dirty streets of Hollywood. It would be hours before the hustlers readied their star maps for
tourists, before the dancing Elvis and Marilyn Monroe impersonators
sweated beneath their costumes, proclaiming their dreams of stardom
next to a lone "Jesus Save Us! I Repent!" sign held by some angry pro-
testor, each praying that one day they'll be noticed.

Had I known what was to come, I would have been on my knees in
the dirt praying for the answers, because the power of money—the loss
of money, the need for money, what we would do for *more* money—

would rip through my family, denying any chance of a resurrection. With each passing day, losing who I was and not knowing who I would become. I didn't know how any of it would happen, how the truth would unravel, and how it would unravel me.

I passed Blake the joint. I thought about the possibility of my father being guilty. "But he wears Tommy Bahama T-shirts," I declared. "My dad. He wears Tommy Bahama T-shirts." Blake and I bent over laughing. Laughing so hard my stomach hurt.

2

Glory Days

My mother and father met in the heart of the aftermath of political unrest in the 1970s, when Washington, DC, was the place to be. The Vietnam War had ended; the civil rights and women's rights movements were breaking barriers leading to a more just and equal society, creating a glimpse of change and promise for a more prosperous future. My mother grew up along the canals of Long Beach, California, running barefoot and drinking chocolate malts from Hof's Hut Bakery. She longed to be a part of history, eventually leaving her beach town life behind to work on Capitol Hill for Republican congressman Robert Lagomarsino. A few months later, she met my father. They fell in love and were married six months after. When I was a little girl, I asked my mother over and over again to tell me their love story.

"Mom, how did Dad propose to you?" I sat on the couch, watching Roxana slide a black St. John knit over my mother's head. Roxana, an exotic Iranian woman who wore clunky gold bracelets and bright red lipstick, was my mother's personal stylist at Saks Fifth Avenue. She always had a Coke and a Snickers bar waiting for me on the coffee table next to the pink lilies.

Our private dressing area had its own kitchen and powder room, and was filled with racks of couture gowns, tailor-made suits, stilettos, jewelry, and purses for my mother to try on. After I was born, my father insisted he was making enough money so my mother didn't have to work. She was now serving on the board of directors at the Columbia Hospital for Women, was vice president of Discovery Creek Children's Museum, and was a member of the Junior League. In her new role as philanthropist, she always needed a rotation of outfits for benefits, meetings, and cocktail parties.

"Honey, you know this story," my mother said, adjusting her bodysuit underneath the dress.

"Tell me again," I said. I was playing hooky. Mara and Chloe were at school. I often lied so I could spend the day with her, watching episodes of *General Hospital*, shopping and running errands. I wanted to talk to her all day long about grown-up things. It was more fun than playing with Poggs and Beanie Babies on the playground.

"Well, I have to tell the whole story," she began, "because of what happened a few days earlier."

My father had been late coming home from law school when my mother showed up at his apartment on Nineteenth and R Streets. She began spending most evenings at his apartment, but he hadn't given her a key yet. My mother was tired and frustrated after a long bus ride home from work and began picking at my father's lock with one of her bobby pins. Without any luck, she pulled out the key to her apartment, intending to use it to continue picking at the lock. But instead, it slid right in, unlocking my father's front door.

"Like fate," my mother said, twirling left and then right in her new St. John knit. After my father arrived home, they had dinner, and when they were reading and lounging on the couch afterward, he said to her casually, with his head still buried in his book, "What do you think about getting married?" My mother had asked if that was a proposal. He looked at her; he was nervous. "Yeah," he said. "Do you want to get married?" Mom smiled at him. "Yes! Let's get married."

"A few days later"—my mother was now standing in her bra and panty hose, waiting for Roxana to bring her an evening gown—"I walked into the apartment, and there was a sock lying in the middle of the living area, which was strange, because your dad always liked to have things clean and neat. I picked up the sock, reached my hand down inside of it, and pulled out a black velvet box. Inside was my diamond ring. But *this* diamond ring." My mother gently lifted the small diamond to her gold necklace resting between her collarbones.

On a trip to Paris, my father had surprised her with a 9-carat-diamond upgrade from Tiffany. She turned her original diamond into the necklace she wore.

"At the time, your dad didn't have a penny to his name. He sold his blue Austin-Healey the day after I said yes so he could buy me this ring," my mother said proudly. "And believe me, he loved that Austin-Healey." My father wanted to make sure she said yes before he sold it.

"But he loved you more than the car," I always assured her.

My father started making what he ironically called "real money" in the late eighties and early nineties. We moved from our quaint town house across from American University, a community called Westover Place, to the white brick Georgian house on Lowell Street across from the Mexican Embassy, where we held Fourth of July block parties and Halloween parties with the neighbors. Local firemen drove their trucks down to let us kids honk the horn and sound the sirens. We attended Christmas parties and birthday parties with guests named (Joe and Jim) Biden, (Arianna) Huffington, and (David) Rubenstein—before they carried the power they do today.

For my tenth birthday party, my mother hired a wild-animal trainer. He arrived dressed in safari gear and brought a wild alligator for us to play with. I didn't care about any of the other wild animals he brought, like the African dwarf frogs and baby goats. I spent the entire afternoon chasing that wild alligator around the playroom in my plaid skirt while the mothers were upstairs in the family room gossiping over bottles of Pinot Grigio, Carr's crackers, and caviar.

When we moved from the city to our estate in Virginia, our birthday parties and Christmases became even more extravagant as my parents' wealth grew along with their position in the social hierarchy of Washington.

One year, the Woman's Club of McLean selected our home to showcase Christmas decorations and interior design as part of the Holiday Homes Tour. (One of the others chosen was Merrywood, the fifty-acre estate on which Jacqueline Bouvier Kennedy grew up.) It was a tour where wealthy women wore booties on their shoes as they walked around the decorated mansions oohing and aahing at the décor with the comfort that the money they donated would go toward a designated charity.

For weeks, my mother and the interior designers spent all day hanging red ribbons and green wreaths from each window above the green boxwood bushes and lush ivy. Candles shimmered in the center of each windowsill. White lights swirled around the Corinthian columns illuminating the front door, making it look like a winter wonderland when it snowed. Inside, the house smelled of cinnamon and vanilla, poinsettias clumped in every corner of every room next to antiques, and mistletoe swung in the loggia. Each room a vision of warm perfection. My mother had come to develop the most sophisticated and exquisite taste, moving further and further away from her laid-back California upbringing.

I was fourteen years old, and I'll never forget the gifts I received that year on Christmas morning. Stacks of presents covered the lower third of our twelve-foot Christmas tree in red-and-white Santa wrapping paper. But before we opened presents, we had already been led by footprints made from fake snow down into the playroom to find a Ping-Pong table and a pool table placed under the hanging green Tiffany lamps. The room was big enough for both.

My father had given me a $2,000 steel watch from Tiffany and had bought me a background role on my favorite TV show, *Dawson's Creek*. He bid the most money during the silent auction at a charity event for the Choral Arts Society of Washington. Eight weeks later, on my fifteenth birthday, my father flew me in his Beechcraft King Air twin turboprop down to Wilmington, North Carolina, where they filmed the show. I hung out on set all day with stars Katie Holmes and Joshua Jackson and had them autograph my yellow North Face backpack.

During those years, we had nannies and housekeepers, painters and gardeners, private chefs and academic tutors. And every six months, it seemed, I'd come home from school to see the newest model of a red or black Porsche being driven off the flatbed of a truck. I'd see Dad standing in the driveway in his white polo and khakis, his arms in the air, directing the landing of the Porsche safely onto the gravel.

My father insisted on buying sports cars with manual transmissions only. "Automatic is for sissies," he would say. My BMW was a stick shift, and when I asked him why he bought me a stick, he said with a laugh, "Because, Bambina, you'll drive all the boys wild. I bet half of them won't know how to drive your car." He was right, except Blake knew how to drive a stick.

When I arrived in Los Angeles a week after my high school graduation, Blake and I would race his friends—the sons of directors, movie stars, and studio moguls—across Mulholland Drive. One of his best friends, the son of an executive at Viacom, flipped his BMW in one of the canyons. He was lucky to have walked away alive. But a few weeks later, he showed up at a party in Bel Air with a brand-new GMC Denali: black rims, blacked-out lights, and tinted windows. High-end cars for the kids who come from "real money" were disposable.

During my summer at the New York Film Academy, I met Steven Spielberg's son, who was a friend of Blake's. He took me to Dream-Works Studios for lunch one day. We ate salmon and Caesar salad and played Grand Theft Auto the entire afternoon in Mr. Spielberg's office. When I got up to use the bathroom and came back, Mr. Spielberg was standing in front of his desk. He looked at me, smiled, and introduced himself. I wiped my hands along my red Marc Jacobs skirt and then shook his hand. He asked where I was from and where I was planning on going to college. I couldn't believe how normal he was. I wanted him to be the vicious director yelling at me through an old-fashioned megaphone. But he was just like any other dad, which thoroughly disappointed me. He had hundreds of awards that followed the entire length of his office. I was oblivious to his being considered the greatest film director of our time. *Jaws* made me nauseous, and *E.T.* scared me so much that I refused to even walk into the family room when Mara or Chloe was watching it. But I wanted to touch one of his awards. So when he wasn't looking, I picked up his Golden Globe for *Saving Private Ryan*.

After we finished playing video games, Mr. Spielberg took us for a cruise around the lot in his golf cart. My father was so excited on the other line of the phone when I called him that night and told him about my afternoon. "My little movie star!" he exclaimed. "By golly, Steven Spielberg . . ." I beamed, knowing how much I'd impressed him. I'd been in Hollywood only three weeks and was hanging out in Mr. Spielberg's office.

I was never conscious of the kind of privilege I was around or the fact that I got whatever I wanted. I was growing and being shaped inside a bubble of wealth where everyone I surrounded myself with appeared to accept it as normal. *Normal.* I believed it was normal. Because it was. It was all that I knew.

3

The Trial

Six months had passed since the FBI arrested my father, and it was now summer. Mara, Chloe, my mother, and I were piled into the Range Rover and heading to the Ritz-Carlton Hotel in Battery Park, where we would stay for the duration of the trial. My father had flown up a few weeks earlier to prep with his attorneys, spending sleepless nights reviewing documents and depositions in the hotel conference room. We drove to save money, and when Mara questioned him before we left about why we were staying at such an expensive hotel, he replied, "Because we got a good deal. Not a lot of tourists want to stay downtown right now."

The financial district was desolate and abandoned as we made our way down Greenwich Street, passing the metal fence encompassing what remained of the World Trade Center. I saw enormous tractor-trailers bulldozing and digging up dirt and construction workers yelling at one another back and forth in their orange hard hats and yellow vests. I thought about loss as I remembered sitting in religion class when the principal called for an emergency school meeting, watching on television the collapse of the second tower into the crescendo of death, and the rumbling of F-16s over my bed that night. Yet, still, I had no grasp of what loss really meant.

For the entire five-hour drive from Washington, DC, to Manhattan, my sisters and I never fought. Instead, we reminisced over our childhoods and all of our favorite memories. It was as if we were searching for all the reasons to hold on to life the way that it was, all the memories of our past, so it would make everything that was happening okay. We remained lighthearted, skating along the surface of any real emotions, hiding behind laughter, too afraid to accept any kind of reality, as everyone was unsure of our family's fate.

Later that night, my father's attorneys paced back and forth with their hands in their pockets in front of the glass window of our hotel suite. You could see in the distance the twinkling lights of Lady Liberty standing dignified with her raised torch of freedom, mocking us.

"No makeup, no jewelry of any kind, simple colors, collared shirts, and conservative skirts," said Mr. David Kenner, one of my father's attorneys. Mr. Kenner was from Encino, California. Exceptionally tan, a silver fox with more hair spray than Dolly Parton, too-perfect teeth, and looked like he had had way too much plastic surgery. He was known for representing Death Row Records and getting Snoop Dogg acquitted of murder charges. I thought it was a good sign. I asked him toward the end of the trial, "So, who killed Tupac, and who killed Biggie?" He looked at me and walked away. He didn't think it was funny.

"It is very important that the jury and the judge like you," Mr. Alvin Entin said. Mr. Entin was my father's other attorney. He was from Fort Lauderdale, Florida, and loved to wear different-colored suspenders. Mara, Chloe, and I sat on the edge of the bed, nodding our heads up and down like three little puppet dolls. Innocent and humbled bait waiting to be fed to the jury and the judge with tears in our eyes. We were being written into their presentation and were now part of the game plan.

My mother sat in the chair across from me; the loss of color in her cheeks was apparent. She wasn't wearing her usual burgundy Chanel lipstick, and she was stripped of any jewelry, except for her diamond eternity band. My father stood next to her. For a minute, I studied his furrowed brow. I could tell he was nervous and trying to hide it. Then I looked back at my mother again, who looked back and forth between us girls. I could tell she was trying to gauge our reactions. She looked embarrassed, and scared, her expression one of an apology. But she never said a word. She wouldn't dare interrupt my father or his attorneys, who were tracking us, making sure we would obey. And we did.

The next day, when we pulled up to the US District Court for the Southern District of New York at 500 Pearl Street, I stepped out onto the sidewalk and gazed up at its enormity. Orange barricades reading "Property of US Government" surrounded the grandiose building. Scattered groups of protestors stomped in circles below the steps shouting things I don't remember. Men with leather briefcases in suits, ties, and tasseled shoes walked by as if the protestors were invisible. We did too, my mother, Mara, Chloe, and I, clad in our khaki skirts and collared shirts, conservative yet bland, intentionally ambiguous and unassuming as we tagged behind my father and his two attorneys, who, in their Brooks Brothers suits, carried brown file folders under their arms.

It was my first time inside a federal courthouse. It felt sanctified, with its high ceilings and Grecian-style architecture, like the inside of a cathedral. But instead of being a place where faith lives, it was where ours would be lost. We breezed through security, having been told to leave everything, including our cell phones, at the hotel. My mother carried our IDs in her wallet in case we needed them. Once we passed through security, we waited outside the courtroom in the empty hallway, where even the smallest heel of a shoe left an echo. The bailiff opened the double doors, and Mr. Kenner directed us to our seats. We sat behind Dad, who made his way to the defendant's table in front of us. We were separated from him by a brown gate.

Mr. Steven Glaser and Ms. Diane Gujarati, the assistant US district attorneys, entered. They wore crisp black-and-white pantsuits.

A law clerk followed behind them, pushing a metal cart with organized file boxes. They looked young, hungry, and ready to impress the judge.

Then the jury entered, and it hit me how powerless we were. My family's fate was now in the hands of twelve strangers.

When they sat down, the room became excruciatingly quiet before the bailiff stood up. "All rise."

The Honorable Denise Cote entered, gliding like a goddess toward her towering podium. She was petite, with short gray hair, and her robe was long like a pastor's except black. I overheard my father and Mr. Kenner talking about her the night before. She was presiding over one of the cases in the WorldCom scandal, at the time the largest accounting fraud scheme in US history. They were paying close attention to her rulings. "No bullshit" was the adjective used to describe her.

"You may be seated."

I was having trouble listening to her opening remarks. I kept wondering about her personal life. Was she married? Did she have children? Boys? Girls? How old? What was she wearing under that robe? Did she have sex? Had she ever been in trouble? Was she ever wrong? I needed something, anything, to strip her of her power and make her human.

"Mr. Glaser, you may proceed," Judge Cote declared. The prosecutor stood up, carrying a legal pad close to his chest. He strolled casually back and forth before the jury as though preparing for a monologue onstage.

> *May it please the court, counsel, ladies and gentlemen of the jury, this is a case about a crooked lawyer and the lies that he told to collect a million-dollar fee. That crooked lawyer is this man, Thomas Prousalis Jr. He is a lawyer who specializes in advising small companies that want to sell their stock to what is called an initial public offering, or IPO. You will learn during this trial that Prousalis was hired by a small internet company called BusyBox to help them sell their stock to the public in an IPO.*

Now, in a written brochure about BusyBox, Prousalis lied to investors about the size of his fee. You see, Prousalis understood that if he told investors that his fee would be a million dollars, given the small size of this deal, that would raise serious red flags for investors.

You are also going to learn, ladies and gentlemen, that at the last minute, as the deal was about to go down, things went wrong. It looked like the deal was not going to happen. So what did Prousalis do? He came up with a secret plan. A secret plan to rejigger the whole deal. Prousalis's plan was bad for the company, and it was bad for investors, and it involved a whole series of lies—lies about how much money the company was planning to raise in this IPO and lies told by Prousalis that he had received approval from regulators to go ahead with this plan and not tell investors about it.

Why did Prousalis do this? Because if the deal didn't close, Prousalis did not collect that million-dollar fee. Why was that million-dollar fee so important to Prousalis? Well, by that time, spring of 2000, Prousalis had lost millions of dollars in the stock market, and at the same time, he was leading a fancy lifestyle. He had a mansion in an exclusive Washington, DC, suburb. He had a two-million-dollar personal jet that he liked to fly around. Prousalis needed the money. So without investors knowing anything about his enormous fee and his secret plan which drained BusyBox of cash that it desperately needed to survive, the IPO went forward, and investors bought stock in this company.

Unsurprisingly, ladies and gentlemen, you will learn that about a year after this IPO, BusyBox declared bankruptcy. Prousalis, on the other hand, did not suffer the way that other investors did. He managed to dump his IPO stock for hundreds of thousands of dollars. And during this trial, ladies and gentlemen, we will prove beyond reasonable doubt that this man, Thomas Prousalis, used his skill, expertise, and his cunning as a lawyer to cheat investors and that he is guilty of conspiracy and securities fraud as charged in the indictment.

Now, ladies and gentlemen, I would like to take this opportunity to reintroduce myself. My name is Steven Glaser. I am an assistant United States attorney here in the Southern District Court of New York.

I wanted to see the look on my father's face. But I could see only the back of his head, which he kept down, staring at the yellow legal pad before him. Chloe picked at her fingernails next to me. I was too afraid to look over at Mara on the other side of my mother, who appeared stoic, like she was prepared for the worst. She didn't seem surprised by the opening statements, and it irked me. I wiped my sweaty hands along my khaki skirt as a flood of rage soared through me, glared up at Mr. Glaser, and thought, *Liar*. He didn't know my father. This was not the story of a crooked lawyer. My father was a good man, a self-made man who would never compromise his integrity, his family, for the sake of a business deal. For the sake of money.

Mr. Kenner rose from the defendant's table and began his opening statements. He didn't have a "secret plan of the government's" to counter my father's supposed "secret plan." He discussed things like SEC filings, registrations, IPOs—number after number, technicalities that he claimed were legal, things hard to understand unless you were a banker, lawyer, investor, a Wall Street type. I resented my expensive education and that I didn't understand any of the issues being addressed. I felt lost in a haze of monotonous math where nothing made sense. I didn't know what securities fraud was, or wire fraud, or money laundering, or any of the things we saw on the news that summer along with the other cases, like Enron—something to do with energy or telecommunications; things that made the world go round—and Martha Stewart. I just knew that a lot of innocent people lost money, lost life savings, lost their jobs. I didn't think it had anything to do with my father—that it was any kind of foreshadowing or indication of what was to come. America was just beginning to reclaim her safety, her security, floating in a decade lost without any kind of an identity, where Facebook still belonged to privileged college students. It would be years before the near collapse of America's financial system, the bursting of its housing bubble, Bernie Madoff, the greatest financial fraud in world history, exposed.

It was one morning in high school: I remember my father was sitting in front of his laptop at the breakfast table, staring at the television screen on the wall in the kitchen. I looked up. A former Enron executive had just committed suicide, and I thought about the Great Depression, and what I had learned in my American history class. Suicide had been a theme, a tragic topic of conversation. Suicide rates fluctuated depending on how the US economy was doing. My father's eyeglasses were slid down to the end of his nose, and the look in his eyes—it was as though he had left our world. I never asked why.

I had given up trying to follow the numbers and charts being shown on the projector screen. Instead, I stared at and observed each member of the jury. All of them appeared bored and uninterested. In the middle row sat a young woman in a red sweatshirt. She looked like maybe she went to New York University or the New School. In another life, we could have been friends. There was no chance she understood what was happening either; I was sure of it. She nodded off at one point, her head slumping over before she woke herself up. I didn't blame her. If my father's life weren't on the line, it would all be such a bore to me. I was convinced that not a single jury member understood what on earth was going on. But I was very aware that my father was teetering on the edge between incarceration and freedom, and I had a hard time accepting that his destiny would be determined by individuals who didn't seem to understand or care.

Until we broke for recess, everyone was bored and lost in "Government exhibit 101, government exhibit 102, government exhibit 103," blah blah blah, and more charts with more numbers projected on a giant screen and words spewing from Judge Cote's mouth like "overruled" and "sustained." The way she said "sustained" was particularly irritating to me: she held the *s* with her tongue, while her inflections traveled upward, like she enjoyed it. Like it was a song to her.

"Bring in the witness," she continued.

• • •

Bernie Carl, who had bailed out my father after the FBI arrested him, was one of the original investors in BusyBox. He filed a civil suit against the directors of the company after he lost more than $800,000 and the company went bankrupt. I don't know whether Bernie knew once the investigation began that all fingers would point back to my father, culminating in the federal investigation and his indictment, but it did.

Having been a lifelong friend of the family's, Bernie did not want to testify against him, but he was subpoenaed and forced to. He walked down the center aisle in his tailor-made Brioni suit, escorted by Mr. Glaser. He glanced at Mara, and a humble smile crossed his face, trying to comfort us from afar and sorry for us all at the same time. When I was twelve, and their family moved to London for a year, Andrew, Bernie's son, wrote me love letters nearly every week. He was ten. I kept them in a little box tucked away inside my yellow balloon curtains so no one would find out.

I could hear Mara sniffling next to Mom. Alex, Bernie's daughter, was one of her best friends, and Joan, Bernie's wife, had stopped returning my mother's calls after he was subpoenaed, so I didn't understand why he was still acting as a loyal friend to my father—even lending him money—if my father had been the reason Bernie *lost* so much money. I decided there were two possible conclusions:

One: Bernie knew he was guilty but supported my father out of a sense of loyalty, or guilt. After all, my father got in trouble as a result of Mr. Carl's civil lawsuit against the directors. And the truth was, even though Bernie suffered over a $800,000 loss, it didn't put a dent in his personal bank account. He was worth hundreds of millions of dollars. Had he not filed suit, the government might never have noticed what my father was doing.

Two: Bernie believed my father was innocent. He believed he entered into business with bad guys and was used as a scapegoat for the deal to get done. And when the plan failed, everyone pointed the finger at the lawyer to save his own ass.

It would be years before I discovered the truth. But I was looking for a reason—any reason—to believe in my father's innocence, and
Bernie was proof.

Mr. Glaser approached the witness stand. "Good afternoon, Mr.
Carl."

"Good afternoon."

"Mr. Carl, were you friends with Mr. Prousalis in the early-to-
mid-2000 time frame?"

"Yes, sir."

"And were you familiar with his hobbies at the time?"

"Yes."

"And what were some of those hobbies?"

"Tom was a former air force fighter pilot, and I think maintained
his interest in aviation. And we both shared a considerable interest in
sports cars and automobile racing."

"Are you familiar with whether Mr. Prousalis ever had an airplane?"

"Yes."

"And how were you familiar with whether Mr. Prousalis had an
airplane?"

"We talked about it a lot, and there were occasions when one of our
children had to go somewhere, and Tom was very kind in getting them
off to summer camp together."

"I'm showing what has been marked for identification government exhibit 202 and government exhibit 200. Do you recognize government exhibit 200?"

"Yes."

"Can you tell us what it is?"

"It is the interior of an airplane."

"Do you recognize government exhibit 202?"

"Yes, sir."

"Can you tell us what it is?"

"It is the photograph of an airplane."

"Do you know what type of airplane?"

"I think it is a King Air C90."

"Are you familiar with the aircraft?"

"Yes, sir."

"And do you know if that was one of the aircrafts Mr. Prousalis owned?"

"I believe he had one of the same type, yes."

There was nowhere else in the world my father would rather be than flying in his airplane. He always said his officer training school days were some of the best of his life. I imagined those days like scenes out of *Top Gun*, where he was Tom Cruise, showing off, doing flips, and rolling in F-16s, driving all the girls wild. I asked him once why he loved to fly so much, and he said, "Because there's nowhere else in the world where you can feel as free."

Mr. Glaser clicked on the remote control and looked up at the screen in front of us. "The government offers government exhibit 201." It was a picture of our home.

"Objection!" Mr. Kenner yelled.

"Overruled," Judge Cote stated wistfully.

"Mr. Carl, do you recognize government exhibit 201?"

"Yes, sir."

"Can you tell us what it is?"

"It is the photograph of a home."

"Whose home?"

"Mr. Prousalis's home, sir." There was a look of shame across Bernie's face. Then he looked at my father as if to say "I'm sorry."

My initial reaction to seeing our home plastered on the screen in front of us was one of confusion. How was showing a picture of our home to the jury relevant in a securities fraud case? I had yet to understand that showing it to the jury would imply we were greedy, that we must be bad people. The trial was no longer about technicalities in legal filings. I was right about one thing. The prosecutors didn't believe the jury would understand it either. So they made it easy. They made it about greed. But I didn't know about class warfare just yet, that the toes of my patent leather party shoes were tipping over the edge before our fall into the underbelly of society. All I knew then was that a seed of shame had been planted underneath the violation I felt by the very institution I thought was there to protect me.

It was 1989, and that morning, my father had piled us into the Volvo station wagon to see our soon-to-be new home.

"Marco!"

In the distance, I could hear the pitter-patter of Mara's feet running through the hallway, the echo of her voice boomeranging off unfinished walls.

"Polo!" I ran up the back staircase with a Hello Kitty beach towel wrapped around my shoulders. We were playing Marco Polo, but instead of in a swimming pool, we were running through our new seventy-five-hundred-square-foot mansion, getting lost amid dirt and plywood, the smell of cedar and paint as it was still under construction.

"Dad, look at my cape!" I cried, twirling around as I followed Mara into the kitchen. My father took out a scroll of floor plans and unrolled it on the granite countertop, while my mother stood next to him, bouncing baby Chloe on her hip. He was showing us his plans for the limestone plaque that would be placed in the center brick wall that adjoined the double staircases descending from the back balcony down toward the swimming pool. On the plaque he would have *Prousalis* engraved in Greek letters with the date 1989 in roman numerals below it. I could see my mother's eyes light up. She had never been inside a house that big before, let alone dreamed of living in one.

"Wait a minute," my father said, looking at me. "You're forgetting something very important, Bambina." He picked up a round rack over the new gas stove, kneeled down, and placed it on top of my head. "Your crown!" Then he turned around and crowned Mara too, to make it fair.

"I'm a princess! I'm a princess!" I cried, holding the rack in place over my head.

In our stovetop crowns, Mara and I giggled while we danced through the black-and-white marble loggia. Behind us, a dozen French doors looked out onto the limestone balcony where the engraved plaque would rest and where weeping willows grew in the distance.

"Mr. Carl, during this time period, the 2000 time period, did you visit Mr. Prousalis's homes?"

"Yes."

"Were you familiar with where his homes were?"

"Yes, I was."

"And where did Mr. Prousalis have homes during that period?"

"He had a home in McLean, Virginia, right outside of Washington, DC, and on the island of Nantucket."

"Mr. Carl, are you testifying here today pursuant to a subpoena?"

"Yes, sir."

"Do you want to testify against Mr. Prousalis?"

"No, sir."

I was about to lose it. My mother shook her head and put a finger up to her lips, indicating for me to remain silent. Chloe was crying. She turned red, and my mother tried to console her, whispering, "It's okay," while rocking her in her arms. Mara tried to remain as quiet as possible, but her breath became erratic, and the tears wouldn't stop until she had to leave the courtroom.

"It is five o'clock. We are going to break here today. Ladies and gentlemen, you have just seen images of some houses. You may not use evidence of a person's wealth or lack of wealth for any improper purpose. Specifically, it would be wrong for you to use evidence of wealth or poverty or financial need to conclude that a person, for instance, has bad character or is not entitled to the protection of the law or has done something wrong. Simply put, it would be wrong to be biased or prejudice for or against an individual simply because an individual has wealth or, conversely, lives in financial distress. Any evidence of wealth or poverty may only be considered by you for a relevant or proper purpose. If you decide it is relevant to the task you have before you, that is to decide whether the government has carried its burden of proving the defendant guilty beyond reasonable doubt with the crimes with which he is charged, if you decide for fulfilling that task that it is helpful for you to consider or understand a person's—specifically the defendant's—motive or purpose in acting a certain way, then you may use evidence of wealth or, on the other hand, financial distress or basically the defendant's financial circumstances to the extent that you find those financial circumstances cast light on his motive or intent. Remember, do not discuss the case. See you tomorrow," Judge Cote said.

"All rise."

The next day, Mara, Chloe, and I were pulled into a private waiting room next to the main entrance of the courtroom. We were told, "Wait here, quietly." The room was empty except for a table, a few chairs, and fluorescent lights. The three of us sat alone but together, in silence. Waiting.

A few minutes later, my mother walked in first. She was crying. Her eyes were bloodshot. She sat down next to Chloe and took her hand and wrapped it in hers.

Then my father walked in with Mr. Kenner and took a seat.

"Dad, what's going on?" Mara asked.

"Girls, your dad has agreed to a plea agreement with the government," he stated.

"What does that mean?" I asked, wanting him to speak faster.

"It means your dad pleads guilty, even though he isn't guilty, so there's no risk having the book thrown at us if we continue the trial and lose." My father always spoke of himself in the third person, as if he were speaking of someone else: a character in a novel, someone separate and untouched, distancing himself from any kind of reality, it seemed—as we did too on our way up to New York.

"What do you mean, 'the book'?" My frustration was growing.

"If we were to continue with the trial, the government is ready to put a very bad man on the witness stand, which could hurt our chances of winning. If we lose, your dad could face up to fifteen years behind bars, whatever the book of the law says for the nefarious accusations made against me. So it is in our best interest that even though your dad is innocent, we tell the government your dad is guilty in exchange for less time, you understand?"

The "man" my father was referring to was Jordan Belfort, the "Wolf of Wall Street," the founder of Stratton Oakmont. Jordan Belfort had become a rat, cooperating with the federal government, testifying against all of his former friends and business associates in exchange for less time in prison. In the mid- to late nineties, before BusyBox, my father had been involved in taking several companies public with Stratton Oakmont, even after Belfort had been barred from the securities industry. Mr. Glaser flew Jordan Belfort from prison in California to New York to testify against him. He was waiting in a jail cell at the courthouse, ready to take the stand unless my father took the plea deal.

"How is that legal? How is this the law?" I cried.

"It's the federal government, Christina," my father said. "They can do anything they want."

"So you're going to prison?" Mara asked.

There was a long pause. The room filled with defeat. He never said yes, because we already knew the answer.

"So what happens now?" Chloe asked, scared.

"You girls are going to help me pack up the house," my mother said.

We were going to lose everything.

4

Ostracism

The bank would be coming in just a few months to take the house. At nineteen, I didn't understand banks and mortgages and how everything worked. I thought when you owned a home it meant that you owned it. And by "own," I mean that no one could take it from you. But it wasn't the truth. We didn't own it. We never did. The bank owned the mortgage, and we paid the mortgage, and if we didn't pay the mortgage, then the bank would take our home. And that's what was happening. Everything was happening so fast when we got home from the trial, there wasn't much time to say good-bye. When I walked into my bedroom one night, there was a note at the foot of my bed from my mother. Handwritten on her embossed stationery. She was always leaving little notes on my bed when I got home from school:

"Want to go to Saks with me this weekend? Homecoming is around the corner! XX Mom."

"I left more lamb's wool for your ballet slippers in your dresser, top drawer! XX Mom." "New Julia Roberts movie opening this weekend! Shall we go see it, movie star? XX Mom."

Each note was evidence of a girl who lived a happy and privileged life. But this note was different.

Christina Bambina,

    Let me know what you do not want to let go of. Make a list. Okay, honey? So we can set it aside. Everything goes up for auction next week.

    XX

    Mom

What I don't want to let go of? I don't want to let go of any of it, I thought as I looked around at my yellow Laura Ashley balloon curtains, where I used to hide my cigarettes, Andrew's love letters, and the occasional bag of weed. My hand-painted MacKenzie-Childs desk, where I spent countless hours crying over chemistry assignments. My bulletin board that carried all my dried-up corsages from prom and homecoming. And my collection of bumper stickers: "Diva!" "Almost Famous!" "Skinny Little Bitch!" (Which I found stuck to my locker one day after first period. I took it as a compliment.) The bookshelf. *Fine,* but that was it. That was all I was willing to let go of. Everything else would be shipped to California; my entire bedroom set. I would take it all with me. If the bank was coming to take the house, then I would keep my bedroom, everything in it, and drag it along with me no matter how absurd it would look, no matter what anyone would think. I wanted my possessions to cocoon me, wrap me up, and keep me safe from a world that was trying to rip it all away. It would become my way of holding on, believing someday I could put it all back the way that it was and the way that it felt when I walked inside my bedroom that night. Because I would never get the chance to say good-bye before it was already gone.

At the time, I didn't know the exact day the bank would be taking the house. I still didn't understand it or how it worked. My parents had stopped communicating with us aside from the occasional note. They were too busy settling their affairs, packing up the house and figuring out where we were going to live.

It would be six more months before my father would surrender to prison, but my mother had warned us that ostracism happened slowly and was often very insidious. More family friends started disappearing.

We were no longer wanted in Washington, DC—shunned, excommunicated, expelled. My parents' plan was to pull Chloe out of Langley High School and follow me back to California. Once Mara finished school, she would meet us there as well. I would be leaving to go back to California in just a few days.

"The cave dwellers," my mother explained, "those are the worst. The one's who've dropped like flies." The term *cave dweller* was coined for the Washington, DC, native. It's those whose old money and manner lurk through the cobblestone streets of Georgetown and Capitol Hill. Cave dwellers are at the top of Washington's social hierarchy. They're members of exclusive clubs like the Alibi gentlemen's club for presidents, senators, and diplomats, or the Sulgrave Club for women, or the Chevy Chase Club for the white Protestant family. They're also in what's called *The Green Book*, a social list that was started in 1930 by Helen Ray Hagner, the niece of Mrs. Theodore Roosevelt's White House social secretary. *The Green Book* lists different social sectors and the names of those "very important people." My mother and father were part of a sector called the social A-list: lawyers, businessmen, bankers, and media moguls, and their philanthropist wives. You make this list based on which social events you attend, how much money you have, and how much money you give away. The cave dwellers and A-listers mingle, but the A-listers have started pushing cave dwellers farther underground. For cave dwellers, it's about politics and class. For A-listers, it's about money. And money trumps all. Then there are the other sectors like the media, reporters and journalists, who associate with the politicians, who have their own social pecking order revolving every four to eight years. Everyone in *The Green Book* is wealthy, everyone is a member of the 1 percent, and everyone has a reputation to protect.

In addition to Joan, Bernie's wife, who threw chic book parties and events at the French Embassy, my mother's friend Faye also stopped returning her calls. Faye was an A-lister, also married to a financier. In high school, I would often come home to find Faye standing at our kitchen island with a glass of Chardonnay in her hand and wearing an aerobics outfit. I'd see that Mercedes parked out front, and before opening the front door, I'd make sure my nose was powdered and that when I stood in front of her my feet were spread ever so wide apart so that my thighs didn't touch. And so that she would see this and, in return, adore me.

Faye liked to gossip, but not about other parents; she liked to gossip about their children. "Did you see how fat so-and-so got?" she'd tsk-tsk, always making sure to note how poorly this reflected on said parents. It was a strange form of cruelty. When our Nantucket house went into foreclosure, Faye bought all of our furniture, reupholstered it, and placed it in her Nantucket home just a mile down the street; the ultimate power move in a competitive friendship, and all too frequent within the world of social hierarchy. A few weeks later, Chloe went to Nantucket to visit one of her friends and Faye's daughter invited Chloe to a party at their house. When she walked in, Faye stumbled over drunk, yelling, "We don't allow criminals in our household!" while Chloe stood between our refurbished toile chairs and family game table. It was a *Game of Thrones* for the desperate housewife.

Back in California, I felt free from the wreckage at home. I had managed to leave Washington, DC, unscathed from any outward ostracism. I was sleeping on an air mattress in an apartment in Brentwood with a few friends I'd stayed in touch with from college. I shared a room for $350 and managed to pay my rent when I auditioned and got the part of "girlfriend" in the Jimmy Eat World music video for the song "Pain." It was the greatest distraction from everything going on at home, and it gave me something to brag about when I spoke to friends, deflecting any attention my father was getting. But when word spread about his trial, Ethan and Abby, two of my best friends from high school, flew out to Los Angeles to visit. I had broken up with Blake, believing I could get myself on track. My life had split in two, and I would forever associate him with reckless abandon, a time that, even though it was only a few weeks behind me, felt like a century ago. I wanted to be close to the friends I felt I could turn to, whom I was comfortable with, who knew my father and my family well, who just might believe me if I told them it was just one big misunderstanding. At nineteen, we were still young enough that the social hierarchy was fast asleep in our subconscious minds. No one had a high-pressure job yet or was a board member of a fancy charity. No reputation was at stake while everyone still danced upon Mom and Dad's credit cards.

When Ethan and Abby arrived, I took them and my roommate Marcie down to my family's beach club in San Diego for the day. The Spanish villa rests on the shores of La Jolla, an exclusive and wealthy beach town. Families stay in suites on the sand, play croquet and tennis and swim, and then dine along the peninsula extending out above the Pacific.

I leaned my head toward the direct sunlight, listening to the rhythmic sound of the waves. Ethan was lying next to me, the book *Writings on an Ethical Life* by Peter Singer was resting on his stomach. He had recently become a vegetarian and spent an hour on the drive down lecturing us on his decision. Marcie was on the other side of Ethan, sitting cross-legged and unscrewing mini whiskey bottles we'd bought with her fake ID. And Abby, with her pale skin and long, dark curls, was on her back tanning.

"Voilà!" Marcie said in her southern drawl. Marcie was from southern royalty, the equivalent to cave-dweller status but from Montgomery, Alabama, with long blond hair and tan, and she loved to drink expensive bottles of red wine while she wrote English term papers. She held out two red paper cups. Ethan and Abby sat up to take one and I took the other.

We held up our cups—"To friendship!"—and then chugged our drinks. I twisted my cup into the sand so it wouldn't fall over. Then Ethan and Abby turned to me. They were waiting for me to speak, as if I had something to say.

"What?" I asked.

They looked at each other, and then back to me.

"*What*, you guys? Stop being weird."

"Really, Christina?" Ethan asked.

"Really, Ethan. What?"

"There isn't anything you want to talk about?"

"Um, *no*?" What did they want from me? I had already given them a few details about my father's trial. I didn't think there was anything left to talk about.

"Do you know what's going on with your dad?" Ethan asked.

"What do you mean?"

"He was on the front page of the *Washington Post* business section today," he said. "My dad told me this morning."

I didn't know. Ethan inched himself closer to me. I flinched back. "Stop," I said.

"We just want to make sure you're okay," Abby said.

I stared down at my empty cup, afraid to say anything for fear that if I did, the tears would come, and they might not stop.

"So your mom and dad didn't tell you?" Ethan was concerned for me now.

"Obviously not, dummy," Abby said, as if I needed defending. Marcie was busy lathering her skin with suntan oil. She didn't know my family well. She had met my mother only on the day I moved into my dorm room. My father had been busy working.

"It says he could go to prison for up to fifty-seven months," Ethan said. I remember doing the math in my head: *Fifty-seven months, fifty-seven months. Twelve times four is forty-eight, so that would be nearly five years. I will be almost twenty-four when he gets out. Why didn't they tell me this?*

"Can I see it?" I asked quickly.

"I don't have a copy of it, but I can email it to you when I'm back at my computer."

I wanted more whiskey. I held out my cup. Marcie pulled out another bottle from her purse and emptied it. I chugged the rest. "I'm going swimming," I said.

I stood up abruptly, and the world went black until I regained my balance. It felt like I didn't have the right to feel what I felt. The stigma and shame of having a parent sentenced to prison was slowly injecting itself into me like poison, silencing me. In a strange way, it felt like a death. I was losing my father, but he wasn't dying. Yet he wouldn't be there on my twentieth birthday, Father's Day, or Christmas. I would have only my memory of him. Unlike death, the loss was ambiguous, not knowing when I would ever see him again and how things would change. I didn't know how to comprehend any of it, and my emotions were isolated—floating and free-falling inside of an infinite possibility of feeling, cementing a trifling numbness in me.

And I couldn't say this to Ethan, Abby, or Marcie. Marcie had lost her father to leukemia when she was five, and I felt ashamed for even thinking about comparing the loss. I couldn't. There were no condolence cards to be sent or sympathy expressed for children of the damned, only humiliating and awkward conversations to be had like this one, yet deep down, the pain somehow felt equal.

I ran as fast as I could toward the freezing Pacific and plowed into the waves, pushing hard against the current. I dove until my adrenaline subsided and the alcohol made its way through my bloodstream, providing some relief.

When I got out of the water, I noticed a woman talking to my friends in the distance. I ran toward them and saw it was an employee. As I got closer, the name tag pinned to her white sweater read "General Manager." *Shit.*

"Are you Christina Prousalis?" she asked.

"Yes?" I said it as a question, as if maybe I wasn't.

"Can you come with me, please?"

"Hold on a minute. What is this regarding?" Ethan sounded stern, like his father, a force to be reckoned with.

"I'm not at liberty to say, but the president of the club would like to speak with you in his office."

"No problem," I said, casually stumbling backward.

"I'm coming with her," Ethan said.

"That's fine."

The general manager stood patiently like a correctional officer while I stepped into my yellow sundress, still sopping wet. I tripped as one of the straps caught my right foot.

Ethan and I trailed behind her and up into the main clubhouse while Abby and Marcie waited with our things.

I grabbed hold of Ethan's arm. "I'm wasted," I whispered.

"I know," he whispered back.

"What do I do?"

"Just don't talk."

The general manager glanced back at us. I smiled at her and then leaned back into Ethan. "It's like that time in eighth grade we were sent to the principal's office for walking to McDonald's."

"*Shhh*," Ethan whispered.

We approached the front door to the president's office. I unlinked arms with Ethan and attempted to stand on my own, the alcohol making me dizzy. I brushed my hair, which was slowly turning into sand-filled dreadlocks, out of my eyes.

"Ms. Prousalis, have a seat."

The president stood tall, with an authoritative presence. He wore a yellow collared shirt and navy blazer with a gold club pin, little criss-crossed flags below his handkerchief.

Ethan stood next to me, and I sat. I could feel my wet butt leaving an imprint on the felt seat cushion. There were gold trophies on his bookshelf. They looked like stupid kid trophies, I thought. My eyes wandered up toward the ceiling as the president accused me of stealing cheeseburgers and Cobb salads. What was he talking about? I had given them our club number. Wasn't he upset that I was drunk? Maybe he didn't notice. I was playing it cool. I stared at the fluorescent lights. I wondered if I stared at them long enough, would I go blind?

"Ms. Prousalis. Ms. Prousalis." The president tried to get my attention.

"Yeah." I blinked heavily in his direction. It was hard to see him. His face was covered by a giant black dot.

"Where are your parents?" he asked.

Where were *my parents?* I hadn't seen or spoken to them in weeks. I knew they must have known that the trial would be written about in the *Washington Post*. They were busy packing up the house, selling family heirlooms, doing things I didn't want to think about, but did they honestly think that I wouldn't find out? They could have at least warned me. It's one thing not to tell me about a Chagall being sold; it's another when Dad is being painted as a criminal in the *Washington Post* for all of my friends and their families to read about.

"Your father owes us money, Christina," the president continued.

It was then I realized he had pulled me into his office not because we had snuck alcohol onto the premises but because my father owed them money. We had been suspended from the club, and I didn't know.

"Unfortunately, you and your family are no longer welcome here. Please exit the property immediately upon leaving my office." The president removed himself from behind his desk and walked to the office door. He opened it like a gentleman.

I sat for a moment; my thoughts clouded with denial. *Is he kicking me out? Why didn't Mom and Dad tell me not to come here? California was supposed to be safe; a place where being sent to prison gives you street cred, not exile. Why didn't they have a discussion with me about Dad's sentencing? What it means, how long he will be gone for. I had to find out that Dad is leaving for prison from two best friends whose parents told them right away—before I even knew the article existed. Mom and Dad could have at least spared me the humiliation; the kind of humiliation everyone spends his or her whole life avoiding, no matter how much money there is in the bank.*

My cheeks felt flushed, and my temples pounded above my ears. My family had always had a veneer of respect and order around money, as we never discussed it—*because it was rude, because it was none of my business, because it was being taken care of.* Sitting in that chair was the first time I became aware of the fact that Abby's father was a partner at a major Washington, DC, law firm. Ethan's father was a senior executive at a Fortune 100 company. Marcie's grandfather was a prominent judge, and her grandmother was a descendant of old railroad money. They spent summers on Jupiter Island, where Vanderbilts, Rockefellers, Fords, Doubledays, and Bushes mingle. Where ordinarily I felt I could tell my friends the truth, this time I couldn't. I felt the divide. I was embarrassed. I had no idea it was just the beginning of a seismic shift that would split me in two. I was about to drift so far away from the only life I ever knew, and the insecurity and anxiety of the unknown left me sitting there with nothing to say.

The president stood in the doorway, waiting for me to exit. I got up and shoved the chair behind me, leaving it awkwardly in the center of his office. Ethan reached for my hand.

"You didn't have to be a prick about it," he said to the president's face. It was the bravest I'd seen him since the night he lit his desk on fire in the ninth grade.

"Yeah," I said. "Nice trophies."

Ethan pulled me through the parking lot. We called Abby on her cell phone, and she and Marcie met us by my car. They sauntered over with our beach bags in tow looking like two bag ladies—if bag ladies could afford YSL. Marcie pulled out a Corona and handed it to me.

"Where'd you get that?"

"Don't ask. Just drink."

I threw Ethan my keys, and we lugged our bags over into the backseat of my convertible.

We peeled out of the parking lot and made our way down the club's elegant driveway, skinny palm trees on either side of us, families playing croquet by a lake filled with swans as we approached the exit gates. Abby threw her hands into the air and howled, "Fuck country clubs!"

Once when we were little, I brought Abby to our country club in Washington, DC. Before we left, she said, "My parents don't mind this country club, because they allow Jews here. The Chevy Chase Club didn't used to allow Jews."

I leaned my head back and closed my eyes. *Fuck country clubs.* So many memories from my childhood had happened there, and it felt as though the president had taken them all back. Like they meant nothing. I tried not to think about my parents when we drove off the private property. I never told them what had happened. What was the use? Instead, I flicked my membership card out the window and kissed that country club good-bye. I didn't belong there anymore. Where I did belong, I didn't know. And I wouldn't know for years.

Ethan put his hand on top of mine as we merged onto the 405 freeway. We would never talk about that day at the beach club. Eventually my friends would go back to their respective universities, and we would all lose touch. They would graduate, climb their way into the upperclass scuffle of corporate America, and make new friends, beginning new chapters of their lives, while I was just beginning to spin backward into mine.

5

Money Laundering

"Meet me at the pink Starbucks on the corner of Sunset and Swarthmore," my mother said. I shifted gears, speeding past the iron gates of Bel Air toward Pacific Palisades. It sounded urgent.

My mother had flown out to California early to avoid watching twenty-five years of her life sold off to strangers and filed away in brown cardboard boxes. She didn't want to be there when the bank took the house. We were staying at her friend Suzanne's house, one of her sorority sisters from her days at UCLA, who owned the local stationery store in town. During the last six months of my freshman year at LMU, I got to know the exclusive beach town just south of Malibu where shiny Escalades, Maseratis, and Range Rovers rest in front of outdated storefronts. Suzanne hired me part-time when she found out about my father's arrest. I sold Christmas cards, Bar Mitzvah invitations, and baby announcements, schmoozing all day with the wealthy wives of agents, producers, and directors, helping them capture their important milestones and memories. The mothers loved me. "Young college student from Washington, DC; daughter of philanthropist and lawyer" was the story I told them, even though I knew it was no longer the truth and wondered if it ever had been.

"Where are you?" my mother text messaged me.

"On my way," I replied.

She had been looking for a rental and needed to register Chloe for high school as soon as possible. Everything back home in Virginia would be gone within the week. What few items were left needed to be shipped to California. Three mattresses, three bed frames, my bedroom set, two couches, the breakfast table, six chairs, five lamps, one television, two desks, two rugs, kitchen dishes, pots and pans, boxes of old family photos, five enormous Louis Vuitton trunks, the Range Rover, and Mom's Jaguar.

I asked my mother how we were able to keep our nice cars if we had no money. She said, "There's a lien against the cars, honey; we can't sell them." I didn't know what this meant. When I learned they were being used as collateral in exchange for a loan, wherever that money had gone, it was gone with the wind, like everything else. How were we going to lease a house or an apartment? How were we going to move everything out to California? My parents were in $12 million worth of debt. The feds were watching. Their accounts were drained.

I arrived in Pacific Palisades and saw my mother standing on the corner in her Christian Dior sunglasses, holding a latte. I parked and walked over to her.

She began explaining to me that we had run out of choices. My father had arranged for a man named Gary in Boca Raton, Florida, who worked at a bank, to wire money into an account for us. "Two hundred thousand dollars," she said. But there was a problem. We needed a name for a bank account that would go unnoticed, a name that would slip right under the radar so that in return, we'd have a roof over our heads and food on the table. Mara was out of the question, because she was back in Texas applying for student loans and financial aid. Chloe was only sixteen. I, on the other hand, was over eighteen years of age and considered a California resident, a struggling actress with a clean record. Who would notice?

"I don't understand. Why do you have to use my name? Why can't we use yours?" I asked.

"Because everything in my name is attached to your father's. We don't have a choice, honey," my mother explained. "The government—they've taken everything from us, and if they see we have more, they'll take that from us too. So we either use your name, or we go to the homeless shelter downtown. Your choice." She had lost ten pounds since the trial, her once rosy cheekbones now empty and gaunt. She was almost unrecognizable the more short fused she became, riddled with anxiety, often forgetting to breathe, and stopping whatever she was doing to rest her hand on her chest to take conscious deep breaths. It was jarring to see her in such a state of desperation; her once calm and nurturing voice whenever I felt anxious under pressure—"How do you eat an elephant, sweetheart? One bite at a time"—now heavy and morose. I wanted to help her. I trusted her. I trusted my father. They would never let me do anything illegal.

"Christina Grace Prousalis, that's a pretty name. Is it Greek?" the banker asked. He was pleased with himself for acquiring a new member of the branch. In five minutes, he'd try to sell me a credit card.

"Yes. My dad's half Greek," I replied, glancing over at my mother, who posed next to me sipping her latte so that we appeared normal. The banker handed back my driver's license with an application to sign.

"Autograph at the X," he said. I used to spend hours in elementary school practicing my autograph on classroom chalkboards, extending the bottom of the a so it looped around, crossing over the t and i's. I wanted my loops to look just like my father's. I had even perfected his autograph, telling all of my friends, "Watch this: I can forge my dad's signature." I remember sitting on his lap at his mahogany desk in the library and asking him to show me how he did it. He put my hand around his as he drew the cursive capital T, looping the o around to the squiggly m.

On the application, I read the statement in small print:

Everything I have stated in this application is correct. You are authorized to make any inquiries that you consider appropriate to determine if you should open the account. This may include ordering a credit report or other report (e.g., information from any motor vehicle department or other state agency) on me. I have received a copy of Consumer Account Agreement, Consumer Account Fee and Information Schedule, and Privacy Policy (collectively the "Account Agreement"), and agree to be bound to the terms and conditions contained therein. I also agree to the terms of the dispute resolution program described in the Account Agreement. Under this program, our disputes will be decided before one or more neutral persons in an arbitration proceeding and not by a jury trial or a trial before a judge.

Everything in the application was correct. The banker accepted the application and handed me the Wells Fargo signature folder. It read "Together We'll Go Far."

We walked out of the bank with our new debit card and temporary checks in hand. Had I known at the time what I had done, I might have felt like Bonnie from *Bonnie and Clyde,* except instead of using a gun, I used white privilege and class. Given the local population, I was just an ordinary girl opening up a bank account with her elegant mother in one of the wealthiest neighborhoods in Los Angeles.

I couldn't quite describe the feeling I had other than it felt dark underneath the bright sun as we crossed Sunset Boulevard toward my car, passing young moms in their Elyse Walker sweaters pushing Bugaboo strollers, their sleeping babies all bundled up like cashmere burritos. My mother needed me to give her a ride to the rental house on the corner of Drummond Street so that we could sign the lease agreement and write the landlord a check.

· · ·

"Mrs. Gilbert, this is my daughter Christina." An elderly woman walked down the front steps of the red and white craftsman home. It was a 1950s picturesque lot complete with a white picket fence right in the heart of Pacific Palisades. Mrs. Gilbert shook my hand. "Nice to meet you, dear. Your mother tells me you're the catalyst for the family's move out to California. That you're an actress." She pretended to be impressed, I could tell.

"I am." I shot my mother a look. *Did Mrs. Gilbert know Dad was going to prison?*

My mother interrupted, quickly sensing my unease. "I've been try-ing to convince my husband to move out here for years, and now that Christina is here, it feels like the right time." I studied her, and if my eyes could speak, they'd have said, "I know your secret."

"That's nice," Mrs. Gilbert said, and she handed me the lease agree-ment. I guessed my mother had told her it would be me signing the lease. *Doesn't this woman think it strange that I'm the one signing the lease? Doesn't she need to verify employment? Run a credit check?* She never seemed concerned. Maybe she needed the money. I signed the lease and handed her back the paperwork. A wide smile crossed her face.

I never questioned the veracity of my own actions. That day was only the beginning of a series of grave mistakes I'd make. We were long-ing for normalcy, longing for a home, a community. A place to belong. I had no understanding of what it took to keep up with the Joneses. That this was what my mother and father were still doing, despite everything. On the outside, on another coast, our situation didn't *look* a whole lot different for us. Not yet, at least. We had the house, the Range Rover, the Jaguar, the designer clothes, and the white picket fence. We looked like we fit right in. But the thing about a veneer is that there's always something rotten underneath. Most of the time, you just can't see it. There was a part of me that could feel it, though—that deep down it was a lie. But my instincts had been disproved by authority figures all around me, like my father's attorneys: "It's the government's fault." The prosecutors: "Do you want to testify against Mr. Prousalis?" Bernie Carl: "I do not." The Wells Fargo banker: "Would you like a credit card?" Mrs. Gilbert: "Sign right here, dear." My mother: "We don't have a choice, honey." And my father: "Everything will be okay." Pointing me only in the direction of whatever it was they needed to believe—for money.

So I must have been wrong to feel that the whole town was a lie, all of those families with their towheaded babies, tree houses, and nannies, acting perfect and happy. They looked just like us. Just like we had been once: happy.

- 6 -

The Partridge Family

My agent called. "You booked it," she said. I had been selected to compete for the role of Laurie Partridge in a new reality television series called *In Search of the Partridge Family*, where VH1 and Sony Television were looking to remake the 1970s sitcom. Other than the fact that money was being laundered in my name, and I had a father going to prison for fraud, I thought this would be a good idea. The reality show would consist of Partridge Family "boot camp," where I would be trained in singing, dancing, and acting by original cast members Shirley Jones, David Cassidy, and Danny Bonaduce, and compete against seven other starstruck girls for the part on national television. To be sure that no one found out about my father, I dropped my last name and used my middle name. I became Christina Grace, innocent and sweet, just like Susan Dey, the original Laurie.

"Is Christina Grace your real name?" the girl asked, flipping through *Los Angeles Confidential* magazine. She had auburn hair, translucent skin, and a husky voice for someone so skinny.

I looked at her, annoyed. "Maybe," I said.

"Or is that your stage name?"

Why is she asking me this? Is my paranoia obvious?

"Grace is my middle name," I replied, trying to play it cool.

"I'm Emily. Emily Stone." Later she would become the movie star Emma Stone. "I'm one of the Lauries." She reached her arm across the table to shake my hand. Her energy felt ambitious and electric.

"Me too, one of the Lauries."

She looked at me with her wide green eyes. "So what's your *real* last name?" *Seriously, what is this girl's problem?* I knew in that moment it was no longer safe to be myself. She looked to be about fourteen or fifteen years old, so I figured she didn't read the *Washington Post*. Besides, no one in Los Angeles read the *Washington Post*.

"Prousalis," I said, a little apprehensive.

"Oh yeah." She nodded her head, indicating I had made the right decision. "Christina Grace. It's innocent and sweet, just like Susan Dey."

"Thanks." I smiled. We gave each other the once-over, the way actresses do, comparing and despairing without wanting the other to know.

Moments later, the rest of the Lauries gathered around us in the hotel lobby at Universal Studios, which was where we were staying for Partridge Family boot camp. It was our first day on set. We looked like Susan Dey octuplets: skinny with long hair, each of us carrying big dreams of stardom. We were driven to Tribune Studios in Hollywood and were greeted by Becky, the talent coordinator with big boobs and a southern accent. She stood in front of the enormous soundstage, holding a walkie-talkie and a clipboard. "Welcome to Partridge Family boot camp, ladies."

We followed her onto the soundstage, which was broken down into different 1970s-looking set pieces with neon green, orange, and red couches. The air-conditioning was on full blast. Straight ahead against a makeshift wall was the craft services table, filled with Red Vines licorice, veggie platters, donuts, chips, soda, hot tea, and coffee. All of it for free. I walked over, shivering in my chiffon tank top and jean miniskirt, contemplating which donut I should eat, when I felt a tap on my shoulder. I spun around.

"You look like you're freezing." A tall boy wearing a USC sweat-shirt stood in front of me holding a wool blanket. "Here," he said.

"Thank you." I took the blanket, eager to wrap myself up.

"They always crank up the air at the crack of dawn because the lights make it so hot in here. I'm Josh." His eyes were the bluest I'd ever seen.

"Christina—"

"Grace," he said before I could finish. "I know. One of the Lauries. I saw your audition tape." Then he started teasing me, singing the *Partridge Family* theme song, "Come On Get Happy," as if we'd known each other for years.

I laughed. "Are you one of the Keiths?"

"No way," he said. "I'm the guy that gets paid to stare at you all day long."

"Uh . . ."

"The camera operator—sorry." He shook his head and blushed. "That sounded creepy."

There was a moment between us. I laughed, and he smiled at me. His cheeks were big and round when he smiled, I could see, still separating the boy from the man. And I got that feeling you get when you meet someone and you know they're going to make their way into the story of your life; it's just that you don't know how yet, only in hindsight could you see.

"Lauries over here, please!" Becky called out across the soundstage.

"Thanks for the blanket," I said.

"Anytime. See you over there."

Emily stood next to me. "Watch out," she whispered.

"What?" I asked.

"That guy over there." She nodded toward Josh, who was setting up his camera equipment. "He's the executive producer's son. We're not allowed to fraternize with crew members—if ya know what I mean."

I blushed. This girl was on it. How did she know this? I started to like how precocious she was.

Fraternizing with crew members was hardly the issue when rumors were floating around that David Cassidy was drunk, Danny Bonaduce was high, and Shirley Jones seemed oblivious to what was going on. Susan Dey refused to participate because fame from the show had screwed her up so badly she wanted nothing to do with the remake. Rumor was she suffered from anorexia, refusing to eat anything but carrots at one point and eventually turning her skin orange. I guess every family has its secrets, even the fake ones.

For the next few weeks, it was a world of make believe, with a strict schedule of singing with David Cassidy, acting with Danny Bonaduce, dance rehearsals, and photo shoots. One afternoon Shirley Jones taught all of us Lauries how to bake a homemade cake at a house in the Hollywood Hills. It felt more like summer camp than a reality television show. Emily and I had grown to become great friends. She nicknamed me Audrey, and I nicknamed her Gilda, for Audrey Hepburn and Gilda Radner, honoring our favorite actresses. She would have me on the floor in the green room, crying from laughing so hard over her Britney Spears impersonation. And whenever Josh walked in, it turned into a scene from *Napoleon Dynamite*.

Josh: "You stayed home and ate all the freakin' chips, Kip!"

Emily: "Don't be jealous that I've been chatting with online babes all day. Besides, we both know I'm training to become a cage fighter."

Josh: "You're such an idiot! Uh!"

It was obvious that Josh and I had a crush on each other. Neither one of us cared to play by the rules, and he had opened up to me about his father being the executive producer. It was his first job after having just graduated from USC's film school. He kept finding excuses to sit next to me during meal breaks.

"Is it okay that we're sitting alone together? You know, since I'm not supposed to be fraternizing with crew members," I said.

"Don't worry, my dad doesn't give a shit. It's Sony we have to watch out for."

Josh looked around. We were sitting at a table underneath one of the tents in the parking lot behind the stage. "We're in the clear."

"So what was it like growing up in LA?" I asked.

"Probably similar to growing up in DC, if you substitute movie stars for politicians . . . so what do your parents do?" Josh asked.

Suddenly utter panic consumed every fiber of my being. No one had asked me this since my father had been sentenced to prison and would be disbarred. I had no answer prepared. My father's attorneys had prepped me for everything else but this: what to say in the aftermath. I had managed to avoid any talk about my family on set. I didn't want anyone to know that once a week, late at night, I had been driving to the rental to give him my per diem money we received on set for food and gas. They needed it to put food on the table until more money was wired into the Wells Fargo bank account.

During my first week on set, after Chloe and my father had moved out to Los Angeles, and the house in Virginia was officially gone, I met them for dinner at the Pearl Dragon the night they flew in. It was a chic Asian fusion restaurant in Pacific Palisades, and my father tried to pay with the credit card, but it was declined. I watched from the other end of the table, the waitress kneeling next to him, whispering something and handing him back the card. So I got up and handed him the few hundred dollars that Becky had given me for the week. "Here, Dad, take my per diem money." He took the cash and paid for dinner while I walked back to my seat. He didn't thank me or look me in the eye—the humiliation was unbearable. But I was happy to do it. I didn't want him to worry.

In the months before my father had to surrender to prison, every day felt heavy with anticipation. My father never left the house. He was nothing short of a recluse, staring at his computer screen all day. I walked by his open computer once when he wasn't in the room and saw he had been reading a document that a friend had sent him about how to survive prison. And all of the things he should be warned about. I didn't know anything about prison except that I believed he didn't belong there. I was too afraid to bring it up with him or ask him about it. No one wanted to talk about their feelings or talk about the truth: that he was leaving us and no one knew when he would be back. I casually walked away from the computer and tried not to think about it.

But as the days got closer, my father appeared either despondent or rageful. Suzanne had hired Chloe to do some work for her at the stationery store too, and when she came home one evening, my father demanded that she give him her paycheck like I had done. Because otherwise, we wouldn't have money for food until Gary pulled through for us with another wire transfer. But Chloe challenged him. I remember my father raising his voice, reeling from her unwillingness, his blood pressure through the roof as though he were some character out of *The Sopranos*, pointing his finger at her, lecturing her on family loyalty. Chloe went sobbing upstairs and into the attic, where she was sleeping.

I looked up at Josh. I decided that since my father hadn't been disbarred yet, it wouldn't be a lie entirely if I said he was a lawyer.

"Dad's a lawyer, Mom's a philanthropist." I picked up a Red Vine and chewed it.

"Cool. What kind of lawyer?"

"IPOs—that kind of thing," I said, shrugging it off and then changing the subject. "Are your parents still married?"

"They are. Been happily married for close to thirty years now. I'm lucky. What about you?"

"Yeah, mine too, really lucky."

A few days before the final competition, I was sitting in the audience. It was the dress rehearsal for the guys competing for the role of Keith Partridge. Emily and I were clapping and singing along, watching our friend Dave belt out George Michael's "Faith" into the microphone, when I looked over and saw Josh's father and Becky standing in the shadows of the wings next to the stage. He had his arms around Becky's waist, his hands moving downward as he caressed her ass. She gave him little kisses on the cheek before they separated quickly. *Oh my God, Josh's dad is having an affair with Becky.* I turned to Emily to see if she had noticed, but she was dancing along with Dave, who was as gorgeous as an Abercrombie & Fitch model, sliding back and forth onstage. I wondered if Josh knew. Thinking about it made my heart break for him. I wanted to be with him even more. I felt comfort in knowing I wasn't the only one with a family full of secrets.

It was the final performance, and I was standing in the spotlight on the enormous soundstage. The cameras were rolling, pink and blue neon lights spinning above and toward me. I walked forward with the microphone and with animated joy declared, "Hi, my name is Christina Grace, and I'd love to be Laurie Partridge. Not that I'm unhappy with myself, but, come on, Laurie Partridge is hot!" I felt numb. I sang the Mamas and the Papas' "California Dreamin'," strutting back and forth onstage, searching for my parents in the audience. But I couldn't find them against the blinding light, and when the judge read my scores—16.0, 16.5, 16.4, 16.2—I knew I had lost.

Todd Newton, one of the hosts of the live show, ran up and pointed his microphone at me. "How do you feel now that you've been cut, Christina?"

"I'm just glad I got the chance to perform; I feel great," I lied. The role of Laurie Partridge would eventually go to Emily, and too much pride hid the pain of rejection I felt along with the other girls who didn't make it. I had always been an actress—acting my way through life depending on who it was standing before me, molding myself into whoever I thought that person wanted me to be. I had no identity of my own unless I had the right props to define me. I craved validation, I craved significance. I wanted to be somebody. But I was so worried about how others perceived me, and I was so worried about my father; I never once stopped to think about who that somebody was.

Before I knew it, David Cassidy was pulling me back onstage, where we would come together once more with our arms wrapped around one another like one big happy family, performing for the last time:

Hel-lo world, here's a song that we're singing

Come on, get happy!

The audience clapped and cheered as I searched for my father in the audience. He looked uncomfortable, loosening his tie, and my mother clapped along because she felt obligated to, and Chloe looked bored. Then I saw Josh sitting in the front row. Tussled brown hair in a Led Zeppelin T-shirt. He wasn't working during the final show, and I remember that, at the end, we locked eyes, and he smiled at me. He was sitting next to an elegant woman in the audience. She had white-streaked hair that reminded me of Cruella De Vil. It must have been his mother. I watched as she clapped and sang along to the music, and I wondered if she knew.

Surrender

It was still dark outside. The rain was loud as it poured through the cop-per gutters along the bay window, creating a drumlike rhythm against the crying and dry heaving that woke me up. I stumbled out of bed and padded down the dark hallway toward the crack of light underneath the bathroom door. I stopped when I heard my mother throwing up, her hands gripping the porcelain toilet bowl. My heart was pounding at the thought of having to ask if she was all right.

I had wondered why, the night before, there was champagne and cake on the table. *Some sick good-bye party this is*. It felt more like a wake for the living dead. All night, my father stood in the kitchen wearing a Santa hat, holding a martini glass—shaken not stirred, the way he preferred it. He was acting abnormally happy, reminiscing about his days at William & Mary, while my mother kept dumping more Grey Goose into her glass, "to take the edge off," she said. I noticed her lost in thought before she turned around and flashed her elegant smile— the smile that all of the mothers of Washington, DC, used to envy. "Honey," they'd say to me, "your mother is so poised, so beautiful."

The morning was January 7, 2005, and my father was leaving for prison.

"Mom, are you okay?" I cracked open the bathroom door. Her cheek was resting on the toilet seat, her eyes wet and closed.

"Diet Coke. Get me Diet Coke," she whimpered before flinging herself back over the toilet with a loud groan. Gracie, her black-and-white papillon puppy, kept yelping and licking her ankles. Gracie had been a gift to fill Mom's empty nest when Mara and I had left for college. She took her everywhere: to the grocery store, to restaurants, and even to the movies, hiding her in her tote bag.

I pulled her red hair back into a ponytail as she spit and cried, unwanted vulnerability ripping her apart at the seams. When she leaned back, her eyes were bloodshot, and broken blood vessels had burst in her cheeks. *Your mother, she's so put together, so perfect, dear.*

"Okay, Mom. Be right back."

I entered the living room to the sound of an Olsen twin punch line. Chloe looked stoned watching an old episode of *Full House* surrounded by cardboard boxes; we hadn't yet unpacked everything. She had snuck out of the "good-bye party" to meet her new friend, Spencer, a sweet Jewish boy who sold marijuana plants out of the back of his pickup truck. Chloe and Spencer met in history class at the public charter school down the street. I went to pick her up one afternoon, and she introduced me to him. He brought me around to the back of his truck, pulled back what looked like a canvas pool cover to reveal hundreds of marijuana plants, and said, "My mom told me I have to be nice to you. Welcome to Cali." Spencer's mother was a friend of Suzanne's and an active member of the Pacific Palisades community. I stood there looking at the odd resemblance between the marijuana plants and the pattern on Chloe's Lilly Pulitzer dress. My sister hadn't made many friends yet except for Spencer, who decided to take her under his wing.

"Is Mara still sleeping?" I asked. Mara was about to be leaving to finish her second semester of her junior year in a few days. It was her winter break, and she had flown out from Texas to say good-bye.

Chloe shrugged, her eyes glued to the television screen, taming her emotions. "Probably."

Mara had informed everyone the night before that she wouldn't be waking up to say her good-bye; it would be too early in the morning for her. At the end of the night, she wrapped her arms around our father's neck, standing on her tiptoes to say good night as if it were just another night before bed.

When I walked into the kitchen, it was filled with an eerie combination of sitcom laugh tracks and my mother hyperventilating in the background as I searched for Diet Coke. Of course, we were out.

"Bambina!" My father, beaming, came walking into the kitchen. He was still wearing his Santa hat. "Mom's not feeling well this morning. What do you and Chloe think about taking your ol' dad to the airport?" I knew that "not feeling well" was a euphemism for "being incapable of operating a motor vehicle because your husband is going to prison."

"Okay, yeah. When do we need to leave?" I asked in a fog.

"We need to leave here in T-minus fifteen minutes."

I threw on my Ugg boots and my blue Juicy jumpsuit. I walked back over to Chloe, who was still lying on the sofa and now wearing her Langley High Lacrosse sweatshirt.

"Get up, we gotta go."

She grabbed the remote and turned off the TV.

Chloe and I waited for Dad by the front door, fumbling with our hands and staring at our feet, not saying a word to each other. We could hear our parents in the bathroom—my mother crying and a few of my father's whispered words as he kissed her good-bye: "It'll be okay. I love you." I tried not to listen, as the thought repulsed me, but I couldn't help but wonder if they talked about things like sex. I wondered if they had a conversation about whether or not they would remain faithful to each other for the next five years while my father was gone. From watching movies, I had heard about conjugal visits. I envisioned a sterile room with a single bed, guards standing outside listening, their right to intimacy now owned by the US government along with everything else.

When my father walked out of the bathroom, I turned to grab the car keys on the table, so he wouldn't think I was eavesdropping. He was wearing khaki shorts and a white polo. When I handed him the keys, I noticed that his usual accessories were absent: he wasn't wearing his Rolex watch, his gold wedding band, or even a belt. He appeared calm. Unemotional. Hands in his pockets.

"Ready to go, girls," he said.

"You don't need any luggage?" I asked.

"Your dad's got his ID and ticket."

"What about, like, toothpaste?"

"Don't worry. Your dad has everything he needs."

The sun was rising, but the rain kept the light in a faded gray, the kind prone to giving me headaches. Pacific Coast Highway was filled with panic-stricken drivers unfamiliar with how to operate their windshield wipers or drive like human beings. Chloe was curled up in the backseat, while I sat shotgun next to Dad. I looked over at the odometer, and next to it I could see that the red Check Engine light was still on. We were in the white Range Rover, and I wondered how much longer the SUV would last before we'd have to give it away because we couldn't afford to fix it.

My father leaned over and opened the glove compartment. He pulled out his gold aviator sunglasses, still in their original case, and handed them to me.

"Here, Bambina, hold on to these for me while I'm gone." They were his favorite pair. The pair he'd worn flying fighter jets in the air force. The pair he'd worn flying over our house when we were little.

"Yes!" I cried, making sure he knew how happy this made me. I put them on despite there not being a ray of sunshine in the sky. I glanced at myself in the side mirror and then looked over at him.

"Movie star," he whispered, letting me know how cool I looked.

I stared at the clock as we pulled up to the curb at Delta Airlines—7:02—and watched the second hand tick by as it crushed another moment in time between us. The windshield wipers were still slapping back and forth. We hopped out, and I headed toward the back of the car before I remembered: no luggage. Dad wouldn't be coming back next week, or the week after that, or any time soon.

He scooped up Chloe in his arms first and told her that he loved her. I couldn't hear whether or not Chloe said she loved him back; she just wanted to get out of the rain and scurried back into the passenger seat, avoiding any kind of real good-bye, her sadness and rage lost somewhere inside of her too.

"Make sure to pick up some more Diet Coke for Mom on the way home," my father said. He stood in front of me, neither one of us holding an umbrella.

"Okay," I mumbled. I was fighting back tears when suddenly he kneeled down, grabbed me underneath my arms, picked me up, and twirled me around the way he used to when I was a little girl after I had fallen asleep.

"Bambina! Time for bed." My father strolled into the family room.

"Carry me, *pleeeeeease*!" I begged, his little damsel in distress all snuggled up on the sofa.

"What do I need?" my father asked, puffing up his chest.

"Spinach!" I cried, cupping my hands and pretending to feed him. My father gobbled up the spinach, and his chest got bigger until he sang, "I'm Popeye the sailor man!" And picked me up in my pink feety pajamas and flew me off to bed.

"Butterfly kiss! I want a butterfly kiss!" I demanded once all tucked in. My father leaned down, brushing his lashes against my cheek before I felt it was safe enough to fall fast asleep.

"I love you," he said, setting me down on the curb. I wasn't ready for him to let me go.

"I love you too, Dad."

I didn't know how I would reach him, or when I would ever see or hear from him again. All I knew was that he was flying to a prison camp somewhere in Nevada, the same camp where Peter Bacanovic, Martha

Stewart's former stockbroker, was incarcerated. There were so many unanswered questions that filled my head, and I felt it was too late to ask a single one.

"Remember, Bambina." My father wagged his finger at me. "The best revenge is success."

And that was it. He turned around and walked through the automatic sliding glass doors, carrying nothing but a plane ticket. I studied him as he entered the concourse, looked left, then right, and then left again. He was figuring out which way to go. It was the first time I had ever seen him look uncertain.

- 8 -

Debt

My father's shoes were dumped in a pile by the front door. Sprawled out on the sofa were his Brooks Brothers suits and ties, still hooked on hangers. The Nantucket tie with little whales on it I gave him for Father's Day one year was on top. His underwear and white T-shirts were in another pile, while his wedding band and Rolex watch were in a Ziploc bag next to it. A half dozen boxes filled with old family photo albums were waiting there too.

"Mom?" I asked. "What is all this?" I could see her sitting at the table in the kitchen, going over paperwork.

"It's going into storage!" she yelled back, as though my father were dead. He'd been gone only a few weeks.

I walked into the kitchen to see what she was doing. There was an open letter from LMU addressed to me on the table. I picked it up. "What's this?"

Dear Christina,

Our bank has informed us of a check returned for "Non-Sufficient Funds." It is the policy of our bank to resubmit checks before returning them NSF. After the second presentment your check was returned. We understand this may be an oversight on your part, and we would like to resolve it quickly.

The check amount was $9,024.99 dated December 12, 2003. We assess a $25.00 service fee to all checks returned by the bank.

Your check may be redeemed immediately by payment via cashier check, money order, cash, Visa, or MasterCard credit card (no personal check). Please remit total amount due of $9,049.99 immediately.

Your Spring 2004 registration will be cancelled if payment is not received by January 9, 2004.

Very Truly Yours,
Collections Coordinator
Student Account Receivable

My father never finished paying my tuition. I had taken a fall leave of absence and was planning on returning for spring semester. It was the third week of January. We'd missed the cutoff. We didn't have the funds.

"Why are you opening my mail?" I asked.

"I'm trying to fix this," my mother said quivering, on the verge of tears.

Then I noticed two American Express cards on the table. One green. One platinum. "These have my name on them," I said. I picked up the statements next to each. One said Christina Grace Prousalis, American Express bank statement balance of $11,994.00; the other, Christina Grace Prousalis, American Express bank statement balance of $32,617.00.

I searched frantically through the pile of documents on the table: Christina Grace Prousalis, Capital One Bank statement balance of $9,029.00. Christina Grace Prousalis, Chase Bank statement balance of $12,360.00. Christina Grace Prousalis, Chase Bank statement balance of $2,250.00. Christina Grace Prousalis, Chase Bank statement balance of $7,176.00.

I stood there, having forgotten suddenly how to breathe. "I don't understand." This was not debt from some reckless shopping spree, as I always had to ask Mom and Dad's permission to use the credit card.

This was debt that had been put in my name without Dad telling me—in just the last year, since the FBI arrested him.

"We're going to take care of this." My mother tried to compose herself. "I'm trying to figure this out, it's just—" She burst into tears. "I'm sorry. I'm so sorry. Your father didn't explain any of this to me before he left."

It never occurred to me that my mother might not know how to pay bills, read bills, read credit card statements, write checks, pay rent. And when I thought about it, I don't ever remember her having her own checkbook. It was always "Honey, go ask your father; he writes the checks." I assumed she would be able to take care of things once my father left. When I was growing up, she was so organized, with her updated calendars, her fountain pens, her highlighters, and her fancy Rolodex. We never missed a doctor's appointment or a piano lesson; she organized benefits and cocktail parties.

I had always thought of my mother as an independent woman, when, in truth, she hadn't looked at a bill in over twenty years. She was free-falling before my eyes—off the pedestal I had kept her on all my life—as she sat there in front of more unpaid doctors' bills, health insurance bills, IRS inquiries, cell phone bills, and utility bills. The checkbook with my name on it from the Wells Fargo bank account was more than halfway used up. We were waiting on another chunk of money from Gary in Boca Raton to be wired into the account to pay next month's rent. After that, there would be one more wire transfer. What money was left would go toward our basic needs: rent, food, gas, health insurance, and car insurance. We were doing our best to stay afloat. But all of the money I made on *In Search of the Partridge Family* was running out. Mara, back in Texas, was fighting to get the financial aid she needed to finish school and landed a bartending job at the local dive bar. My mother took my place at Suzanne's stationery store in the Palisades working part-time, miserable waiting on all of those mothers whose lives reminded her of what was and what would never be again. And Spencer helped Chloe get a job at the skate shop on weekends, the trendy clothing store up the street from Suzanne's. We might be able to use a little of the money coming in from Gary to pay off some debt, but not anywhere close to covering more than $80,000 plus interest. Working for minimum wage wouldn't even begin to cover it.

The financial pressure turned into an unparalleled state of paralysis. Because I never knew what it was like to struggle. I never once pondered the possibility of not being provided for; I was going to be taken care of by my father. He told me I would never have to worry. I was never told how a credit card worked. It was never explained to me. I didn't learn it in high school. I didn't learn it my freshman year of college. I didn't learn it by watching the news or reading any kind of story. This was my introduction into the financial world of credit cards and loans.

If I was lucky, the creditors wouldn't call me on my cell phone. They would call the rental—those companies whose employees sounded like robots yet managed to instill the most heightened of emotions in me. They called from places named GC Services Limited Partnership, Collection Agency Division, Nationwide Credit, and Risk Management Alternatives. And the lawyers—the lawyers representing the moving company that my father used to ship everything out to California, the reason we had to open up the Wells Fargo bank account in my name to begin with—would not stop calling and threatening to sue me if I didn't pay up.

My father left me in nearly $100,000 worth of debt and didn't tell me before he left. I didn't know where he was. I had no way of getting in touch with him because he was somewhere in a holding facility waiting to be transferred to his designated prison. I didn't have an address to write him a letter. I would have to wait for him to write or call me. It could be months before I heard from him. I felt abandoned in the middle of a financial ocean where I didn't understand anything about money, credit cards, or debt; there was so much mystery beneath it that with my initial rage, I wondered and doubted if my rage was even real. My father, before, had never betrayed me. Betrayal was a foreign feeling I couldn't make sense of; I didn't know if it was honest or not. I wanted

only to speak with him because I believed he would tell me the truth—
that only after we spoke would I know what to feel.

A few days after I discovered the debt, an unknown number called my
cell phone. I was the only one home. Praying it wouldn't be a creditor,
as it usually was, I picked up. A female operator began speaking: "You
have an incoming call. This call is from a federal prison. You will not be
charged for this call. This call is from: Tom. To accept the call, dial five.
To decline the call, dial nine."

"Dad?"

"Bambina! Are you a movie star yet?"

"Dad!"

I was so excited to hear from him so soon that I had forgotten, for
a moment, the reality of all that was happening. My father let me know
quickly that our phone call would be timed. No more than fifteen minutes, and if for some reason his minutes ran out for the month, the phone
call could be cut off at any point, and he wouldn't be able to call me back
until the beginning of the next month. He told me he was at a camp on
an air force base, and I listened and pretended like everything was okay.
He asked about Mom, and I told him that she was working at the stationery store and Chloe had found a job just down the street. He asked
about my auditions, and I made it sound better than it was, to make him
happy, to make him not feel so bad. A few minutes into the conversation,
I mustered up the courage to ask him about all of the credit cards.

"Dad," I said, "I'm being threatened by creditors, by lawyers of the
moving company, because we haven't paid them. I don't know what
to do." I didn't yell at him and was careful about expressing any rage
because just hearing the words over the phone—"This call is from a
federal prison"—scared me. All I could think about was how vulnerable
he must feel. I had this heightened sense of empathy, where I became
more worried about my father's feelings than my own.

"Ignore them," he said. "Don't you worry, I will take care of every-

thing as soon as I'm home, which will hopefully be soon. We're filing an appeal, Bambina. It's looking good." He sounded so calm and sure on the phone. Yet I still didn't understand all that was going on. I didn't know what an appeal meant, and how could I just ignore people trying to sue me?

"And help out Mom as much as you can, Bambina. I know this is not a happy time, but it could be worse. I could go to Fallujah for a year and come home in a box. So we should thank our lucky stars." He was referring to the war in Iraq. I suddenly felt guilty for bringing up the credit card debt.

"Okay, but Dad—" *Beeeep!* I threw the phone to the floor and grunted with frustration. He'd run out of minutes. I had to tell someone what was going on. I couldn't handle it on my own, and my mother couldn't either. I called Josh.

Josh and I were officially a couple. He had taken me on a date to the movies a few weeks before my father left, and by the end of the night, an unexpected outbreak of hives had me pumped with an IV full of Benadryl in the emergency room at Cedars-Sinai Medical Center.

"Stress," the doctor suggested when I told him I wasn't allergic to anything but penicillin. I hadn't taken any penicillin. He asked Josh, standing next to me, what his connection to me was, and he said, "Boyfriend. I'm her boyfriend."

When Josh carried me out to the car, I looked at him googly eyed, drunk off Benadryl, and told him that I loved him. He knew I was having a hard time about my father by then. I had told him the truth on Halloween night. He was dressed up as Napoleon Dynamite, and I was dressed up as groupie Penny Lane from the movie *Almost Famous*. He wore a blond curly wig with a "Vote for Pedro" T-shirt, and I wore an old brown suede jacket of Mara's, plus round sunglasses and a feather boa. At the end of the night, he drove me home and kissed me in the car

as we listened to the Beatles' "I Saw Her Standing There." I tried not to ruin the moment, but I had to tell him.

"I want to tell you about my dad, but I'm afraid to," I said.

"Christina, I grew up in Los Angeles; it's hard to scare me."

"He's going to prison. He was indicted for securities fraud and was forced to enter a plea agreement with the government." My heartbeat felt suspended in time until he responded.

"I'm so sorry," Josh said without any judgment. I felt relieved, but I also felt the sudden need to defend my father.

"The government's just making an example out of him. He's filed an appeal, so hopefully he won't be gone for long."

"So he's not guilty?" Josh asked, slightly skeptical.

"No. I mean, I don't think so. The government forced him to enter a plea deal; otherwise, if he lost, he'd go to prison for a very long time. I had a really happy childhood, like a fairy tale."

"Well . . ." Josh paused. "If it makes you feel any better, I did too, and now I think my dad is fucking Becky." I didn't tell Josh that I already knew; I was glad to know the truth was out between us and didn't feel the need to tell him. After all, it was hard for me to talk about the truth of what went on around me. The commonality of each other's new-found pain and our once-perfect childhoods would glue us together with an intensity far too great for either of us to understand at such a young age. We fell madly in love.

Josh took on the role of "man of the house," helping my mother get situated, sometimes surprising us with sushi or pizza for dinner in the gaps when we weren't sure how we'd put food on the table. Josh had met my father a few times before he left for prison. They bonded over their favorite directors, such as Martin Scorsese and Terrence Malick. My father would send us letters from prison talking about Scorsese's latest film, like *The Aviator*, which was the last movie he saw before he surrendered. We had gone to see it on Christmas to distract us from the bleak and friendless holiday, with only a few presents that my mother bought from Santee Alley downtown, where street vendors sell knock-off designer purses and shoes.

Overwrought with anticipation, I ripped open the first letter I received from my father in prison. It was addressed: Movie Star! And Future Porsche Driver. His handwriting was written in flawless cursive. He told me once his father would make him practice words, letters, and sentences over and over again on lined paper until his writing became, itself, a work of art.

The very first thing he told me to do was send him a copy of *The Aviator* screenplay. He would write our story, he would tell the whole world about the injustices our family was facing. And I was happy to help. He let me know that he was safe. That his stay in prison was like a big Boy Scout camp with fighter jets flying over your head. "It's funny—they expect me to climb in an F-16 and take off, not polish it," he wrote. He reminded me to help out Mom as much as I could and that we should be grateful. Then closed with, "Hurry up and become a movie star and buy me an airplane. I would like a Gulfstream V, white with blue and gold stripes and tan leather interior. XXXOOO Dad."

When I told Josh about the phone calls from the lawyers and creditors, he didn't understand it either. Josh had grown up in the heart of Beverly Hills, a West Coast version of my own upbringing: raised around celebrity instead of politics; never having to worry about money, with a trust fund waiting for him. He thought that maybe the partner of his father's business manager could help us.

Ralph Adler agreed to meet my mother and me the following weekend. We drove to his palatial home, and my mother rang the intercom on the iron gate. "Hello?" a chipper voice answered.

"Hi, it's Gayle Prousalis and my daughter Christina." My mother's voice was soft, the way she sounds when she's nervous, giving me the feeling that if she spoke too loud, something might break.

A loud buzzer sounded, and the gates opened. We drove down the long driveway and parked next to a Maserati.

A maid wearing a gray dress and white apron opened the front door. We entered the foyer. The walls were covered with framed photographs of politicians, famous bands, musicians, and other celebrities with Ralph. I was staring at all the celebrity faces on the wall when Ralph bounced toward us. He was hyper and a bit disheveled.

"Ralph Adler, nice to meet you." He smiled as he shook my mother's hand. He had a clunky braces on his upper and lower teeth and tan rubber bands that stretched in between them, making him look like a skinny walrus. He gazed at my mother a little too long for my liking, and when he led us into the kitchen and family room, he stared at the sequins on the back of her jean pockets. My mother had started dressing more "LA" lately, which I found unsettling. I preferred her in a St. John knit, or jeans and a navy blazer.

We took a seat on the couch and pulled out the letters from the creditors, credit card bills, and IRS documents. Only recently did my mother find out that my father owed more than $500,000 in back taxes.

"Why don't you start with telling me what happened." Ralph sat on the ottoman. My mother told him our sob story. That my father left, and we didn't have any idea what a financial mess he had made until he was gone. Ralph placed his hand on my mother's knee—to express his compassion.

Then I showed him all of the bank statements and letters. Ralph looked at me with serious concern and asked, "Are you close with your father? Do you have a good relationship with him?" he asked. Why was he asking me this?

"Yeah, I am."

"Because the only way to clear the debt is to sue him. Are you willing to sue your father? Otherwise you can write letters to the creditors telling them it's not your debt, and see if they'll lower it, but there's no guarantee."

I sat on Ralph's sofa with my sweaty hands between my legs, feeling like I wanted to cry; not wanting to look at Mom, paralyzed with fear. I had never heard of credit card fraud before, and Ralph, gauging my reaction, careful with each word he spoke, never actually said the word *fraud*.

So I couldn't believe he was asking this. There was *no way* I was going to sue my father for the sake of money. I told myself there had to be another way. I had no tangible proof of my own that my father deserved to be in prison. And I didn't want to believe anyone else's. It was an impossible situation where, no matter how I looked at it, as a family, we couldn't win. There was no light at the end of this tunnel.

"I don't want to sue him," I stated calmly, as if I weren't responding to the most painful question anyone had ever asked me.

"What about your sisters? Are they in any debt?" Ralph asked.

"No," I said. Well, that wasn't true. Mara had a bill from one collection agency in the amount of a few thousand dollars, mostly from unpaid doctors' bills for treating her depression. She had told me over the phone a few days earlier. I told Ralph again that I would do anything except sue my father. So instead, he helped me draft a letter to each credit bureau and helped my mother draft a letter to LMU explaining our circumstances without incriminating my father any further.

> *To whom it may concern,*
>
> *I am writing this letter in an effort to explain that my credit score and previous debts have not been a result of my own irresponsibility. My father was sentenced to five years in a minimum-security prison. In an effort to protect my parents from further debts, my father placed several credit cards in my name, leaving me, at the age of eighteen, in over $80,000.00 worth of debt. As you can imagine the unbearable pressure at such a young age, I would like to request the understanding that these debts were not my own, and I continue to work hard at making sure payments are sent in on time. Thank you.*
>
> *Sincerely,*
> *Christina Grace Prousalis*

Loyola Marymount University
Office of the Controller

To whom it may concern,

    Fourteen months ago, my husband, Christina's father, was indicted by the federal government for securities fraud. He subsequently went to trial in June 2004 in New York, lost, and is currently serving fifty-seven months at Nellis Federal Penitentiary. At my husband's sentencing, the federal government required restitution of $12 million, which will stand until paid. Furthermore, the SEC has sued him civilly for an additional $12 million, which I believe he has defaulted on. We are under dire financial circumstances, which have prevented Christina from returning to LMU at present, I am writing this letter on her behalf. All of our financial assets were exhausted as a result of the trial. My husband has been disbarred and will be unable to resume his legal career when he is released from prison.

    We have lost our home in Virginia, and I have recently moved my other daughter into a rental in Los Angeles, so that I can be close to a support network of family and friends. I am currently working for minimum wage part-time while trying to reenter the workforce after twenty years of raising my children. I am trying to keep both Christina and her sister, Mara, in college. Their younger sister, Chloe, hopes to attend college as well. I hope that she will be able to do this. All three girls have pitched in, taking part-time work when they can find it, but we are rapidly running out of the small funds we have left, and I may have to move us in with friends.

    Thank you for giving every consideration to Christina and her request for assistance. Please don't hesitate to contact me if you have any further questions.

    Sincerely,

    Gayle Prousalis

After we went over the letters, Ralph demonstrated how to use an accounting software called QuickBooks in order to help us budget and keep track of incoming and outgoing monies—especially with the last wire transfer coming in from Gary. But I felt so intimidated by it. I'd never learned about managing money in high school, simple things like balancing a checkbook, nor had I learned about it my freshman year of college despite being offered numerous credit cards in the mail and around campus. And I wondered why it was so rude to talk about money. For fear of looking closely and seeing the reality of our financial situation, it was easier to live in the ambiguity of money rather than the specific details of it.

While Ralph showed us where to input all the numbers, I nodded earnestly at his computer screen, feigning enthusiasm and pretending to understand it—even though I knew my mother and I would never use it.

Before we left, Ralph said we could call him at any time with questions or concerns about anything at all. "Keep me posted on any responses you get from the credit bureaus or LMU, okay?" I began fantasizing about Ralph becoming a surrogate father figure. It felt comforting and familiar having a man take charge, showing us how much he cared, infusing my need for my father to come home, to protect me, to take care of me.

Sinking in Delusion

Rent was $7,000 a month. That's what it costs to keep up with the Joneses in Pacific Palisades, yet we were sinking fast, living in the delusional conceit that we could maintain a lifestyle of privilege and comfort. I was able to pay off about $12,000 of one of the American Express cards, $2,000 of LMU debt, and a couple thousand on my car payments because of Gary's wire transfer. The rest I would default on, and my credit score would continue to crash. There was still a lien against my BMW, so I couldn't sell it. The bank held the title. The Range Rover eventually gave out and died. My mother defaulted on the payments to her Jaguar, and the bank said it was on its way to claim the car in just a matter of days. And that was it. We would be on our own until my father came home. (That's what I told myself, anyway.) The four of us were hanging on by a thread.

The greatest news was that Mara was able to receive some financial aid for the rest of her time at SMU. My mother continued working at the stationery store and had began taking classes part-time in hopes of starting an interior design business. Perfect sense, since she had spent the last fifteen years decorating our home in Virginia.

Meanwhile, Chloe would come home each day from school and complain about how much she hated it even though her grades were better than they had ever been. She was making straight As.

"Well, what the hell else am I supposed to do other than study? It's not like I have any friends."

"What about Spencer?" I asked. "He's your friend."

"Spencer doesn't count."

Chloe came home one day crying because she had heard someone talking about a student who got stabbed in a fight the previous year. She was scared to go back after that, threatening to drop out and get her GED. I avoided being at the house as much as possible. And as much as my mother tried to re-create a home for us with the furniture we had left from the sale, it felt cold and lifeless. I knew we wouldn't be able to stay there much longer. We couldn't afford it. My mother said I needed to find another place to live as soon as possible because she and Chloe were going to have to move into a two-bedroom apartment.

I received a phone call from Emily, who had just finished filming the pilot episode of the *Partridge Family* remake. She invited me to come live with her at her apartment in Park La Brea, an enormous apartment complex that had been built in the heart of Los Angeles at the end of World War II. "Yes!" I told her. I wanted so desperately to have fun again, to be around friends again. These were supposed to be my wild college years, but I knew that leisure of mine was over. Maybe I could focus on acting more, and living with Emily would help inspire that. But I was worried about rent. I'd had only a few job leads. Josh's parents made a phone call to the manager they were friends with at an upscale restaurant called La Scala in Beverly Hills, but I hadn't heard back yet. Emily said that as long as I could manage $500 a month, I could have the smaller bedroom. I thanked her and told her it was a deal, and prayed that I would get hired for the restaurant job. In the meantime, my father had written a letter asking me to help him with a few things.

He had begun to write the screenplay of our life, but that it would remain top secret until he finished. He raved about *The Aviator*, obsessively, as his inspiration before he told me that I must go in search of his computer to download documents to a disk. "There are very, very important documents and information in this area and I am afraid I might lose them if something happens to the computer. Once the download is complete, please keep the disk in a safe place . . . Break a leg on your auditions . . . XXXOOO Dad."

Josh was busy working on a new reality television show about flipping houses, so I went to the storage unit on my own to find my father's computer. I pulled up to the bleak building underneath the Santa Monica Freeway, punched in the code to the garage, and parked my car.

There were no windows inside. I walked down the fluorescent-lit corridor, passing numbers on consecutive metal doors, and wondered if prison looked like this. I turned the lock and yanked on the metal door, kicking up the smell of dust and old memories. My father's suits dumped on top of the brown boxes, just as I'd seen them in the front hallway a few weeks back. My mother hadn't bothered to cover them up. It was like she just wanted them to rot away with time. His wooden airplane propeller was leaning against the wall in the corner. He kept that propeller next to the giant globe in his library, which would light up when you touched it. It was the propeller of a prop airplane, and he refused to sell it with the estate sale, while the globe sold fast.

I threw his pile of suits to the side so I could get to the brown boxes. I searched, digging down for his computer. My mother had dumped all of our old framed family photos in these boxes. I found the photograph of my parents sitting in a booth together at Martin's Tavern in Georgetown, the landmark restaurant and frequent hangout for presidents like Nixon and Kennedy, where plaques with their engraved names hang above their designated booths. The picture used to be in our family room on the console next to the fireplace. My mother in her signature burgundy lipstick and gold Tiffany mesh bracelet, and my father in his pin-striped jacket and red Hermès tie; they were laughing, and they looked so happy. I set down the pictures in a neat stack. I couldn't look at them anymore.

I was coughing from the dust when finally I found the box with his computer in it and other work files. "BusyBox" had been written in black Sharpie on the side. I remember my father was so excited about the prospect of BusyBox. He had just finished talking to Steve Madden, the successful shoe company bearing his name. Only later would I learn that in 2002 Steve Madden was sentenced to three and a half years in prison for money laundering and securities fraud. I had bought my first pair of platform shoes from Steve Madden and was ecstatic at the thought of my father and him doing business together. My father also mentioned he was speaking with the Nantucket Nectars guys, Tom and Tom, about other potential businesses. We had boxes of their juices in the kitchen pantry. But BusyBox was what excited my father the most. It had something to do with selling digital pictures and videos online. He told me he was going to meet with Bill Gates about possibly investing. There were piles and piles of BusyBox pitches on the floor of the library, and every time I carried my juice box near them, he would yell at me and tell me to finish my juice before I entered so I wouldn't spill it on anything.

Most of the documents were leftover court papers and depositions full of legal jargon I didn't understand. I couldn't bother to keep reading all of it. I grabbed his computer, put the boxes back, and tossed his clothes back on top. I just wanted to get out of this storage unit. It was dark and felt haunted. I locked the door, and on my way home, I stopped off at Staples to pick up a disk so I could save all the necessary documents he'd wanted.

When I got back to the house, I closed the door behind me, sat on the floor in front of the TV, and opened up his laptop computer. I scrolled through "My Documents," searching for something, but I didn't know what. I was curious. I found information on General Edward Ratkovich, my father's mentor, a decorated air force general who would visit the house with bags of Tootsie Rolls and Nerds when I was little. He was the director of intelligence in Stuttgart, Germany, for the US European Command. I didn't know it at the time, but the

general had recently died. My father had never mentioned it. When I
scrolled through the information, it said that he was the one who purchased MVSI Inc., a company taken public by a firm called Stratton
Oakmont Inc. It said that he was the one who purchased Socrates Computer Systems, and when I Googled it, I wasn't sure if it had anything
to do with the earlier Project Socrates: a classified US Defense Intelligence Agency program first started under the Reagan administration
to determine America's economic competitiveness. *"It's the government's
fault, Christina."* So I kept scrolling through.

Then I came across a folder titled "Albania," and I clicked on it.

I remembered the purple orchid in the front hall. Classical music was
echoing through each room in the house, and my mother had been
anxious that morning, more uptight than usual. Behar and his wife
were coming for dinner, and a translator would be present. Behar was a
businessman running for office in Albania, and he and my father were
orchestrating a deal to build an American university there. I was told to
be on my best behavior that night. I was sixteen. My father had showed
me the floor plans for the university a few nights earlier in the kitchen
after school. I don't know how the deal was related to IPOs and the
stock market. I never asked. I never asked my father about his work.
The only time I did was in middle school. My religion teacher had
asked me what he did for a living—I don't remember why she asked
me this in the middle of class—but I told her he was a securities lawyer;
not the kind that went to court. And I realized I had no idea what this
meant. So that night at dinner, I asked him, and he explained to me
about IPOs, the stock market, and taking companies public. But when
I started asking too many questions because I didn't understand what
he was talking about, he grew frustrated with me and snapped, "That's
enough; finish your dinner," making me feel that I wasn't smart enough
to understand it—that I was better off not asking questions.

"Christina, darling, we're in the living room!" my mother called.

I was wearing Mara's floral Betsey Johnson dress, one she left behind while studying in Switzerland. I always knew when my mother was faking it; when she was trying hard to exude European charm. When she showed us off, her voice extended into drawn-out vowels and ascended into a higher register that bugged me. I walked over to say hello and sat down on the yellow sofa in front of the Brie cheese and crackers as I watched Behar and his wife, in their black suits, sip Kir Royales in crystal flute glasses. They asked me about my "studies." The translator, wearing a plain gray suit, sat quietly next to them.

I felt stiff the entire evening. I was pretending to be in another century with manners I didn't even know I had. The aura between us, foreign, the crystal chandelier dimmed to spotlight on lamb chops, green beans, and crescent rolls. I chewed with my mouth closed the entire time.

It was an old email exchange. The document opened up on the screen, and all I saw were words from Behar: "The deal off—the American university—everything off." Someone had been killed. *Stabbed* was the word I saw printed in Times New Roman font. And it had something to do with money. Of course. I can't remember if the date was before or after the trial. It must have been after, because that was when my father was despondent, right before he left for prison. I thought it was just because he was afraid to leave. But maybe it was because the American university deal was the only one he had left. Now nothing was left. Any hope for a future business and making money for our family was gone.

I grabbed the new disk next to me and shoved it into the computer. I didn't believe what I saw, or I saw what I saw but didn't believe my father's business could involve violence. I slammed his laptop shut. I felt paralyzed by what I'd just seen. I couldn't erase the words from my mind. But I could bury them in an empty part of me where they would sit, and they would wait, while I told no one, while the possibility meant everything and nothing—a lie I would tell myself through sheer omission, because the terrifying truth was unacceptable.

I started spending most nights at Josh's parents' house in Beverly Hills. It felt like the West Coast version of our former home. Perched halfway up Coldwater Canyon, it was a Spanish-style house with big glass windows, an alarm, a housekeeper, a fully stocked fridge, a swimming pool, and a mom who loved to cook. It was easy to live vicariously through them, as though nothing was changing for me.

When I fell asleep with Josh that night, that's when the first night terror hit.

I was standing, staring at the walls of the Yellow Oval Room in the White House. The same color yellow as our living room, my mother had said. Not too bright, not too dull, just right. Crystal, crystal vases, crystal service bells, crystal trinkets, crystal glasses, crystal bowls, and crystal statues engulfed me. My chest felt constricted, but the room itself was airy. The French doors opened to the balcony with towering willow trees whose branches grazed limestone columns and lace curtains drifted out in the humid air. I was stuck, paralyzed. I couldn't breathe. I couldn't cry, my tears and breath clogging my windpipe like lava. My young reflection stared back in the gold Louis XV French mirror, while the acanthus leaves curled around beveled glass. I was eleven years old and wearing my choir uniform. And when I turned my neck, General Ratkovich appeared before me like a ghost on the Persian rug. My patent leather shoes would not step near him. My uniform, green, like Kermit the frog. His uniform, blue and gold, like war.

He shook his head at me with great disappointment. My right arm was heavy as it reached for my mother's crystal rabbit. The general's eyes burned mine. When I grabbed the rabbit, I pitched it hard over and over until he disappeared. Then I pitched the vase, the service bell, the bowl, praying for relief from the sound of shattered glass, but nothing would break. I paced back and forth in front of the fireplace, wanting to cry. But I couldn't cry. I couldn't breathe. I was suffocating and shaking, my arms gripped when suddenly my unwavering screams, steady and deep in their grunt, woke me up. I shot up drenched in sweat. Josh grabbed me tight. We rocked back and forth as I sobbed, disoriented, in his arms. Until it was safe to look around the room, to remember where I was, Josh kept kissing my forehead and purring, "Shhh, it's okay. You're okay." I held on to him as though I were falling off a cliff. "Don't let me go, just don't let me go."

Post-traumatic stress disorder is what shrinks call this delayed unconscious feeling of terror. It appeared only in my dreams. Josh suggested I see a psychiatrist. I had never seen a psychiatrist before. "I don't need one," I told him. "I'm fine." He was seeing one for his parents' separation. His father had just leased an apartment down the street and was still seeing Becky.

"I like having a therapist. She gives you a safe place to unload all of your thoughts and feelings without being judged," he said. But I was firm with him and held my ground. "No. I don't need it. I'm not interested." My father was the one who had kept me safe.

Wearing my pink feety pajamas, I held on to my father's hand as we followed the beam of his flashlight down the back staircase.

"Show me where the monsters are, Bambina," he said as we set foot into the playroom. The white bookshelf was filled with Shel Silverstein books, Nancy Drew novels, and Hans Christian Andersen fairy tales.

"In there," I whispered, pointing to the door of the electrical room. This was a nightly routine, checking for monsters. I wouldn't be able to sleep otherwise.

My father opened the door to the humming of air-conditioning pumps. "Nope. No monsters!"

When he carried me up into my room, I made sure he checked my closet too. I would watch as he rummaged through winter sweat-

ers, shoes, and Halloween costumes. "Nope. No monsters, Bambina!" Once we were in the clear, he tucked me into bed so tight I could barely move my arms underneath the sheets. It was the way I liked it, cocooned in tight covers. Safe. Then he would plop down next to me, and I'd watch him put his arms behind his head and close his eyes. But before he would doze off, we listened to the engines of commercial airplanes descending into Reagan National Airport along the Potomac River running just behind our house. My father would predict each plane that soared past us—"747, 727, Cargo 737 . . ."—until I was fast asleep.

"Christina! Today is your birthday!"—the first without my father—"rather than send you a silly card, I thought that I would write you a letter." They were hunting for me, the creditors and attorneys. I was in tears from the pressure, having locked myself in the bathroom for fear they would literally find me; I sat on the cold floor with my back up against the door holding the letter in my hand while the phone kept ringing in the other room. It was another attorney threatening to sue me over the American Express credit card balance, yelling things I didn't understand into the answering machine. Creditors and more creditors followed thereafter. And the only thing I could think about was how I was going to make the $58 in my bank account last until I found a job. Digging myself into a deeper grave, a few days earlier I had received a notice in the mail informing me that, as expected, the letters I sent to the credit bureaus didn't work.

> *Dear Christina Grace Prousalis, thank you for contacting Transunion. Our goal is to maintain complete and accurate information below in response to your request. Re: dispute status. After reviewing your correspondence, we were unable to determine the nature of your request. To investigate information contained in your credit report, please specify why you are disputing it (for example, "this is not my account," "I have never*

paid late," "I have paid this account in full," etc.). Unless you provide
us this information, your request will be considered frivolous under the
federal Fair Credit Reporting Act, and we will be unable to initiate an
investigation.

Specifying would have meant admitting that my father had stolen
my identity by taking out the credit cards in my name. Even the credit
bureaus were calling out my ambiguity; my inability to see clearly or
truthfully. The only way I justified it—the only way I managed to pick
myself up off that floor and take the abuse from the creditors—was
by believing my father's words: "I'm really hoping to leave this place
this summer. . . . We're going to make a huge recovery! Success is the
best revenge . . . within 24 months after I vacate this air base, believe
me, we will be on <u>Top</u> of the world again. Also because you're going
to be a big film star, I will have a beautiful new Gulfstream to fly us to
Paris for lunch! . . . I'm glad your BMW is waxed. Try not to leave the
top down in the sun—it's really tough on leather—except, of course,
when you're driving in your aviators . . . xoxo Dad." He was so optimistic about coming home early, minimizing our financial avalanche,
I wanted to believe in him because I had no comprehension of what or
how it would cost me.

I took a deep breath and stood up, my head light and my body heavy
with the weight of the world as I glided toward the ringing telephone.
I grabbed it and then threw it as hard as I could against the wall until it
shut up. In a few hours, Josh would be taking me to dinner to celebrate
my birthday. He was trying to make me happy, but most days I couldn't
see him as I struggled to stay present, walking through each day more
afraid of the next. All I wanted to do was climb into bed that night and
pray that I'd never wake up.

First Job

There was no use for my name anymore. Dried up and used, it would remain on the "most wanted" list in computer systems at all the credit bureaus and bank law firms. Meanwhile, my mother had to figure out a way to negotiate a deal with the new landlord so that she and Chloe could keep a roof over their heads. They were moving into a two-bedroom town house, and my mother needed to convince the landlord to rent to her and Chloe despite their not having anyone to cosign the lease.

"An entire year's worth of rent. Up front," the landlord told her.

"This is crazy, Mom. It's too expensive!" I tried to talk her out of it. I knew the rest of the money from Gary wouldn't last much longer; it was his last wire transfer, and my mother had no plan in place for what she would do once it was gone.

The town house was in the Highlands, an isolated community high up in the Santa Monica Mountains, and hard to find if you aren't a native. It had one bedroom on the bottom floor, a kitchen, a living room and eating area, and a second bedroom on the top floor. It was only a few thousand dollars less than the rental in the village. We had been looking at apartments all day in Hollywood, West Hollywood, and Westwood, but none would suffice. My mother's anxiety flared up, she was short tempered, and we had stopped speaking to each other by the end of the day for fear of an outburst. Humility was not an option.

"I'm taking it," my mother reiterated. "I will not lose my dignity, goddamn it." She said it was imperative to stay in town because of the school district. She didn't want to have to pull Chloe out of Pali High and place her in a school farther east toward the city. I sat there, flaming with anxiety, watching my mother write a check in my name for thousands of dollars. And I don't remember my mother running the decision by anyone: not Ralph Adler, not her friend Suzanne. Money still remained a dirty secret, and how we used it would continue wrapping me in shame. I knew it was a reckless mistake and that there had to be a better, smarter way, but I couldn't argue with her anymore. She wouldn't listen, and I didn't have the answers.

My father had been moved from the camp on the air force base in Nevada to a new federal prison in Herlong, California, way up in the cold and windy northeast corner of the state. He claimed the prison had determined that he was a threat to flee because of the nearby fighter jets. It had been a few weeks since anyone had heard from him. Mara would occasionally check in with us from Texas. She had landed a job at the Chanel makeup counter at the mall and promised that as soon as she graduated the following year, we would get an apartment together in Los Angeles.

Within the same week as my mother's move, I made my last trip across town with my things before settling into Emily's apartment. I had landed the job at La Scala.

In the beginning, it wasn't so bad because Ralph Adler would come in to check on me. His office was down the street. He would wrap me up in a bear hug and ask me how my budgeting was going and if I was using my QuickBooks. I'd lie and tell him it was going great because I didn't want him to think I was stupid and couldn't figure out the damn thing, which I couldn't.

La Scala is an Italian restaurant where movie stars like Warren Beatty and Jane Fonda dine; also agents, lawyers, and studio executives. They stroll in at one in the afternoon for the Hollywood lunch hour and, without fail, complain about needing a booth. They will actually die if they do not have that full, round booth. Not a half booth—the booth where only one side is a booth, where only one or two people get to sit, and then the others have to, God forbid, sit in chairs—no, they need the full, round, red-leather booth where everyone's ass gets a cushion, or they will die. And if I do not give them that booth, they will humiliate me in front of waiting tourists and other angry guests behind them, their entitlement always traveling backward like a disease to each and every other guest, who are now thinking they can pull the same shtick.

I wasn't making nearly enough money to put up with their bullshit booth problems. So I started lying, to save myself. "Oh, I'm *so* sorry, that booth is taken," I'd say. Even though it wasn't. So they would tip me off—mostly twenties, but if I was lucky and it was a busy night, they'd whip out the Benjamins. It worked for a while, until one night it was slow, and a few customers refused to tip me. "We'll just wait for a booth to open up, then." They knew I was lying. The manager, who wore a pin on his blazer, as if this were a country club, came over and asked me why the customers hadn't been seated. I didn't have an answer for him. I managed to last there for about a year before I was fired.

I wondered if we, as a family, had acted as entitled as some of the customers who came in to La Scala. A few times my father had complained when we weren't given the finest table in the house. He'd cause a scene until it was handled and we were sitting where he wanted. And *never* near the bathrooms. *Never.* I remember our first family trip to New York, when I was ten. It was 1995. Doormen in white gloves stood beside the gold revolving doors of the Plaza Hotel, moving toward us as our limousine pulled up. Chloe hopped out first, running up the red-carpeted steps, hyper, excited to be in the Big Apple. I ran up behind her and then turned around. "You guys, hurry up!" I wanted to run inside, explore the hotel. *Home Alone 2* had been released a few years earlier. Ever since, we had been begging our parents to take us to New York.

"Girls, hold the bus!" my father yelled, trying to turn on the video camera. Mara stood with her arms crossed. She had entered her Bush and Nirvana grunge phase; she wanted to be at the Chelsea Hotel downtown, smoking cigarettes. She held up her hand in front of the lens. "Don't film me," she said.

"Oh, Mara, stop being such a sourpuss," my father replied.

"Daddy! Daddy! Film me! Film me!" I cried, craving his attention.

Doormen pushed our mountain of Louis Vuitton trunks inside toward the front desk.

"Reservation name?" the front desk clerk asked.

"Prousalis." Dad took out his wallet from inside his camel blazer.

"I'm sorry, sir. I do not have a reservation under the name Prousalis. Could it be under a different name?"

"Negative," my father said. He was always using flight terms when dealing with "pedestrians."

"I'm sorry, sir. I do not have a reservation under that name." I looked up at my dad and felt the energy of his rage brewing.

"Girls, come with me," said my mother, sensing a scene coming between my father and the front desk. "I want to show you Eloise. Do you know who Eloise is?" She ushered us into the hallway of the lobby. As we walked away, I could hear my father demanding to speak with the general manager. I knew what his face looked like: his furrowed brow, his blood pressure shooting through the roof as he raised his voice, like whenever Mara and I would fight during a conference call.

I held my mother's hand and stared at the gold-framed portrait hanging on the marble wall.

"Eloise was the little girl who lived on the tippy-top floor of this hotel," my mother explained. I stared at the disheveled blond girl with the red bow in her hair and her blue suspenders and wondered if she ever got lonely.

"I want to be like Eloise!" Chloe cried. Mara sat on a chair a few feet away from us with her head leaning back against the wall, sighing loudly so that everyone could hear her exasperation.

Twenty minutes later, my father walked over with the general manager.

"Let's go, girls." He was satisfied and calm.

The general manager led us into one of the elevators. A bellman followed with our trunks. My father stood tall, with a smirk on his face. "Girls, are you ready for the surprise?"

I watched as the general manager whipped out a special card and inserted it above all the elevator buttons. We watched the PH button light up in all its glory.

"Tom, you're joking!" my mother gasped. She couldn't believe it.

"The presidential suite," my father boasted.

Chloe and I shrieked, and Mara even smiled. "No way, Dad."

"*Way,*" he replied. My mother kneeled down to Chloe, and her eyes grew big and wide. "Guess what! We're staying on the tippy-top floor, where Eloise lived!"

Chloe danced around in circles and hugged her waist.

The elevator doors opened, and we made our way down a private hallway. The general manager took out a gold key from his pocket and inserted it into the lock of the double doors while naming all the celebrities who'd previously slept where we were about to: "Michael Jackson, Nicole Kidman, Princess Diana."

"Wow! Wow! Wow!" I repeated, making my father chuckle.

The bellman stopped in the foyer and asked my father where we would like each suitcase.

"Here is fine," Dad said, and took out two $100 bills as a tip for their service.

"Thank you very much, sir," the bellman said, tipping his hat.

"Enjoy your stay, and welcome to the Plaza," the general manager said. "A butler will be arriving shortly to take your dinner order."

The private dining room was already set with crystal glasses and Spode china.

"Girls, how about some lobster!" my father yelled as we trickled off to explore the suite. It was two floors with four bedrooms, each room a different color and style, with floor-to-ceiling silk drapes and a view of all Manhattan. It was now dark outside, and the city lights twinkled like millions of stars in the distance.

My mother sat down at the black grand piano in the gold-and-red-colored living room and played the ballad "Greensleeves," allegedly composed by Henry VIII for his lover and future queen Anne Boleyn. I stood next to her, watching her fingers pound in passionate fever, concentrating on the notes, and slowing down for each high note as if it were her lullaby.

That night, we ate pounds of fresh lobsters in our nightgowns, my father in his blue flannel pajamas. We slurped on chocolate milkshakes for dessert, each one delivered on its own silver platter, with extra cherries on the side, and my father surprised us with tickets to see *The Lion King* the following night. It was a family slumber party in the most famous suite of the most famous hotel in America. We were on top of the world.

Maybe my father never made a reservation at the Plaza. Maybe he convinced the general manager that an employee had fallen short on the job and made a grave mistake. Maybe it was a gamble he felt worth taking. What were the odds that the presidential suite would be occupied? The thought occurred to me, but I didn't dwell on it. I didn't know it at the time, but the manipulating and rating of customers would serve me well in nightlife. I had been schmoozing since the age of eleven. I thought La Scala was where I first learned how to hustle, but I had no idea what hustling meant.

Michele and Arianna

I felt my mother was splitting into two different women: one I longed for but could find only in my memory, and the other, alive yet with the life in her dimmed to that of a distant stranger.

"You want to know how disgusting it was? How sick it felt being there, seeing him like that? Jesus Christ, Christina."

I'd asked my mother what it was like visiting my father in prison. She and Chloe had gone to visit him up in Herlong. I didn't go with them because I couldn't afford to miss work. And when I tried to ask my sister what it was like, she quipped, "Christina, are you *trying* to ruin my day?" They didn't want to talk about it. It was after this visit to the prison that my mother's drinking escalated, and things started getting worse.

Josh's family had invited us to the Screen Actors Guild Awards. By the end of the evening, my fantasy world of limos, photographers, and Hollywood's most glamorous movie stars burst when I realized my mother was about to power barf three feet from the cast of *Good Night and Good Luck,* leaving her on her knees in the bathroom at the Shrine Auditorium in her Christian Lacroix gown—the same gown she'd worn to President Bill Clinton's 1997 inauguration ball. Josh had to scoop her up in his arms and carry her out to the limo, with her head resting on his chest and her gown bunched up around his face, like he was cradling a sleeping toddler in a princess dress. For the next four days, she was bedridden at Josh's parents' house. "Bad food poisoning" is what she insisted it was when she finally woke up.

A few nights later, Chloe called me hysterical because Mom had hit the curb on the corner of Pacific Coast Highway and Sunset Boulevard in her Jaguar, blowing out a tire after another night of drinking. The bank never came to repossess the car, and I presumed it was simply because they couldn't find her. "She's passed out in her clothes with her shoes still on, lying on top of her bed," Chloe cried.

The $200,000 from Gary was gone.

Many years later, my mother would admit to having had a nervous breakdown. After the SAG Awards, one of her best friends flew in to take care of her for a few days. During her first marriage, Michele had been front and center in the Washington scene. After a bitter divorce battle, she remarried an investment banker and spent most of her time in Houston, far away from the A-lister, cave-dweller lifestyle, yet still wealthier than most. She and my mother remained friends through it all. And after Michele saw my mother in the state she was in—frail, glazed eyes, anxious, depressed, in debt, drinking too much—she flew her out to Colorado to stay at her country home for a week of rehabilitation.

My mother didn't tell anyone where she was going, so when she returned, Suzanne had fired her from the stationery store. I never could get a straight answer as to why specifically she was fired, as Suzanne and my mother had been lifelong friends, but I knew there were many days when she just couldn't get out of bed, showed up late, or not at all. My mother started taking antidepressants after that, although, she said, "They give me the shakes." It was one of the side effects, but the pills helped her get out of bed each morning.

I tried my best to encourage her to find work with higher pay. After all, she had a degree in history from UCLA and had worked on Capitol Hill. But my mother wasn't so optimistic. She had just turned fifty, and whenever I brought up the subject, she got confrontational with me, letting me know I was too young to understand her grave circumstances. "No one is going to hire a fifty-year-old woman who's been out of the workforce for nearly twenty years. No one," she said despairingly.

But when my mother returned, Arianna called. She invited us for tea at the Peninsula Hotel. Two of the few loyal friends, Nancy and John Palmer (the late NBC News journalist), reconnected us. Nancy and my father wrote to each other, and she would remain the constant thread tying me to the life I wanted back and the life I wanted to forget all at the same time. At first, I assumed that the Palmers stayed in touch with us because we were a "good story," but through it all, they remained kind and gracious.

My parents met Arianna when her oldest daughter, Christina, and Chloe went to elementary school together. At the time, Arianna was still married to Michael Huffington after he'd defeated my mother's old boss Bob Lagomarsino for the Republican seat. Chloe was always coming home and bragging that a manicurist had come to their house for mani pedis, and how Arianna would create their own personal spa. I remember the first time I met Arianna. I went with my mother to pick up Chloe at her big stone house in the Wesley Heights neighborhood of Washington, DC. It was Arianna's daughter's birthday party, and Arianna handed me a goodie bag even though I hadn't attended the party. She was always so warm and took a liking to us because of my father's Greek heritage. "Greek girls, like me!" she exclaimed in her famous accent. Arianna adored my father. They would flirt with each other at holiday parties, talk about being raised Greek Orthodox, and laugh about their overbearing Greek parents.

I thought that Arianna could help my mother reconnect with her political background, as Arianna had just run for governor of California. Maybe she could help her find a job. So we pulled it together and headed to the Peninsula Hotel in Beverly Hills for tea with Arianna, Christina, and Isabella, her youngest daughter. Chloe had managed to come up with some excuse as to why she couldn't come with us.

We pulled into the semicircular driveway of the luxury hotel. Gleaming black Mercedes and town cars were parked out front. My car was dirty, but I didn't have the money to get it washed, and my mother asked me to drive because her car needed servicing. I wore a mock Chanel jacket, pearls, and my jean skirt, while my mother was back to her Escada blazer and Chanel ballerina flats, looking very "DC."

We sat on blue-green silk couches and sipped English breakfast tea. Enormous fireplaces lit up either end of the tearoom, and orchids curled in every corner. Arianna was as vibrant as I remembered her, in a sleek black pantsuit, her hair short and red like my mother's. People kept walking up to our table to say hello and kiss her on the cheek. After one man came over, Arianna leaned into the center of the table, whispered, "That was Oprah's producer," and winked.

I studied my mother, who remained quiet and reserved until Arianna asked about my father. "Gayle, how is Tom doing? He's such a wonderful father," she declared, and then, genuinely concerned, asked, "How are you and the girls holding up? Seriously." It was evident she knew all that had happened. I wanted my mother to tell her the truth, to say we were really struggling, that she needed a steady job and steady income. But she clammed up. She got stiff, the way she does when I ask about her father. She smiled. "You know, we're great, doing fine." She didn't want to ask for help. She was somewhere else. Until that moment, I'd felt maybe we still belonged; it seemed we'd taken back our past for just those few moments, until my mother refused to speak our truth. She wanted to go home. She wanted to lock herself in the bathroom or pull the covers over her head.

The rest of the afternoon, we talked about school, and what Christina's and Isabella's plans were for college, and whether or not Chloe liked Pacific Palisades High School, and how my auditioning was going. "Great. Everything is fine."

Before she kissed us good-bye, Arianna told us about a website she had been working on launching, which would become the multimillion-dollar news website the *Huffington Post*.

When we left the hotel, we felt deflated; the balloon of potential empty and airless. There was nothing but missed opportunity and whiffs of a life to which we were no longer entitled. Maybe we never were. I saw from my mother's response to Arianna's question that it was still not safe to talk about money. I told myself it wasn't because my father was a criminal but because even if we did explain it to Arianna or to anyone else—about all the debt we were in, about our family's financial crisis—they wouldn't understand. *It was for love; it was for the family.* And maybe my mother was right about women her age. Arianna's position was rare. But I didn't want to believe that what my mother had said was true: that it was impossible for a fifty-year-old woman to rejoin the workforce after having raised her family for the last twenty years. I was beginning to see the facade of the women I grew up around: the facade of their independence. I didn't understand that most were being fully supported by their husbands' money. The mothers and wives seemed so busy "working"—putting together event after event, board meeting after board meeting. As the veil of truth was lifting, I could see my mother, afraid to emancipate herself from within while learning about the barrier that keeps us unequal from men, crushing her all at the same time.

"Furlough"

"Honey!" Madeline yelled from her bedroom down the corridor. I was hanging my clothes in Josh's closet. I'd spent all day rearranging my shabby-chic childhood bedroom furniture among Josh's gold soccer trophies and *Star Wars* posters. The lease had ended at Emily's apartment, and I was planning on living with Mara when she graduated, but there was a six-month gap where I needed a place to live. Josh had moved into an apartment at the bottom of Laurel Canyon, and we weren't ready to move in together yet, so I figured his mother was a better choice. Besides, Madeline had that huge house all to herself; she wanted the company.

"How do I look?" she asked, removing the ice packs from her black-and-blue swollen eyes. She had arrived home from the hospital, opting for liposuction and lifting her eyelids. She opened them about halfway to look at me, propped up in her four-post California king-size bed, French doors opened to the backyard swimming pool.

"You look just like you do in the picture in the hallway," I told her, trying not to look nauseous. The photo in the hallway was of her in her early thirties, holding Josh on the playground.

"When I woke up from the surgery, the woman told me to put on this girdle. To keep everything tight, you know?" She put her hands around her skinny thighs. "Extra small, the woman told me. And look, it even has its own pee hole!"

"You look so . . . *young,*" I said, sitting next to her on the silk bedspread, wanting to comfort her more but not knowing how. A few weeks earlier, in the kitchen, she had asked me about Becky, about how she was on set of *The Partridge Family*, and how old she was. She was only a few years older than me. Madeline cried, and I tried to remind her how beautiful she was. She told me she'd thought she and Josh's father would grow old together; that when he retired from showbiz, she would go back to school and become a therapist, and it would be her turn to work. But now she was having to do it on her own. She had dedicated her life to this man, and for what? To be left high and dry for the old Hollywood cliché. I thought about my mother too. I could see why they had become good friends: not just because misery loves company but also because each had lost a man who would no longer take care of her, and now they were having to figure out nearly thirty years later how to become independent women. I was glad I didn't move in with Josh. I made a promise to myself that night, despite having been fired from La Scala, that I would pull it together as best I could, that I would find a better-paying job, that I would work, and that I would never depend on a man for money or give away my life to him.

I met a girl through Emily who worked for a fashion designer. She knew everyone in nightlife. "You gotta go in for the interview looking sexy. Not like Laurie Partridge, and none of that East Coast BS. No pearls," she warned me and then handed me a pair of YSL fuck-me pumps.

My interview was at nine at night at the most exclusive nightclub in Hollywood. Unless you were Paris Hilton, Leonardo DiCaprio, a supermodel, or a Wall Street banker willing to throw down $2,000 for a bottle of Grey Goose, you weren't getting in.

I stood behind the red rope in my little black dress, gold hoops, and pumps trying to flag down the security guard. "Excuse me!" I kept trying to get someone's attention until I realized I was being too polite. Fed up, I ducked under the rope and walked toward the front door until a security guard grabbed my arm. "No trespassing," the man snapped. He was nearly seven feet tall and must have weighed about three hundred pounds. "Christina Grace. I'm here to see Anna Shapiro," I declared and then looked at him with *Do not fuck with me, I need this job* eyes. He let go. "Oh, right this way." Anna Shapiro was the prom queen of Los Angeles nightlife, the boss and woman responsible for weeding out the ugly and bringing in the beautiful.

The security guard opened the double doors, and I walked into a modern, open layout filled with white leather couches, glass tables, and disco balls. Bartenders by night and models by day were cutting fresh fruit while bottle-service girls by night and actresses by day were pulling up their fishnets and curling their hair in the women's bathroom. Josh liked to call them MAWs: models/actors/whatever.

A young hipster in round glasses and skinny jeans approached me, carrying a clipboard. "Are you Christina?" he asked.

"Yes."

"I'm Fred. Anna's busy, so I'm going to interview you."

We sat down on the white leather couches, and he handed me the clipboard.

"So this is the checklist you mark while collecting guests' email addresses." I looked down at the sheet of paper. "*M* is for model, *S* is for socialite, *P/H* is for pretty/handsome, *A* is for average, and *NC* is for not cute. So for each person you meet, you have to rate them. It's very important because all of this goes into our database so we can determine who we allow or do not allow in our nightclub. Do you think you can do that?"

This kind of information collecting would, years later, turn into algorithms used to monitor the hottest nightclubs in America. Where cameras eventually replaced clipboards and paperwork, hidden in front entrances in order to take a snapshot of a face and calculate the measurements of what is considered "beauty," and, based on how well you score, you will be either accepted or rejected. And if you're fat, don't even bother, because the owners look at it as taking up the space of what could potentially be two buyers instead of one, the potential difference between $1,000 or $2,000: two drinks or four.

"Yes," I said. "I grew up in DC. I got this." *Cave dwellers, social A-list, politicians, media.*

"Good," he said. "And don't let anyone see the list. It's fifteen an hour. Anna wants to take a quick look at you. Come with me." I did the math again in my head: *The club is open only from ten to two. Fifteen times four is sixty, and I'll be working only five days a week, so that's sixty times five, which is three hundred a week times four, which is twelve hundred a month. Not enough to live.*

I stepped into the back office, where stacks of $100 bills were being shuffled inside a money machine. Anna walked over, with her short, Anna Wintour–style bob and bright red nail polish. She looked me up and down. I stood trying to appear taller than my barely five-foot-three frame, with my hand on my hip and my legs crossed like all the young starlets pose on the red carpet.

"You're cute," she said and then turned to Fred. "She can do the job."

The front doors were about to open, and Hollywood hopefuls covered in Ed Hardy and Chrome Hearts stood behind the red rope, eager to get in. Mike, the doorman, would tell them to keep waiting for a few more minutes, but he'd never let them in. It looked good to have random people waiting outside. Made them feel special. Made the brand important. Hostesses stood under heat lamps, chewing blocks of Orbit gum while waiting for a celebrity or socialite to come claim a reserved table.

It was one of my first nights of work, and I was standing in the all-encompassing stainless steel kitchen, clocking in, when one of the bottle-service girls approached me.

"Hey, hon." She wore a white corset, a miniskirt, and fishnets, and had long blond curls and false eyelashes. "Can you zip me up? I can't get it all the way." She pointed to the zipper in the back, her breasts bursting over the frilly rim.

"Sure." I pulled on the zipper as the bussers ran in and out of the kitchen with buckets of limes, lemons, and ice.

"Can I ask you something?" I said.

"Yeah, doll."

"How much money do you walk away with a night?"

"Depends on the night. A bad night is usually around four or five hundred, and a good night can be up to two thousand. Do you have experience?"

"No." I couldn't believe how much money you could make without having to take off your clothes. I needed that job.

"Well, you gotta get experience, you gotta hustle, you know what I'm saying? I don't know about you, but I got a little girl at home to feed and a mortgage to pay." I got the zipper up and then watched her fiddle with a walkie-talkie attached to her waist. "For security, like, if a customer is comin' on too strong, you know?" she explained. "Gotta run, doll. Good luck."

A little girl at home? A mortgage to pay? How did she do it? Come to work each night dressed in patent leather thigh-high boots with men groping at her waist and breasts, lines of cocaine sprawled across glass tables, then go home, sleep, and wake up her daughter for preschool the next morning. And not only that, but she had a mortgage to pay. With inconsistent pay from the nightclub, I wondered how that was even possible. I didn't know the whole story, and I wasn't one to judge. Each night, I rated clubgoers based on looks and social status because I needed money so desperately I was willing to do anything.

Later that night, as I was standing around near the DJ booth, a girl sauntered over to me, shouting over the music, "Can you add me to the email list?"

"Sure," I yelled back and handed her my clipboard. Her eyes, full of hope that maybe she would get the chance to come back into the club again. She scanned the paper then looked up at me. "Are you rating people?" she asked, shocked.

I looked at her, speechless and guilty, then plucked the clipboard out of her hands and ran as fast as I could into the kitchen.

"Watch it!" one of the busboys shouted. A young man with a square jaw and dark hair slicked back into a low bun squeezed by me holding two large buckets of ice, beads of sweat along his forehead.

I was clearly in the way.

"Sorry, I'm really sorry," I said, scooting over a few steps.

"Do you work here?" He dumped the buckets of ice on the floor and looked me up and down in my "club outfit."

"Yeah, um, I'm the list girl."

He let out a laugh, indicating that my position and ranking for employees at the club was on the bottom of the list. "What does that even mean? You mean bottle-service list girl?"

"No, I was hired to collect email addresses and . . ." I leaned in and whispered shamefully, *"rate people."* I showed him my clipboard.

"Oh, man!" He shook his head. "Sounds like prison."

Shocked that he had said the word *prison*, I replied, "My dad's in prison." It just fell out of my mouth, begging to be heard. No one I knew wanted to talk about prison.

The young man took a step back.

"Oh yeah?" He looked me up and down. "You sure don't look like a girl who has a dad in prison."

"What do you know about prison?" I asked.

"I know a lot about prison."

"Tell me."

"What's your name?"

"Christina. What's yours?"

"Jesse." He stuck out his hand. A word was tattooed on his forearm, but I couldn't make it out. The letters looked gothic in style.

"Nice to meet you."

"Here," he said. He pulled over another bucket of lemons and handed me a knife.

I held the knife and stared at the lemon. "Um . . ."

"You never slice a lemon before?"

"No."

No, I had never sliced lemons before. I had never even made my bed. I never had a summer job. I never had to clean up after myself. I didn't know anything about *work*.

Jesse shook his head, ashamed of me. "Like this." He took the lemon and sliced off each end, demonstrating. "Then down the middle like this, then one slice, two slice, three slice, four." He dumped the slices in the bucket. "And careful, your fingers."

I took a lemon and carefully sliced as he sliced next to me. The bottle-service girls ran in and out carrying frosted bottles of Grey Goose and sparklers that looked like mini fireworks as they strutted through the club to their designated tables. Jesse and I continued talking that night, and for the first time I felt safe opening up about my father being in prison.

"I did some time," Jesse said. He kept his eyes on the lemon, his voice real low.

"What did you do?"

He kept slicing the lemons. "You're not supposed to ask that."

"Oh." I was not aware of any "prison etiquette." "Well, my dad's in prison for fraud." I didn't care what the etiquette was. I felt relieved to have met someone with a connection to prison too.

Jesse looked around the kitchen. "Assault . . . drugs, you know," he said. "But I'm straight. I don't do that shit no more."

Jesse and I continued talking, and after I told him about my debt, he told me he was eleven the first time a gun was put in his hands. His older brother was a member of a gang and had been in and out of prison his whole life.

Jesse looked at me. "You know, your dad loves you. Just because

he's locked up, it doesn't mean he doesn't love you." I never told Jesse
I thought my father didn't love me, and it made me uncomfortable the
way he said it—as though he could see some kind of pain in me that I
couldn't.

I turned around and saw Fred walk in and dropped the knife.

"Where the fuck have you been?" he yelled.

"I was just—"

"Get out there! Paris Hilton and Lindsay Lohan just walked in."

I grabbed the clipboard and ran out the kitchen door back toward
the dance floor. Fat Joe and Lil Wayne's "Make It Rain" was playing.

I weaved through all the bodies on the dance floor, which smelled
of vodka and sweat, when all of a sudden a trust-fund kid whose father
owned a cement company or something started "making it rain" with
$100 bills. I made my way to the upper-level VIP area and saw the blond,
blue-eyed baby holding wads of cash in rubber bands as he released
them over the dance floor. It felt like a suction of drunken hipsters,
this force of gravity, pulling them toward the dirty floor covered in wet
money   like mosquitoes to light. I made sure Fred wasn't looking, and
I dropped to my knees like everyone else, gathering as many bills as I
could get my hands on. I stuck three $100 bills in my bra and stood up,
when I got elbowed in the face. Blood gushed from my nose toward my
upper lip. I ran back inside the kitchen to find my new kindred spirit,
Jesse, all bloodied from chasing the rain.

"You all right? You all right?" he asked, handing me a clean rag. I
looked at him, and before I could say anything, I began to cry.

It was like standing in the twilight zone: rays of light projected outward
around my father's head when the front door of the town house swung
open.

"Bambina!" he exclaimed, swooping down to give me a hug. He
appeared skinnier, and his hair was gray. I guess he had been dying it
black all these years. *Did he escape?*

My mother had called me the night before. "Your father's back," she said, irritated. "I need you over at the house for dinner tomorrow night."

"*What*?" I blurted out, confused.

"He was granted a furlough."

"What's a furlough?"

My mother sighed, always exhausted by my questions these days.

"I don't know; he gets to come home for a day," she said, exasperated. I thought furloughs were granted only under extreme circumstances such as a death in the family. There were no deaths.

My father was being moved from Herlong to a minimum-security prison in El Paso, Texas. On February 24, 2006, he wrote a letter to Nancy Palmer: "I've been assigned to La Tuna (Spanish for desert flower of some sort) in El Paso, Texas. It's the worst of places, and I'm going to the prison, not the camp . . . the Bush administration is making a concerted effort to close the remaining camps. La Tuna is 85 percent Latino . . . my Francois will take me far . . . I hope to see Gayle and the girls during my travels . . . Mum's the word on that event."

He was able, somehow, to buy a plane ticket and fly across the state of California as a convicted felon currently serving time in prison. Probation had given him a bus ticket that would have taken a total of about two days to travel from Herlong down to El Paso, Texas, and my father decided he'd use that time to see his girls instead.

So there he was, in his khakis and white polo, grilling steak and holding a martini—like Leonardo DiCaprio in *Catch Me If You Can*. Chloe was downstairs in her bedroom, presumably doing homework, when I knocked on her door.

"Hey," I said. She was sitting on her bed when I walked in. "This is weird, right?"

Chloe leaned toward me and whispered, "Yeah, he just, like . . . *appeared*. Mom didn't even tell me he was coming until, like, an hour before she went to pick him up from the airport." Chloe and I were both so uncomfortable, we didn't know what to do other than laugh at the absurdity of it all. And besides, what could we accomplish with Dad being home for just a few hours? He couldn't fix my credit in that amount of time; he couldn't make us thousands of dollars to live off of. He was there to fill the gap because he felt Mom slipping away from him. I was hopeful that his being home even just for those few hours would make us feel like we could be a family again. But after a few martinis, my father was cruising around the TV area looking at all of the family photos on the side table. There was only one picture of him. I don't remember which picture—maybe the one of my father kneeling between Mara and me, still in his pin-striped suit and red tie. We're on the sidewalk, standing under hundred-year-old trees along Lowell Street. It was my third birthday party. I'm wearing a blue floral party dress, blue and white ribbons in my hair, and I'm holding a blue balloon. And Mara, on the other side of me, is posing as she sits on his knee, laughing in her pink smock dress.

"How come there's only one picture of me in the whole house?" my father asked my mother, who was preparing the salad for dinner.

"I don't know, Tom," Mom said. "Why *is* there only one picture of you?" She challenged him, wanting him to answer his own question. But when Chloe and I entered the kitchen, they dropped it.

That night, I didn't ask my father about prison. I didn't ask him about my credit. I didn't ask him about anything. I felt frozen from the jolt of his sudden presence, the tension between the words he exchanged with Mom. This was his night of "freedom." But all I remember from that dinner was watching him—the way he chewed his steak, sipped his red wine—wondering how in those moments he measured freedom in between the hours and the days that he had been locked up. He would soon be locked up again—trapped—wondering if he, or any of us, even knew what freedom meant.

Josh and Christina to Washington, DC

I was staring at the champagne and crudités on the table, her mother's sundress, and her father's bow tie. I'd flown back to DC with Josh for a high school friend's twenty-first birthday party, held on the top floor of a chic restaurant, and her parents were sipping bottles of Pellegrino while discussing the Duke University lacrosse team rape case. I hadn't kept in touch with most of my friends from high school, but they knew that my father had gone to prison. I never spoke about the debt, or what was happening at home with my mother and Chloe. I had the steel Tiffany watch that my father had given me clasped around my wrist, and Josh on my arm to shield me—insecure from the thought of any of them finding out.

I suppose I needed to go back there to prove to everyone that I was fine. I thought I was; so sure I was moving in the right direction. But while I sat there at the round table drinking champagne and listening to my old friends talk of their internships on Capitol Hill, at think tanks, law firms, and investment banks, their wild and hilarious stories of frat parties and sorority balls, I was beginning to see all that I had taken for granted: my education, my background, my parents' connections to the world at large. And I wondered if there was an answer to understanding privilege without having to lose everything, without having the rug ripped out from beneath you. How to become conscious of it when it's all you know, or if privilege is destined to circulate and perpetuate itself insidiously down through generation after generation—an inevitable doomed and stagnant fact of life where change within oneself and, therefore, the surrounding community, is just not possible.

I fiddled with the clasp of my watch and had the sudden urge to take it off and hide it, bury it, smash it, feeling like a fraud. But instead, I kept playing the part—good manners, looks, possessions, and charm—while asking myself: Which was it? Was I from a wealthy family? A poor family? Did it matter? For the first time, I felt the gap, lost in some kind of a divide within myself, not knowing how to be, squirming in my seat, "Pass the champagne, please, thank you," turning to Josh and kissing him on the cheek, hoping no one would notice how uncomfortable I was. Through my new pair of eyes, my friends appeared to have everything, when before, I'd never even noticed. Were they aware of it? And it was that word again: *everything*. What did it even mean? I knew only one thing: I had taken everything I ever knew for granted, but I could never say it out loud. I couldn't admit it to myself—and certainly to no one else, not even Josh. I wanted to go back. I wanted to close my eyes and wake up in my bedroom and start over.

I took Josh with me the next day. The foreclosure sign was still stuck in the grass, now tall, uncut, and sprouting weeds. It was muggy outside, and the swirling hiss of cicadas grew louder as Josh and I hopped out of the car. It had been seventeen years since the ugly insects merged from underground. I was only three years old and in my car seat when I saw them for the first time. My mother was pregnant with Chloe, and Mara insisted she carry them with us wherever we went, like pets. It drove my mother crazy. These giant bugs were everywhere: in between car seats, in our shoes, and crawling on our sippy cups.

We parked down the street for fear of running into any old neighbors. Lois, the mother of the boy who tried to blow up our house with
a Coke can, was the neighborhood gossip, strolling the streets with her
pet ferret on her shoulder. I wanted to be spared the humiliation of
running into her. I looked down the street until the coast was clear,
grabbed hold of Josh's hand, and led him up the stone walkway. It was
more chipped and loose than I remembered it to be from years of hop-
scotch and jump rope. Josh stopped in the middle of the walkway and
looked up at the estate. "Wow, you grew up here?"

It was bigger than I remembered. Overgrown ivy weaved around
each window in between shutters, and along the gutter, and the once
white Corinthian columns framing the front door were now faded,
chipped, and weathered, paint peeling away with the wind. In my
mind, it all still belonged to me, not the bank. Every brick, every stone.
I turned the knob of the front door to see if maybe it was open. No luck.
Josh stood back while I pressed my face up to the beveled glass. The
house was empty, even the dining room chandelier had been ripped
from the ceiling, loose wires poked down toward the floor. It must have
sold at the estate sale, and I wondered how it was for my father packing
up the house all alone. I wondered which door he walked out of on the
last day. The front? The back? The garage? I needed to get inside the
house. I wasn't leaving until I did.

"Follow me." I grabbed Josh, remembering the garage doors. My
parents always kept them unlocked, even when we went to Nantucket
for the summer. Josh and I shuffled down the green hill to the three-
car garage beneath the house. A frequent act I did in high school when
I'd come home late from a party after forgetting my keys. I could see
through the windows that the alarm was off.

I yanked on the garage door handle. It was locked.

"Oh, wait." I searched my purse.

"What are you doing?" Josh asked. I could see the paranoia growing
in him as he looked left and then right.

"My key. I still have my key."

"Yeah, right. You don't think the locks have been changed?"

"It's worth a shot," I said with a shrug.

I pulled out the key, dangling it at him. "I haven't taken it off my keychain yet." What was I supposed to do with such a key? The key to every childhood memory I desperately wanted to hold on to? Just throw it in the trash? Give it away with everything else? By holding on, I could at least assert some form of control over something, over the nightmares, the dreams, the memories. I ran back to the front door. Josh kept watch behind me. I stuck the key in the keyhole, and with a quick *click* to the right, the front door popped open.

"Holy shit." Josh laughed. "It worked."

I was home.

It was hot and musky, the odor reminiscent of the way it smelled when we arrived home from Nantucket at the end of August. It was as if the air, our air, had been trapped for all these years, waiting for the right moment to be released. I inhaled as much as my lungs could take. Josh strolled ahead of me through the foyer, taking in the high ceilings, crown molding, and arched doorways. I had never noticed those details before. I followed him through the loggia, the marble corridor with a dozen French doors still wrapped in lace curtains that opened up to the limestone balcony and our garden full of weeping willow trees.

"This is where we used to dance with Mom and slide in our feety pajamas," I told him.

The pink rug still covered the front hall staircase. I walked Josh through the vacant living room and into my father's library. His entire encyclopedia collection was still in its alphabetical order, abandoned in the mahogany bookshelves to the right of the fireplace, covered in dust. I sat on the floor and opened one of the bottom cabinets along the wall where he kept his BusyBox documents. It was empty. Then I opened the cabinet next to it where he kept our arts and crafts. I peered into the empty cabinets, making sure no memory was left behind. I thought about Kate, my best friend in middle school. I remembered the first time she came over for a playdate.

"Is your dad a judge? Is he in the Mafia?" She was the daughter of two psychiatrists.

"He's a lawyer," I told her.

"He sounds like a mystery man." I had never thought about it before.

Josh walked over and said, "Let's keep going," sensing I was on the edge of a spiral. I was putting together the pieces.

"Show me your bedroom."

It looked exactly the way it did before I left, except empty. The walls a faded yellow, and my blue and white striped rug was still there. I showed Josh where I keyed my name into the edge of my bathroom sink when I was eleven, and the window perpendicular to the window of Mara's bedroom, where when we got in trouble we'd talk to each other, sometimes throwing CDs back and forth.

I sat down on the floor and crossed my legs. The sun was setting and thunder rumbled in the distance, silencing the cicadas. A summer storm was coming. I closed my eyes and asked myself, what if none of this had happened? What if I was just in a terrible nightmare? I wanted to open my eyes and be sitting on my floral bedspread staring at my dresser against the wall, my bulletin board hanging next to it with my prom corsages and my bumper sticker collection, and I wanted to hear Popsicle, our yellow cockatiel, chirping in the kitchen, and my father banging around the pots and pans preparing for Sunday morning pancakes. There were holes growing inside of me with every passing memory.

Josh wrapped his arms around me and then let go, grazing his hand along my neck, his thumb caressing the bottom of my jaw. He kissed my forehead, then my cheek, my eyes, my nose, my lips. His eyes never left mine after we undressed each other, and I had to remember to breathe, breathe, as he swayed into me, my bare back against the dusty rug, the rain suddenly showering like the pitter-patter of stars falling from the sky. And I held on to him tighter this time, with my eyes open, and our lips loose, exchanging heavy breaths, louder and then softer each time the carpet burned my back. The room grew dark with no electricity, we were sweating and laughing, and he came and I came, relieving me from all of my memory as though each hole in me now was just a blip in time.

Suddenly a loud bang jolted us.

"What was that?" I whispered.

"It sounded like a door slamming." Josh reached for his boxer shorts.

"Shit, shit, shit!" I grabbed my scattered clothes, getting dressed as fast as possible, using our cell phones as light.

"If we get arrested, it's all your fault," Josh grumbled.

"What is your problem?"

"I'm just saying. This was your idea."

We tiptoed down the hallway and into Chloe's old room, the windows of which overlooked the street. I saw a familiar car parked out front. A blue Jeep Grand Cherokee.

"Wait, I think I know that car," I said.

Holding our breath, we tiptoed down the front staircase, when I heard distant laughter coming from the basement.

"This is so fucking scary," Josh whispered. "We are *so* going to jail."

"Shut up!" I whispered back.

We finally made it to the front door, when suddenly the back door opposite us swung open, and crashed into the wall.

I spun around. A body stumbled into the hallway, shining a flashlight on my face.

I squinted with my hand above my eyes. "Chloe?" She wore an old bikini top and shorts and held a Miller Lite in her other hand.

"Dude!" she said, just as shocked as I was. Then she took a swig of beer. "What are *you* doing here?"

Her ex-boyfriend and a group of his friends came around behind her, reeking of cigarettes and pot.

"What am *I* doing here? What the fuck are *you* doing here?"

I had forgotten that Chloe would be in DC visiting her best friend from high school and that our trips would overlap a few days. Given the way we hardly communicated, it wasn't surprising we each forgot.

Chloe pulled out a gold Baldwin key and dangled it in front of me like a carrot. Stumbling forward, she bragged, "I still have my key."

I paused for a moment. Of course she did. So did I.

Chloe and I sat at the grand piano, pretending to be concert pianists, when my mother turned on the surround sound.

"Walkin' on, walkin' on bro-ken glass . . ."

It was a lazy Sunday afternoon, and I could smell the macaroni and cheese and hot dogs cooking in the kitchen.

My father was off flying his airplane for the afternoon.

Mara was in the family room, wearing her headgear and reading *The Baby-Sitters Club*.

Annie Lennox's "Walking on Broken Glass" blared through each room. I could see my mother from where I was sitting, dancing in the kitchen as she grilled our hot dogs.

"Mom! Turn it down!" Mara cried from the couch. My mother didn't care; she turned it up and kept dancing. Then she ran out into the loggia to find Chloe and me, pretending to pound on the piano keys to the song's rhythm.

My mother picked up my red feather boa, threw it around her neck, and then pulled me up from the piano bench to dance with her.

We strutted across the marble floor together, doing twists and turns. Chloe slipped into our mother's red high heels, which we'd stolen from her closet earlier, and as the song crescendoed, my mother grabbed Chloe's hands and sang at the top of her lungs. Mara came into the loggia, and my mother tossed the book out of her hands and pulled her in to dance with us.

"I'm living in an empty room with all the windows smashed . . ."

Mara let go, and sang, in full headgear and pointing her finger with attitude while I sang at the highest pitch possible. And then the four of us threw our hands up in the air—free, singing, slipping and sliding— like superstars.

Ralph Adler

A few weeks later, I was pulling out of the parking lot at Warner Bros. studios after auditioning for "cheerleader #3" on the TV series *Heroes* when Ralph Adler called. Why was he calling me? The letters to the creditors didn't work. I wasn't using QuickBooks to budget. I was broke; there was nothing to budget. The last time I had seen Ralph Adler was while I was working at La Scala.

"Ralph Adler's office."

"Hi, this is Christina Prousalis, I'm returning Ralph Adler's call."

"One moment, please."

When Ralph picked up, he sounded frantic and out of breath. "Hey, hey, how are you?" he asked.

"I'm good! How are you?" I said nervously. I had a terrible feeling it was about my father.

"Good, good." I could hear a door shutting in the background. His voice quiet and low, he said, "I want to ask you something . . ."

"Yes?" I said, my heart pounding.

"So, sometimes, on weekends, I like to do these triple-X video shoots, and I was wondering if you would like to assist me. I'll pay you five hundred dollars—cash—under the table, because I know you need the money . . ."

I almost lost control of the car. I had trusted him. I had sat in his living room with him, spilling my darkest secrets. He was a man my father's age—asking me to be in a porno! And not only that, but to have the audacity to offer me only *$500*? And what did the word *assist* mean? I imagined a dimly lit studio somewhere deep in the valley of Van Nuys. We're out in the backyard by the open swimming pool, the brown Burbank Hills in the distance. Ralph's standing there, wearing an open bathrobe while his flaccid penis dangles free, and I'm on my knees, naked, with a giant feather in my hand, tickling his little penis inches from my nose because his wife won't fuck him at home. And I can see his face smiling down at me, those clunky braces on his lower and upper teeth reflecting the sun as he opens his mouth to cum, the stretching of the rubber bands lengthening like roaring walrus teeth before he moans with pleasure and calls out my name: *"Christina!"*

"I . . . I . . . I . . . *No!*" I dropped my cell phone, pulled over to the side of the Cahuenga Pass, a narrow road along the eastern end of the Santa Monica Mountains beside the Hollywood Freeway, swung open the car door, and threw up.

A flood of employees leaving Universal Studios and Warner Bros. slammed on their horns and flipped me off as they screeched by in their black Priuses. I pulled myself back inside the car. There was a two-day-old Coke still in my cup holder. I took a swig and called my mother.

"Ralph Adler is a pedophile!" I screamed in ever-escalating hysteria. My mother scoffed, as if this information was the most ridiculous thing she had ever heard.

"Oh, honey, you have to realize he thinks you're sexy, that's all. You're over eighteen now. Get used to it."

Get used to it?

Where was my mother? The woman who would do anything for her children? Who would kill for them; die in order to protect them.

"You are never allowed to see that man ever again!" I shouted back.

"Well, that's not going to happen," she said. Her serenity was unnerving.

"Why?"

"Because he's dealing with our taxes and helping me find a divorce lawyer."

Her words were too painful, overloaded with information. I felt too much and understood too little of how the reality around me was cementing itself into a story I didn't want to tell. I hung up on her. The reality of my parents. The reality of my age and my mother's implication that because I was legal, I was "up for grabs" by powerful men, so I'd better just accept it. My mother said the word *divorce* so casually, as though she wanted to quickly erase twenty-five years of a marriage. The possibility had crossed my mind a few times, but like every child wants to believe, I never thought my parents would ever divorce. I was convinced that all of the things they did were the things that happy couples do. They took vacations alone together! My mother wore sexy lingerie to bed! My father squeezed my mother's ass when he walked in from work each night! This, I thought in all of my naivete, was love and marriage, never having been privy to what was actually inside of it.

My tears turned to rage, with no words for the volcano awakening inside of me. I screamed so hard at the steering wheel that I thought the veins in my neck were going to explode.

I rang the buzzer to Josh's building, mascara stains across my cheeks— the role of cheerleader #3 gone terribly wrong.

When Josh opened the door, he wrapped his arms around me. "You want me to go over there and beat the shit out of Ralph?"

"Forget it," I said.

I didn't insist because I knew that Ralph Adler's business partner handled Josh's family's money and that they had developed a lifelong friendship. When I told Madeline about it, she said, "I'm very surprised, honey; that does not sound like Ralph." I was up against thirty years of money and friendship. I was not going to win that battle. And when I told Josh that my mother had said she was filing for divorce, he brought up therapy again. His family had started going to therapy together, and he said it was making him feel better. I finally caved and asked for a referral. Josh said he would call his mother and get one for me as soon as possible.

I changed the subject, and then I noticed another letter and a paper airplane from my father on his desk. He and Josh had started corresponding with each other apart from me. He was teaching my boyfriend how to make expert paper airplanes. It started a year earlier, just before Father's Day, when he started sending paper airplanes with each letter he wrote. I walked over and picked up the letter. "Enclosed is another rendition of N1TP. When I sat down to make it, I had not done so since I was 12, about 27 years ago. As I folded the wings and made the tail, it came back to me like it was yesterday. . . . If the airplane wants to dive, adjust the trailing edge up slightly, which will bring the nose (attitude) up and enable it to fly from LA to Herlong, if you do it right. I will look out on the Southern horizon for it! Best, Tom."

The paper airplane was made out of yellow legal pad paper. My father had written "N1TP" (Number One, Tom Prousalis) on the side of the tail, which was the tail number on his King Air. Josh and I took the airplane out to the apartment balcony overlooking the courtyard swimming pool. "Would you like to do the honors?" Josh asked, handing me the airplane. Before I took it, I thought about the first time I flew in the copilot's seat with my father, searching for clues.

My Keds wouldn't reach the metal pedals and instead were dangling in the air. My father tightened the headset around my head, and I stared at all the buttons and gadgets, and the million little lights, red, yellow, blue, orange in front of me. He said words to the air traffic controllers like "Alpha," "Bravo," and "Charlie." The steering wheel in front of him moved on its own. Left, and then right, up and down, like a ghost playing tricks. I tried to lift myself higher so I could see out the window, but I was too short.

"Dad, go sideways. Go sideways!" I yelled. Even at the age of seven, I was an adrenaline junkie. My father knew I got it from him. He loved it.

"All right, Bambina," he said, "Better hold on tight to that steering wheel!" I leaned forward to grab hold even though I knew he was in charge. Until he let go.

"Dad!" I shrieked with excitement.

"You're flying, Bambina!"

"Oh, my, God. Dad, I'm flying!"

Before I knew it, my nose was pressed up against the glass window, my stomach flipped upside down, and I was wide eyed. We were flying sideways, just as I'd asked. The earth below me, like *Mr. Rogers' Neighborhood*, with little cars zipping down highways, and suburban houses in cul-de-sacs with swimming pools, when suddenly I felt a wave of nausea. I looked over at him. He was flirting with the female air traffic controller.

"Is N169 out of the question?"

"It is never out of the question."

"Do you have any restrictions?"

The air traffic controller giggled. Her voice was annoying and robotic and had a slight southern accent.

"You're putting on a great show."

"Dad. Dad . . ." I tried to get his attention. "Dad!" I felt my heart pounding louder and the back corners of my mouth getting watery until finally, "Dad, I don't feel so well—"

I sat and watched what was once my mother's homemade tuna fish sandwich ooze in between the colorful buttons.

"Roger that. This is N1TP approaching MNZ, I'm going to need a crew of men with buckets, mops, wipes, anything you have down there on the ground. My seven-year-old just barfed all over my control panel."

I exhaled with relief as the wheels hit the ground. Yellow buckets and mops and crewmen from Manassas Regional Airport stood by ready to clean the mess I'd made. Flushed with embarrassment, I turned to my father. "I'm sorry, Dad."

"It's okay, Bambina. You're just not ready to be a fighter pilot yet."

I snatched the paper airplane from Josh's hands. I pinched the bottom in between my pointer finger and thumb, closed one eye, and thrust the plane out over the balcony. We stood there amazed at how far it soared: twenty feet maybe, before it went careening sideways and plunged into the swimming pool.

A few days later, I was staring at a list of doctors, their metal signs plastered on the wall, one above the other with a button next to each. I was ten minutes early and had been thinking long and hard about what I would say to my mother. She had agreed to a therapy session. I thought about how I would convince her that she was still in love with my father, and that she would need to stop all communication with Ralph Adler; I didn't care that he was helping her pro bono. I pressed the button and watched the red light turn on.

Sheryl was a friend of Madeline's, petite with frizzy hair, and she sat on top of a square pillow to make herself higher while she held a yellow legal pad and folder in her lap, to scribble down our insanity as proof. I sat down on the gray couch across from her and waited to the sound of a ticking clock before ten minutes from the start of the hour had gone by.

"Do you know where she might be?" Sheryl asked, concerned.

"She'll be here. She's just late for everything," I explained, even though it wasn't true. My mother was never late for appointments.

I checked my phone. No messages.

"Would you like a piece of candy?" Sheryl held out a bowl of Jolly Ranchers.

"No thank you."

The sound of a ticking clock.

Ten more minutes had gone by, and the sun had set. Sheryl stood up to light a scented candle on her desk. I dialed my mother's cell phone for the third time.

"Hi. You've reached Gayle Prousal—"

I hung up. The pit of my stomach was twisting and turning. *She's not coming . . .*

"Well, I guess it's just you and me, dear," Sheryl said.

I looked down at my phone, praying one more time that I would see "mom cell" pop up on the screen. It was the moment that solidified the severance of our relationship—the moment I realized that she was gone, checked out, moving on. The betrayal hit me with such force. Intellectually, I understood that our new worlds were pushing us in different directions for our simple need to survive, but, still, I didn't want to accept it; I wanted to *correct* it. I thought that if I could remind her how much she loved my father, if I could remind her how happy we were once, she might just hang on a little longer until he came home. I was so determined to get her to prove to me that my childhood perception of them was real, so that I could hold on to a part of the illusion of all that was true and listen to the denial that was keeping me afloat.

When I told Sheryl about Ralph, she suggested that I take action and tell his business partner the truth. I Googled "accountant code of ethics." I compiled a list of every moral and ethical code that I thought Ralph broke. Then I picked up the phone and called his business partner. I would stand up for myself if no one else was willing to. The man was flabbergasted, speechless, flustered on the other end of the phone. He stuttered, "Well, well, no, that can't be. I've known Ralph thirty years; he would never do something like that." *Why does everyone think I'm making this up? If I wanted an excuse for attention, I would play the "Daddy's in jail" card.* I insisted I was not making it up. I listed the codes of ethics I believed Ralph had broken and said it was also sexual harassment.

"I will look into it," his partner said before hanging up abruptly. A few weeks later, I received a letter in the mail written by their legal team. Something along the lines of "We are sorry that you are unhappy with our services and feel that it is best that both parties part ways." I flushed the letter down the toilet right after I read it. Ripping it to shreds in sheer rage, I had never felt more isolated, more voiceless, and repressed by blatant lies. There was no hope, no use in keeping it. I thought I would never see Ralph Adler again, or his business partner; there would never be a lawsuit, there would never be any kind of real admission or apology, and I never ever wanted to think about that day or be reminded of it ever again.

I had read that this was typical: the reason why so many women do not report sexual harassment, for fear that no one will believe them. And that is exactly what happened.

When my mother called me back a few days after my first therapy session, she apologized. "Honey, I forgot. I'm so, so sorry."

I never believed that she forgot the therapy appointment. I knew she didn't want to sit there in front of Madeline's friend and spill all her deep, dark secrets. "We'll go another day," she promised. Whatever innocence was left inside of me died that day. I gave up. I didn't care anymore because I didn't think anyone else did. My instinct to want to protect myself had been dismissed so that each time I tried to do it, or thought about doing it, it felt wrong. I had normalized Ralph Adler's behavior and anything like it. Just like my mother did.

- 1 5 -

Hustle

Hustle was what I learned to do when the need for money became greater than the need for self-respect. The creditors were still looking for me, and I needed to earn more. I had just turned twenty-one, and I started thinking long and hard about the things my mother had said to me: "Get used to it." "We don't have a choice." My father had been arrested when I was at an age where your identity is still a blank slate—where teenagers go off to college and get to reinvent themselves.

I had been a "good girl" growing up, with the exception of the occasional bag of weed and sneaking in a beer or two at parties. I didn't drink and drive. I didn't have anything to hide from anyone, no shame to bear that I was aware of. But in Los Angeles, the line between right and wrong seemed to be fading every passing day, insidiously making its way through my impressionable self. When the nightclub wouldn't promote me to bottle-service girl because I had no prior cocktail waitress experience, I created a fictitious resume, went online, and found a job on Craigslist.

I parked my car in front of the pink dilapidated Mark Twain Hotel: half of it used as a flophouse, the other half for struggling artists who want to kill themselves—or so it looked. With my resume and headshot in hand, I marched up to Sunset Boulevard in gold hoop earrings, a black miniskirt, necessary Wonderbra, and spaghetti-strap tank top. Over the phone, Jerry had warned me that the office door didn't have an address on it. Jerry was the owner. The office was in between a bar and a newspaper stand that carried plastic Academy Awards and mini-license-plate key chains with random people's first names organized alphabetically.

When Jerry opened the door, he looked like a dirty sailor. His handlebar mustache curled upward from a ball of wax. He sat down in a swivel chair and leaned back to catch the breeze from a revolving floor fan, revealing his happy trail and beer belly. He wore a Corona beer T-shirt and asked me about my experience as a cocktail waitress. I lied to him about all the restaurants I worked at in DC and embellished my job at the nightclub. He asked me what I would do in different scenarios, such as: "If a customer asks you to take a shot with them, what do you do?"

"Well, I would ask you first, but I imagine the answer would be yes, since I would charge him for two shots instead of one."

"Great." He winked at me. "And flirting helps."

I would start the next day.

The bar was in a run-down shack in Hollywood that smelled of beer, dirty sponges, and cleaning fluid. Modelo beer balloons and sports team pennants hung across the ceiling. It was home to drunken tourists who wore trucker hats and sleeveless jerseys. A girl named Kayla was the first to train me. She was a no-bullshit bitch from Southie (Boston) who flung a Corona belly shirt, apron, and rag at me on the first day and sneered, "Hurry up, princess, we're opening." Kayla was black Irish and had five older brothers. Her dad died when she was five, and she was raised by her Irish immigrant grandparents. It was like she could smell the good breeding on me. I asked her where the bathroom was so I could put on my new belly shirt. "Red door in the hallway," she said, counting cash and smacking Bubblicious gum. The bathroom walls were bright green. It smelled like a Porta-Potty, the aura of shit combined with the kind of cheap air fresheners hung in cars. I breathed out of my mouth as I heard Bruce Springsteen's song "Born to Run" come on the jukebox.

"Shoot this every hour," Kayla said, handing me a shot of tequila. "The night goes by twice as fast." I took a swig and shoved a lime slice into my mouth.

"And this is Jimmy, our bartender." Jimmy looked like a rugged version of Brad Pitt's character from *Thelma and Louise*; a toothpick see-sawed up and down in between his teeth.

"Nice to meet you." I shook his hand, and it felt sticky.

"Does lil' miss here know the deal?" Jimmy shot Kayla a look.

"Gonna take her out back right now."

Kayla pulled me into the back alley by the dumpster and whipped out her black checkbook full of cash.

"Do you need money, or what?" Kayla was impatient.

"Um, yeah, I need money," I said, not understanding what she was getting at.

"Here's the deal: Jerry sells Patrón, but it's really Jose Cuervo, upcharging customers for shit tequila. Also, we don't get legal breaks here, and we work seven- to eight-hour shifts. The whole place is a complete fraud. But, if you're like me, Jimmy, and the rest of the girls here, and need money, and can't afford to look for another job, then this is the deal: when your customer sits down, you walk up to them, and you ask *up front*: "Cash or credit?" If they say *cash*, go to Jimmy, whisper the order, then pocket the cash. We pool it at the end of the night, and split it with Jimmy. You dig?" This was a rhetorical question.

"So . . ." I was about to reiterate what she said to me in simpler terms, but then stopped myself when she took a long, hard look at me. "Yeah. I got it," I said. I wasn't conscious that what I was doing was wrong regardless of whether the entire business was fraudulent. It was as though some giant blank spot inserted itself into my brain, creating a moral blackout for the sake of survival, not wanting to have to choose between a meal and putting gas in my car.

"You fuck this up in any way, and your ass will be fired before you finish training. Get to work."

For the next week, I emulated each girl that trained me. After Kayla, it was Colleen. A bleach blonde from Missouri, she was grieving the death of her older sister, who had been killed by a drunk driver. Colleen could drink any of us under the table and when she did, that's when she'd talk about her sister. Then there was Alana. Tan and from the Bronx. She loved telling me about her boyfriend and how the only reason they were together was because they were serial cheaters. She drove a motorcycle to work. The last girl to train me, Fiona, was tall and lanky, and raised on a marijuana farm up in Humboldt County, California. She always brought bags of brownies with her to work. "Here, you want one?" she'd ask. I'd shove it into my purse and save it for a hard night. She wore neon glowsticks around her neck. I was always surprised at how much cash she reeled in.

I watched how each girl teased and flirted with the male regulars, tickling them under their chins, taking shots together, sitting on their laps when it got slow. I understood quickly why taking a shot every hour helped get you through each night. At only 105 pounds, I managed to shoot nearly seven shots a night, gliding past tables, teasing and throwing my head back and running my hands through a customer's hair, believing that I could make more money by using my femininity and sexuality. I felt an intense power when I did, but I was naive and had no understanding of *false* power—that even power could lie. But how could it when it felt so real?

Exacerbating my disillusioned life, I received a letter from my father at around the same time. It was about a tequila company he was starting from prison. How apropos, I thought. Instead of Patrón, it would be called "Matron Tequila: The Mother of all Tequilas." They already had 170 acres of agave plants near Puerto Vallarta. He even enclosed a map, as if it were my own personal treasure map, with arrows and a dot leading to the property. It was paper-clipped to an old Patrón ad, cut out from a magazine. He crossed out the *P* and wrote *M*. Below "The World's #1 Ultra Premium Tequila," he wrote: "The Mother of All Tequilas." And at the bottom where it gave the website address, he put a line through it with his pen and wrote "MATRON.COM." He told me I'd be able to buy a house in Beverly Hills before I knew it. I owned 2 million shares of common stock in the company, which would be doing its public offering (IPO) in about eighteen to twenty-four months. And it would trade between seven and eleven dollars a share, which meant that if it were to trade at its highest—at eleven dollars a share—we had the potential to earn $22 million dollars. And if that were the case, Dad said he'd buy a new airplane and keep it in a hangar in Santa Monica next to Tom Cruise's, "We can sing Scientology songs with Katie and Tom!" But first, in order for this to happen, he needed me to be his "law clerk" for a few things. "The first thing you need to do is get the disk . . . download 'My Documents.' Then you need to do the following . . . Find the 'Certificate of Incorporation,' and make three different Certificates of Incorporation for me." My father enclosed an edited document in his letter, an example, of the changes I needed to make. "Pay close attention to my edits and notes . . . send me four copies of each edited Certificate of Incorporation. You'll also need to find the 'cover letter' or 'Delaware cover letter.' Edit the letter as I've indicated . . . Oops, I almost forgot, also, send me a copy of the 'Business Advisory Agreement' . . . P.S. In case you didn't know, 'MCC Trust' represents the first initials of you and your sisters . . . With a little luck, I'll soon be flying you and Josh to Aspen for lunch! . . . XOXO Dad."

I couldn't remember where I had put my father's disk—whether or not Josh had it somewhere or if it got lost in the storage unit. I was late for work the day I was looking for it. Most days and most nights, I was somewhere else. Floating through fantasies, through fields of agave in Mexico, dreaming of the Mother of All Tequilas while serving my patrons Patrón. Once on a busy night, a jock in a New England Patriots jersey walked up to me and said, real close to my face, "You are the worst, most horrible cocktail waitress I have ever had. Ever. In my life." Later, when I picked up the bill, instead of leaving me a tip, he left a little note that read "Suck It, Bitch," and below it, a PS with a tiny drawing of a penis. I was slacking and lazy and trapped in my entitled thinking that my father was coming home to save me. I knew I was a bad waitress. Sometimes I would hustle and work hard, and other times I just faded into the fantasy of a future with my father and all that he was promising. I never brought in as much money as the other girls did. It was as if I was genetically predisposed to failure and a bad work ethic—one half of me believing that when my father would come home, everything would go back to normal; and the other half uncertain, desperate, and unaware of how I craved love and attention, flirting with endless strangers under the guise that it would make me feel financially safe.

As a result, my relationship with Josh was falling apart. He would come into the bar with friends, and I couldn't help but want to make him jealous, pushing the envelope on purpose, testing his love for me. And Josh was picking up on it. "I feel like you always need attention from other guys, Christina. Am I not enough?" I couldn't explain it other than it felt like he was becoming, in some way, a threat to my survival. I wouldn't be able to hustle with all of his questioning and jealousy. Yet I wanted him to prove to me over and over again that he loved me in spite of my unconscionable behavior; even though it would never feel like enough.

I didn't know what the meaning of love was without the need to be saved, and I knew Josh couldn't save me. It was the push-pull of wanting to be saved and wanting to take care of myself all at the same time. My moral compass was spinning in unknown directions, and a war was beginning inside me between love and independence. I didn't believe the two could coexist together.

I drove to Josh's apartment after work one night and told him I needed a break. I told him how jealous he was acting, how he made me feel trapped, that I was miserable and needed to free myself.

"Oh yeah, Christina?" he fired back. "Is being with other guys part of your *liberation* process? You were never as invested in this relationship as I was. I have given you and your family my heart just so you can throw me away." He was right. Josh had given us so much. Helping my mother out around the house, holding me through night terrors, making me laugh, paying for meals—taking care of me. Loving me wholeheartedly while I had one foot out the door, ready to run.

I yelled back and told him I couldn't do it anymore. With the loss of my identity, projections of love, and trying to figure out how to become an independent, young woman, there was nowhere in my severed and rewiring of brain circuits that I could fathom committing to anything but whatever it would take for me to survive. I felt we didn't have a fighting chance at staying together as we—on top of everything else—continued watching our parents' marriages fall apart with zero evidence of lasting, healthy love.

I slammed the door of his apartment. In tears, I walked outside in the pitch-black night and wondered if I was making the right decision.

Mara's graduation weekend was a President Bush lovefest, with Texas pride swarming the Southern Methodist University campus. The elephant in the room for us was palpable: our father wasn't there, and not because he was dead—which is the only reasonable excuse for a parent to miss a child's graduation—but because he was in prison. And God forbid anyone brought it up. There were moments when I had the urge to blurt out "My dad's in prison!" Just to stir everyone, to see how they might respond. It was a dare I told myself to do, but in the end, I was too afraid to do it.

In the months leading up to Mara's graduation, she had called me to ask how I would feel living with her and her boyfriend, Brian, in Los

Angeles. We realized that with our combined bad credit, the two of us wouldn't qualify for a lease. I had missed Mara so much—through all the years we had been apart since she'd left for boarding school when I was just a freshman in high school. I agreed, and a few months later, I was moving my cocoon of childhood furniture for the fourth time into a lovely two-bedroom apartment in Beverly Hills. Brian generously said I could pay only $600 a month in rent because he knew I was struggling.

Brian was preppy. Didn't smoke, didn't drink. That was the first thing I noticed different about my sister when she moved to LA. She was known to date the artist, the musician. She knew how to roll perfect blunts and smoke out of a six-foot bong. She handed me my first Adios Motherfucker (a cocktail) in the Swiss Alps at her high school graduation party. She took me to my first Veruca Salt concert when I was eleven and helped me crowd surf onto the stage. I wanted us to become close again. But now the stark reality was hitting me: she wore plaid dresses, collared shirts, didn't drink or smoke, and made broccoli casserole dishes for dinner. Brian had landed a job at a corporation, she had landed a job at an online start-up, and our schedules were exactly the opposite. She would come home from work just as I was leaving for work. We hardly communicated. A few months in, I was beginning to feel like she was trying to create some semblance of a perfect life, but different from the one that I wanted. Hers was filled with Brian's strict and rigid rules, and nowhere did I feel I fit in. She was acting more like him than herself. I was watching my inner battle unfold in her, in front of me, where we allowed ourselves to disintegrate into whatever we could hold on to, with whomever or whatever was right in front of us, no matter the truth of how we felt about it. We began to bicker more and more when we were home together, over minute things like taking out the trash and doing the dishes. But beneath the surface, there was a whole lot of rage boiling up between us about how we were individually changing. I was rebelling against domesticity, commitment, and responsibility, while she was playing Betty Crocker.

. . .

On a whim, I decided to drive to San Francisco to see my cousin Alex. Her father, my uncle Larry, is my mother's brother. We didn't grow up knowing each other. I met Alex for the first time at my grandmother's funeral the summer before the FBI arrested my father. Alex grew up in Jacksonville, Florida. Far from the life my parents had built, and it created a ripple of resentment and divide between families, keeping my mother and brother apart until grief brought them back together again. Alex and I stayed in touch, and as soon as she "got the hell out of Jacksonville," we had promised to see each other again.

Alex and I were slumped over at a karaoke bar after hours called Bow Bow Cocktail Lounge in the heart of Chinatown, dimly lit to a warm color red, dangling Chinese lanterns everywhere. I started thinking about it again: privilege, money, the things that kept Alex and me from growing up together despite being family. I began to wonder if I was a bad person for having grown up with money. Leaning into her, I slurred, "Did you hate me? Did your mom and dad hate us? Tell me the truth." The bartender, who looked like she'd fallen out of an old newsreel from the Great Depression, set two shots of Patrón in front of us.

"Put them on my tab," Alex said, knowing how broke I was. We'd already had three shots of Patrón at Columbus Cafe in North Beach.

"Come on," she said, petting my arm, "you know Gayle and Larry are both at fault. My dad had trouble holding down a job, and your mom needed things to be a certain way." We started calling them Gayle and Larry, as if they were caricatures we could look down upon as our once-beloved parents continued falling off their designated pedestals. Alex took her shot and slammed it on the bar. "I mean . . . we can just blame *them*. Fuck them for keeping us separated for all these years!"

I took another shot and changed the subject. "Listen," I whispered. "What?"

"I think I own land in Mexico."

Alex laughed so hard that she almost fell off the bar stool. *"What?"*

"Two *million* shares of stock in the Mother of All Tequilas."

"Why am I paying for all these shots, then?"

I took another shot, and my cell phone resting on the bar began to vibrate.

"Your phone's vibrating." Alex pointed to it as she wiped away tears of laughter. She thought I was joking.

I looked down at the caller ID. It was Chloe.

"It's just Chloe." I pressed Ignore. But then my sister called again.

"Maybe you should get that." Alex seemed concerned.

Annoyed, I picked up. "What? What happened?" Chloe's tears were sobering. "Mom's still not home," she said. "She left the house at six o'clock."

I looked at my phone: 3:53 a.m.

"I've called her ten times, and her phone keeps going straight to voice mail," Chloe cried.

"Okay, okay, calm down," I said, trying to gain control and sound responsible. "I'll try calling her. I'll call you right back."

"What's going on?" Alex asked as she flagged down the bartender yet again.

"It's Gayle. She's gone missing." I dialed my mother's number. "Hi. You've reached Gayle Prousalis. Please leave a message." I dialed again. "Hi. You've reached Gayle Prousalis. Please leave a message." Each time I heard her voice, I imagined her trying to kill herself a different way: driving drunk down Benedict Canyon and wrapping her Jaguar around a tree. Or maybe she'd gone to hang herself in a room at one of those cheap motels below the Santa Monica Freeway. Or maybe she'd gotten a gun and shot herself. The intrusive and morbid thoughts were not uncommon, and I had been having them more frequently. Then—finally—I got a ringtone.

"Hello?" My mother picked up, out of breath.

"Mom!" I cried.

"Oh, *hi*, honey." She sounded fake friendly.

"Where are you?"

"What?" Pretending not to hear me, she was avoiding my question.

"Where are you?" I asked again.

"I'm . . . with my . . . my . . . gay . . . friend." *Gay friend?* I heard laughter in the background and her shushing someone.

"Call Chloe. She thinks you're dead." I hung up and threw my phone across the bar and then just stared into space.

"My mom's seeing someone," I said.

- 1 6 -

Richard

He reminded me of my father: bushy eyebrows, blue eyes, and thick, wavy hair. But older. And British. Working-class British. Instead of flying airplanes, he rode Harley-Davidsons and sounded like the voice-over guy from *The Fabulous Life Of*, the old VH1 show about greedy celebrities. I'd met Richard only a few times before my mother declared they were moving in together. It had been only a year and a half since my father left for prison. And we never spoke about the divorce. My mother and all of us living, breathing, and communicating in our own separate stratospheres.

My mother and Richard met through an online dating website for people from a certain socioeconomic background, which led me to believe she had joined it not long after my father left—when there was still a lot of cash in the Wells Fargo bank account. It wasn't long before she started wearing cowgirl boots and biker jackets, acting subservient and picking up after him. It was hard to watch, because when I was growing up, it had been the opposite. My father always doted on my mother, bringing her a glass of wine while she lounged on the chaise, or a bowl of ice cream if we were curled up watching an old Audrey Hepburn film. On the weekends, Richard was throwing her on the back of his motorcycle for rides along Mulholland Drive—my father hated motorcycles; each time we drove by one he made sure to comment on how dangerous he thought they were. I could quickly add it to the list of my morbid thoughts—the possibilities of how I thought my mother might die.

The first time that Mom invited Richard over for dinner, I was surprised to see him sit down at the head of the table, which was our father's spot. Mara, Chloe, and I looked at one another in mutual disdain as we took our seats. I remember staring at his face, watching it morph in between my father's and his until I had lost my appetite. I had convinced myself that my mother's and his relationship was just going to be a fling; that maybe this was just an "arrangement," and my mother would come to her senses when my father came home from prison. But when I looked at Richard sitting there where my father had sat just a year earlier during his "furlough," slicing his steak and sipping his red wine, it felt permanent.

My mother had invited Spencer and his mother, Cindy, too, to serve as buffers and ease the tension. They sat on one side of the table with Chloe, while Mara, Brian, and I sat on the other side, and my mother sat opposite Richard at the other end.

Richard tried to be polite. He asked me questions about my acting, like, "How does it feel being rejected so much?" I figured his intentions were good, and I was willing to give him the benefit of the doubt. I wanted to like him, because I was so afraid of losing my mother to one of my morbid thoughts that I was willing to accept anything that made her happy—for the time being. But dinner took an unpleasant turn when Spencer decided to tell us a story.

"So this kid, right? This fuckin' kid . . ." I knew the story was going to be a good one, because whenever Spencer had a good story to tell, he jumped in his seat. "He comes up, and he's banging on my fuckin' door, and so—"

"Excuse me!" Richard interrupted, raising his voice, startling everyone. All heads turned to the head of the table. "I find your language to be disrespectful and offensive, and I will not tolerate it at my dinner table." ("*My*" table?) "If you cannot remove the F-word from your story, I'm going to have to ask you to stop talking." The room fell to utter silence.

Chloe's chin quivered as she stared at her barely eaten plate of steak and potatoes. Mara's mouth hung open from shock. Brian stared at his dinner plate with his hands between his legs. Cindy's eyebrows were raised, so shocked that this man whom she had never met before had the audacity to reprimand her son right in front of her. My mother continued chewing quietly, and Spencer turned bright red with embarrassment. I couldn't stop staring at Richard and his untapped rage.

The story, of course, was now moot.

"Would anyone like dessert?" my mother asked, clearing her plate as if nothing had happened. Chloe threw down her fork, the sound of silver scraping china like nails on a chalkboard, humiliated in front of her best friend and his mother, whom she had come to adore as her second family.

"I think it's time to go, honey," Cindy said to Spencer, setting her cloth napkin on the table.

"I'll call you later, Chloe," Spencer said as he glared at Richard, ready for a fight.

After Spencer and Cindy walked out, Mara said, "Excuse me," stood up, locked herself in the bathroom, and sobbed for twenty minutes. Then Chloe ran downstairs to her room and slammed the door shut. I stared at my bloody steak.

Richard set his napkin on the table, and I felt him look at me, but I kept my eyes steady on my plate. I felt if I opened my mouth, I might burst into laughter or burst into tears. It was a toss-up. He got up and joined my mother in the kitchen, where she'd started doing the dishes.

"I think it's best I leave for now," I heard him whisper to her.

"No, honey, you don't have to."

"Really, Gayle, it's going to take some time."

I heard them kiss, and then Richard walked out the front door without saying good-bye.

I sat on the couch in the TV area, waiting for Mara to come out of the bathroom so we could leave. We had taken one car. Brian still sat awkwardly at the dinner table, scrolling through his phone. My mother walked over carrying a glass of Chardonnay and sat down next to me.

Then Mara stormed out of the bathroom. "Does Dad know about Richard?" she demanded.

"Well, no, not exactly," my mother replied.

"Jesus, Mom! What if Dad calls us? What if he asks about you? Or where you are?"

"Just tell him . . . you don't know." My mother took a sip of wine.

I could see she was trying not to place us in the center of it, though not realizing that she already had.

"Someday you girls will understand." Her voice started to quiver. "Richard really loves me, and I'm trying to make this as smooth as possible. I didn't want to drag you girls into it. I want you to be able to have a relationship with your dad all on your own."

"Who's paying for the divorce if you don't have any money?" Mara quipped.

"Oh, you didn't know?" I said sarcastically. "*Ralph Adler!*"

Mara stood in silence, shocked. The day I called her to tell her about the porn shoot, I had been so upset that I forgot to tell her our mother was using Ralph for the divorce.

"That's right. *Pro bono!*" I stormed off toward the front door.

"That's not true," my mother tried to fire back. "He did my *taxes* for free, and he's *referred* me to a divorce lawyer." She took another sip of wine.

Mara followed behind me. "Brian, let's go."

"Where are you going?" my mother pleaded.

"We're leaving," Mara said.

Before I walked out, I turned around and looked at my mother sitting alone on the rose-colored sofa, a look of fragile desperation across her face. Desperate for a man to be by her side; how incomplete she felt without one. And none of us girls knowing where to turn without our father, without a man to help us—no matter who he was, how imperfect he was—never realizing that the man in and of himself would never be sufficient. Would not make us whole. Would not provide security.

I wouldn't understand it until later how the choices I watched my mother make were seeping into my subconscious no matter how hard I tried to fight them, continuing to feed my desire to use my sexuality, to use victimhood, as power to get what I needed: money, protection, love. And how those things would entangle themselves so tightly in me I wouldn't be able to separate one from the other.

Chloe started coming home with tattoos symbolizing a lost past: weeping willows, and Greek letters inked across her back. She dropped out of high school after my mother announced that she was moving in with Richard. My sister didn't want to be anywhere near them when they were together. She had made it clear to my mother that she didn't feel comfortable when Richard was around the house and that she didn't like it when he slept over, but my mother allowed him to do it anyway. My mother would say that Mara and I were lucky, because we were older when my father left. She couldn't control Chloe because of the guilt she felt, because of how young Chloe was when everything was taken from her. What my mother couldn't see was that *everything* wasn't about Chloe needing a big house, needing new clothes, or a car on her sixteenth birthday. The things she felt guilty for not giving her—all of those gifts we wrapped ourselves in to make us feel that we were safe— were not the things that made us safe. They were the things that were keeping us from loving one another and being there for one another, in the right way.

It was the contract and Richard's new house that sparked Chloe's running away. Richard was buying a house in the canyons. And he considered Chloe untrustworthy because of her outbursts. He presented her with a contract of rules to live by while under his roof. With my mother's credit score at a lowly 300 or so, her name wouldn't be going on the house. The house would be Richard's and Richard's alone and Chloe would be his "guest." This was written to a girl who, just one year prior, was making straight As, was a star athlete, and who used to have more friends than anyone could count. Chloe was gone within days after that. Left with a friend of Spencer's for Santa Barbara and would never look back.

Mara and I knew it would only be a matter of time before our father would find out about Richard. Every other weekend, my mother and Richard were jetting off to some new location. Mexico. Napa Valley. The Caribbean. I wasn't even sure how they could afford it. Richard had money but not the kind of money my father had once. He worked at a furniture manufacturing company, and before he bought the house in the canyons, he'd lived in an apartment in Redondo Beach. If my mother were in a relationship for safety and security, it would have been a lot more convenient and secure had she married a multimillionaire who had plenty to share. But her instinct to survive would lead her to settle inside a lifeboat; a fantasy with someone she barely knew.

One afternoon, when they were in Mexico, Mara and I drove to Ikea to buy new silverware and plates. I had promised that once I made enough money at the bar, it would be my contribution to the apartment, since they had provided everything else. We were strolling through the plate section together talking about how I had the password to Josh's Facebook account and that I'd been checking it obsessively every hour, when sure enough, my father called looking for my mother.

"It's Dad," Mara said.

"So pick it up!" I said, not wanting to miss the call. We never knew when he would be able to call us again—three weeks later, maybe four.

She pressed the speaker button so I could hear her. "You have an incoming call. This call is from a federal prison. You will not be charged for this call. This call is from: Tom. To accept the call, dial five now. To decline the call, dial nine." *Beep!*

"Dad?"

"Marsie!" Marsie was Mara's nickname because sometimes we would find her spaced out staring into nothing, like she was on Mars.

"I'm with Christina; we're at Ikea."

"Christina Bambina!" my father shouted with excitement.

I was happy that he called while Mara and I were together, which almost never happened. For a moment, it felt as though our family was still one nucleus.

"Listen, girls, I don't have a lot of minutes left this month, and I don't want us to get cut off. I've been trying to reach Mom for a few days now, but her cell phone seems to be turned off."

Mara, panic-stricken, mouthed, "What do I say?" My heart started pounding. Were we really about to be the messengers? Responsible for breaking the news that his wife of nearly thirty years was in Mexico with a man who was buying her a house in the canyons?

I had noticed that my father never mentioned the divorce in his phone calls, which made me wonder if he knew at all that my mother was planning on divorcing him or if he just sensed that I didn't want to talk about it. So when my mother finally admitted that she was dating Richard, I'd asked her if my father knew. "No, it's not the right time to tell him," she said. But she never said, "Keep this a secret between us, and heads up, he doesn't know about the divorce." It was left up to me to decide whether or not to bring it up when I spoke to him. It was too overwhelming to think about: Richard, the divorce. I felt paralyzed, my world spinning, bombs dropping, change happening all too fast for me to comprehend any sort of reality. I never thought about the consequences of being put in such a position until it was happening.

Equally panicked, with no answer to give, I mouthed back, "I don't know! Jesus!"

Mara hung up. Pretended to lose the call. It was the only thing she could think to do. Then she flung her cell phone across the linoleum floor toward the kids' bedding section and fell down on her hands and knees, a panic attack coming on, rocking back and forth to the sound of her own inflections. "Oh God, oh God, oh God . . ."

- 1 7 -

Prison

I was sitting next to my mother at the glass octagon-shaped table, pressing my thumb back and forth against the corner. Kids in my fourth-grade science class were talking about the O. J. Simpson murder trial, repeating things their parents had said, and I was curious to know about prison.

"Dad, what do they make you eat in prison?" I stared at my uneaten, now cold and soggy brussels sprouts.

"Bread and water, Bambina. Now eat your brussels sprouts."

"Every day?"

"Every day," he said. "Now finish your dinner." His voice was stern.

The memory was visceral as I stood in front of the mailbox in the lobby of our apartment building. *Children always know things.* It was three in the morning. A wad of uncounted cash bulged from my black knee-high boot, and a new run in my stocking that climbed up toward my thigh let the world know I had not made it out of the bar unscathed.

I flipped through the mail, and my heart skipped a beat when I came across the return address: "Federal Correctional Institute La Tuna." It was a letter from the Department of Corrections. I ripped it open. Josh and I were cleared to visit.

Within months of Richard's arrival, it seemed that Josh and I would get back together and break up every five days. Filled with confusion about the course my life should take, the trust I once had was slipping away from me: trust in Josh, trust in myself. I was jealous and needy when he gave me space, and when he tried to love me, I became distant and cold. I didn't know how to seep into the gray with him. I didn't know how to love him. I just knew that I needed him now more than ever.

I ran upstairs to call him despite how late it was. Which, before, wasn't uncommon. To check in after work, to fall asleep listening to the sound of his voice on the other line, making me feel like I was safe.

I sobbed, holding the phone tight against my ear. "I'm sorry, Josh." Below my swollen eyes, I wrapped an old brown scarf around my neck, hiding the black and blue hickey given to me by a man at the bar who offered me a $300 tip if I went with him to the Standard hotel in West Hollywood after work. It was half my rent. I remember walking into the mid-century building and seeing a young female model sleeping inside of a glass cage in the lobby, not far from two clear plastic swings that were in the shape of half bubbles hanging from the ceiling. "I just want to swing in the swings with you, that's all," the man told me.

"You're pushing me away, Christina," Josh said, exhausted on the other end of the line. Exhausted from me. Exhausted from it all. "My mom suggested we go see Sheryl together."

"What?" I said, irritated by the suggestion. Couples therapy in our early twenties?

I had seen Sheryl a few more times but still didn't think she was "working." After our sessions together, I would crawl back into bed and sleep for the next three hours until I had to show up for work.

"We've been cleared to visit my dad. I just got the letter. That's why I'm calling."

"Call Sheryl, Christina. I don't want to talk to you until then." Josh hung up on me. He could see that I needed help; that I was far beyond his reach. I didn't want to hear it; I believed that every problem remained outside of myself. But I knew that if I wanted him with me, I'd have to call the therapist and make the appointment. And my father wasn't going to let me visit him alone. He said it was too dangerous. I was a girl and far too young.

"I threw up when I got back to the hotel room." Mara warned me of how it was visiting Dad in prison for the first time. She stood in the doorway of my bedroom, brushing her teeth before bed wearing an old Nirvana T-shirt.

Mara and Brian had driven cross-country from Dallas to Los Angeles after graduation. On their way out west, they had stopped in El Paso to visit Dad. I didn't ask for any details about her trip, maybe because I figured I wouldn't get the whole truth, just as my mother and Chloe didn't want to talk about it. So I began an obsessive internet search. It kept me awake most nights before Josh and I left. Much to my chagrin, we'd seen Sheryl together, and he had agreed to come with me. I wanted to know everything. I needed to outsmart the fear I had about going to prison, and if I knew what to expect, I figured it wouldn't hurt as much. I wanted to know what it looked like beyond the visiting rooms. The cells: Did they sleep in bunk beds? The cafeteria: Were inmates chained to the tables? Did they really shower naked together like in the movies? What did solitary confinement look like? Were they locked in cement dungeons like in medieval times?

I had come across an old news article about a prison riot. I read about rival gang members creating weapons called shanks made from pencils and pens, sharpened lids from cans, tied locks to socks; each used to swing, slice, and stab one another until those few not left injured or dead were all facedown and handcuffed along that cafeteria floor. Guards outnumbered by hundreds. And I imagined blood everywhere—the smell of sweat, salt, and copper—grown men moaning and crying for help, crying for medical attention where there was none to give. And I thought about my father. I thought about him being nearly sixty years old, barely five foot ten, never owning a gym membership in his life. He didn't have a violent bone in his body. The fear hadn't dissipated from my research. If anything, it grew, and my heart sank deeper for him.

It was the night before Josh and I were scheduled to leave. He was picking me up the following morning for a seven o'clock flight. My father claimed that moving to the minimum-security prison in El Paso, Texas, was for the best. The federal government had set up a program where you could see a psychiatrist, say you're an addict, and complete a series of drug and alcohol classes that would knock off a few years of your sentence. I had never seen my father drunk or known him to use drugs.

Mara took the toothbrush out of her mouth and waved it at me like a conductor, lifting her chin so toothpaste wouldn't spill out. "Luk as ugly as possible. Covu up you entaya body, oh those fuckas will tun you away. Gotta go spit." She walked across the hall to her bedroom and closed the door behind her.

It felt strange standing in front of my closet, pushing silk shirts and spaghetti-strap tank tops out of the way, searching for something to wear, my empty carry-on bag on the floor next to me. I never thought there would come a night where I could say to someone "I'm packing for prison." I had no idea what to bring or what to wear. I never knew anyone incarcerated. Prison was just a distant, imaginative hell that belonged only to villains in movies or serial killers on the news. It was never supposed to be connected to me personally; it wasn't supposed to be bound to my life in any way. But here and now it was, and tomorrow—would be forever.

I settled on my baggy "fat" jeans and a baggy sweatshirt that would do a good job of hiding my body. I pulled out my black-and-white Converse shoes and placed them next to the bed. I didn't even bother packing any makeup or a hair dryer. I felt relieved. It didn't matter at all what I looked like, as Mara's words "look as ugly as possible" clung to me for dear life.

"Girls, over here! Dad wants to get a family photo!" my mother called, waving her arms back and forth in her shell Moschino sunglasses and new Princess Di haircut. We were strolling the sidewalks of Lahaina, shopping for the day. It was spring break, and I had just turned four-teen. We were staying at the Four Seasons Resort on the shores of Wailea Beach in Maui.

I ran over in my red-and-pink skort and my blue Ralph Lauren bikini top my mother had bought me a few weeks earlier. Mara and Chloe followed behind me, all three of us crowned with pink plumeria leis. My father stood in his Tommy Bahama T-shirt photographing five parrots—red, yellow, blue, white, and red—as they squawked, bobbing their heads back and forth while dancing on wooden perches inside a giant green cage. The owner, an old man with weathered skin, wore a straw hat and had an old 1980s oversize boom box on the ground next to him. My father had convinced the owner to let us take the birds out of the cage so we could get a family photo with them. "We've got a cockatiel at home; I assure you my girls won't be scared."

"No problem," the kind man said. "Their wings are clipped."

I kept thinking about that family vacation while Josh drove, and I sat in the passenger seat with my feet up on the dashboard of our silver 2001 Toyota Corolla rental that smelled of vanilla air freshener and McDonald's french fries. To shut out the memories, I turned on the radio, scanning for a decent station but settling for Christian rock for lack of anything better. We didn't think to bring an iPod or any mix CDs. There was nothing celebratory about this "vacation," nothing to sing about, nothing to laugh about, nothing to dance about here in El Paso. I looked at the clock, and it was almost noon. Josh and I needed to speed if we wanted to make it in time for the rest of visiting hours.

The freeway was fast and clear, and I rolled down my window to get some fresh air. Passengers in passing vehicles wore cowboy hats and vests; crosses, some with Jesus Christ, dangled from rearview mirrors. Faith felt dark as I looked out toward the border of Juarez, Mexico, just a mile to my left. Some journalists call it the most violent place in the world outside of declared war zones. And I could see it. I could see the rolling hills of black and brown dirt where dilapidated bungalows stood, and I could feel its passive anger as billows of distant smoke evaporated from piles of trash into the round blue sky. As I looked to my right, I saw the veneer of a safer place, a seemingly innocent place—America, where freedom rings, where endless rows of identical pink brick tract homes lined the vacant freeway. I was shaken by the juxtaposition of extreme poverty paralleling cookie-cutter suburbia. I was lost in the divide of it all, when Josh asked for Bob's letter. "Did you remember to bring Bob's letter, Christina?"

Bob, Mara's godfather, had sent us a letter with directions to the prison attached. It was a be-forewarned-let-me-prepare-you-for-this letter. It had been years since we'd seen or heard from Bob, and only after my father left for prison, did we reconnect. He and my father were air force buddies and had remained best friends ever since. For my father's fortieth birthday, Bob gave him a gold plaque that read "If You Ain't a Pilot, You Ain't Shit." My father displayed it behind his desk in the library.

Just under two miles ahead is where your dad is. When you go in, leave everything in the car except your driver's licenses, your car keys, $2 or $3 of change (for vending machines). You can't take anything to him. I offered him a Life Saver yesterday, and he couldn't take it. Don't take your wallets. These guys are on a power trip and depending on the individual, they will enforce the above to the letter. It's just easier to play

*their game. You will get the back of your hand stamped and then you will
proceed outside and through 3 gates to get to the building. Once through
the first gate, you will have to pass the back of your stamped hand under
an ultraviolet light (same when you leave). Once in the last building,
you will walk across the room and hand your sign-in paper to the man
at the desk. He will then call for your dad. There have always been other
visitors in front of me at the last sign-in site, and these guards have no
interest in expediting the process. When you tell him a time, don't be late.
He's not going anywhere (as he would say). I hope so much you have a
wonderful day with him. It will mean the world to him. I look forward
to the next time I can see you and your sisters.*

Love,

Bob

Josh veered off the freeway onto a long dirt road. The road felt pointless
against miles and miles of flat land around us as we accelerated toward the
prison entrance. "Low La Tuna Federal Prison" was painted on a series
of consecutive brown rocks. I could see the building. At first glance, it
appeared beautiful and historical-looking, which I found unsettling, like
an abandoned, maybe once-elegant medieval Spanish villa still with its
original molding and arched windows and doorways in the middle of a
vacant desert. Only now it was forgotten about: saddened by the out-
skirts of brown wooden power lines and barbed-wire fence where tiny
boxed windows were carved out of white cement walls—no breathing
sign of vegetation. Isolated and cold. As it should be.

"How you doin', kiddo?" Josh glanced over at me. I stared out the
window as I felt the truth retract from my throat. How could I possibly
answer such a loaded question? We were rushing into one of the most
physical acts of survival, other than war. It was prison. There was no
time to feel. Yet I found myself fixating on the word he used—*kiddo*—
endearing but patronizing, close but distant. In our session with Sheryl,
Josh had agreed to come with me to prison, but that didn't mean we

were getting back together. I couldn't help but wonder what we were doing there together. I wanted to say "So what are we, Josh?" I fixated on anything but the truth, which was only that he was there to protect me, to take care of me, to support me. And I resented him for that because it meant that I was fragile, that I was unstable, which I could never admit to myself was true, though it was. Anything Josh said to me I would find a reason to twist, turn, and spit the words back at him as if he were the cruelest human being on earth, as if it were his fault.

"I'm fine," I said.

"You sure?"

"Really, I'm actually okay." I smiled at him.

We pulled alongside a beat-up security house. There we came face-to-face with an overweight correctional officer dressed in a uniform similar to that of the US Marines. His combat boots added an escalated element of fear, and his belt was complete with a gun, other various weapons, and handcuffs, which were buckled appropriately to his waist. His hand was clinging to his belt.

"Remember to call him 'sir'; call him 'sir.'" I nudged Josh, reminding him what my father always told me when I first got my driver's license: "If you are ever pulled over by a cop, Bambina, it's 'yes, sir,' 'no, sir,' or 'yes, ma'am,' 'no, ma'am.' They like to be treated with respect."

"Driver's license," the guard demanded.

"Here you go, sir," Josh said.

"Is this a rented vehicle?"

"Yes, sir."

"Rental car agreement and vehicle license plate number." His face expressed nothing. He was apathetic. Numb. There was no please, no thank-yous exchanged, no "Hello, how's your day going, must suck having to visit your dad in prison today" conversation. It was no place for empathy, no place for compassion, no place for feeling. I was nothing but a speck of annoyance in this man's day—just another notch on his belt, another statistic added to the United States Federal Bureau of Prisons. *"Here's another one, boss. Poor baby, welcome to prison, sweet girl. You are not special; just collateral damage now"* is what ran through my mind as I was officially handed someone else's shame.

I smiled again.

"Straight ahead into that lot, then get in line." He signaled for us to drive through.

Per Bob's direction, we left everything in the car except our driver's licenses and a roll of quarters for the vending machines. I felt confidently ugly in my oversize sweatshirt, baggy jeans, and Converse shoes, my hair tied back in a loose bun, and wearing no makeup. Josh wore a gray hoodie, jeans, and his Converse shoes too. Despite our best efforts to fit in, we still looked out of place for prison. We were the only Caucasians other than some guards. We stood at the end of the line, and I noticed that Josh was also one of the few men. The line consisted mostly of Hispanic women and children—mothers, daughters, and a few young sons—walking hand in hand upstairs to another holding area that looked similar to a bus stop. There sat a young girl who looked like she was my age. She was pregnant and reading a novel. She'd been there before, it seemed. A pretty girl, with curly black hair. She was calm and cool, exuding peace and acceptance. I didn't know it then, but I envied her fearlessness.

We continued waiting like cattle until we were called through the first gate of the prison. There we had our right hand stamped. Then we proceeded toward the second gate, where I placed my hand under the ultraviolet black light, just as Bob had said. Next, we arrived at the official security booth, where we had to pass through metal detectors. I watched the families before me pass through first. Every time the buzzer went off, indicating something metal or illegal, it echoed throughout the waiting area. A few white-painted benches stood along the wall, but not one person sat down. All of us remained silent, cooperative; eager to pass through as efficiently as possible.

I was next in line when the guard whose job it was to motion individuals through stopped the woman in front of me. She was heavyset, with gray streaks in her hair; she looked like she was wearing her Sunday best. The guard wagged his finger at her, motioning the woman to step toward him. As she did, he felt below her breast, staring at her with intimidation. He didn't blink. The woman's young son—or grandson; I couldn't tell—was standing behind her, watching.

Through the fabric of her dress, the guard stuck his finger underneath the underwire of her bra. Then he flicked it.

"You either take this bra off and leave it right here, or we are going to have to cut out the underwire," the guard said, leaving no room for negotiation. There was a sudden wave of humiliation across the woman's face, as she turned back to acknowledge her young boy, waiting with the rest of us.

"But," she pleaded, "this bra . . . this bra is Victoria's Secret. It cost me a lot of money, sir. I am not hiding anything. It is just a bra."

I knew the type of bra she was talking about. They cost anywhere from $50 to $65, easily the cost of a tank of gas to get to and from work for the week. And if she took off the bra, it would deem her inappropriate, and she would be turned away, forced to come back wearing something else. By the time she returned, visiting hours would be over.

"Step aside, ma'am," he replied. Until she could make a decision, she was of no use to him. She meant nothing. She was nothing but another speck of an annoyance, like me. An inconvenience in this man's workday, and he could dismiss her because recreant power allowed him to do so.

I placed my hand beneath my own breasts and sighed with relief, thanking God I'd remembered to put on a sports bra. I didn't want this man coming near my body, let alone touching any inch of it.

Josh and I passed through the metal detectors alarm free. We waited in front of a series of dark-tinted windows next to what looked like a large automatic metal door. I felt eyes on me but couldn't see them. It smelled of metal too and disinfectant—the way a hospital smells. The floors were dusty, scattered with folded gum wrappers and dirty tissues. Testimonial laziness is what I'd call it.

"*Clear!*" the guard yelled. My heart pounded, and I told myself,

Breathe, just breathe. I felt as if I were a criminal, as if I'd broken the law—that I too deserved punishment, indicated by the way they treated us because we were bound by an inmate's blood. All of us were collateral damage. And this was my initiation into the United States prison system. This was my golden ticket for blame, for sorrow, for madness, my mind swaying from humiliation to fear as we passed through the windowless hallway. Guards stood with their legs spread apart at either end. The door behind us jolted shut and locked. There was no way out now. Images of the riots fluttered through my head, and I turned to look at Josh, who seemed unusually calm and steady for his typically neurotic and emotional self, reassuring me that it would be okay despite the unbearable anticipation.

His head of gray hair was the first thing I noticed. And also how skinny he was. He'd lost about fifteen pounds since I saw him a year earlier during his "furlough." I figured it must have been all those endless games of Ping-Pong he played. He was by far the oldest among the inmates lined up next to him in the front of the visitor room.

They marched in a single profile line, and then stopped and faced forward. But they weren't looking at us. They weren't allowed to until permitted. They wore identical khaki jumpsuits. I wondered what the other inmates' crimes were. Drug dealing? Burglary? Rape? Murder? My father kept his chin down, and his eyes locked on one of the guards. Then he glanced down at his feet. He was wearing tan Timberland boots. These boots were popular among the boys at my high school; they'd wear them unlaced, with their khaki pants hanging down in the middle of their ass so you could see their boxer shorts. Not a good look.

My father walked over with a mischievous smirk on his face, marching toward me like an unwound toy soldier. It was the look he gave when life wasn't supposed to be taken so seriously, like the time he mooned our old neighbor, Mr. Anderson, in a dispute over the property line.

"Christina Bambina!" he cried and then swooped down to give me a hug. His silly walk and smile helped restrain the lump of tears in my throat. I wasn't going to cry. I held on to him, and he smelled of Dial soap. We were prohibited from hugging for too long. All inmates were. If you showed any great length of affection, you were at risk of being kicked out—or worse, blacklisted altogether from visiting privileges. When he put me down, he grabbed both my hands to look me over. His hands were calloused and rough, and I had trouble looking him in the eye.

Josh stood up and shook his hand. "Hello, sir, it's nice to see you again," he said, nodding his head. "Despite the circumstances, of course."

"It's my Mexican resort!" my father blurted out, trying to make light of the situation. He chuckled while patting Josh on the back and led us outside to one of the concrete benches in the courtyard. "For more privacy," he said.

"You look great, Dad," I lied, hoping he wouldn't notice how startled I was by his weight loss.

"I'm down to my old air force weight!" He made it seem as if it were on purpose. As if he was on a diet by choice.

"So. Bambina," he continued. Not one of us wanted to talk about the fact that we were inside a federal prison. In fact, we were not in prison anymore; we were at the Four Seasons, waiting for our drinks. "How's Mom?" he asked, eagerly. "How does her hair look? Is it still *fire engine red*?" The way he said "fire engine red," it was as though he owned her; as though her trademark was his trademark. Still his young wild thing that he was madly in love with. All my father wanted to do was talk about my mother.

"You know, the first time I met Mom, she was wearing the most god-awful dress I had ever seen: some kind of California mumu. We were at a party, and I was in law school at the time—piss poor—and my neighbor Debbie would invite me over and feed me apple pie. She made the best apple pies. And one night she had a party, and Mom showed up, and I could not, for the life of me, understand why this total knockout of a babe was wearing this . . . mumu. And she ignored me the whole night!" My father leaned back on the concrete bench, laughing so hard at the memory of her, his cheeks flushed a rosy color red.

Josh and I laughed with him, more out of discomfort than humor. I could see the fear across my father's face: the fear he felt of losing her, neither one of us wanting to believe she was already gone for good. Although I knew, of course, that my mother was now with Richard, a part of me wanted my father to keep talking about her: because indulging in their love story fueled my belief that *maybe* he could win her back. I wanted to believe in true love. I wanted to believe that my parents were meant to be together—"like fate," I remembered my mother saying.

It was inevitable that the subject of Richard would come up.

"Dad—" I said, about to tell him that Mom and Richard were moving in together. But before I could speak, he put up his hand and waved it in front of his chest. "Ah-ah-ah," he said. "Don't say his name, Bambina. We refer to him only as *Le Asshole*." He leaned across the table. "How much *money* do you think this guy is worth, eh? What kind of *car* does he drive?" I turned to Josh for help.

"All right, all right, all right." My father waved his hand again. "I don't want to talk about *Le Asshole* anyway."

"Do you want anything from the vending machines?" Josh asked, attempting to change the subject. "We brought a roll of quarters."

"Oh, that's good; yeah, that's a good idea," my father said.

"I'll go, I'll go—what do you guys want?" I stood up from the table, desperate to get some space.

"I'd go with you, Bambina, but the mullahs won't let your old dad near a roll of quarters or a vending machine. Grab me a Snickers." He looked at Josh. "My favorite."

My father had started referring to anyone working for the American government as "the mullahs" to imply our country's hypocrisy, ignoring America's rampant oppression of minorities and the poor, and its mass incarceration crisis.

"You want anything?" I asked Josh.

"I'm good," he replied. "You want me to go with you?"

"No, no, I'm fine. Be right back."

When I walked through the courtyard, I couldn't help but look around at all of the other inmates and their families. Underneath the shaved heads, tattooed necks covered in gang signs, and hardened bodies, I saw vulnerable men sitting with their mothers, girlfriends, sons, and daughters. One of the inmates I saw while I stood in line for the vending machines looked younger than me. Maybe all of eighteen years old, with an innocent, round face. He bounced a baby in his lap. She wore a pink dress, and a matching pink scrunchy headband encircled her soft bald head. Her tiny hands patted his plump lips with excitement as he whispered nurturing words to her in Spanish, laughing occasionally, and looking to the woman next to him, who appeared to be his mother. She kept resting her head on his shoulder.

I felt embarrassed suddenly at how obvious my "prison outfit" was. Based on all the violence I had seen and read about on the internet, and had seen in the news and in Hollywood films about villains and prison, I had assumed that all inmates were somehow exempt from the human condition. But here I was, watching men with families like mine: mothers, daughters, sons. And the men themselves were fathers, sons, grandsons. I had been so misguided, believing that because of where and how I was raised that it made us separate from one another, and I was beginning to see how wildly untrue this was because there was a depth I saw, a commonality of pain that I saw. Everyone had a story to tell. I wanted to know what it was, how each inmate ended up here, and what had led them astray.

I grabbed the Snickers bar, a bag of Fritos, and a Coke, and headed back to the courtyard. Josh and my father were quiet. I figured they were probably talking about me. I set the Coke and Fritos on the table, handed my father the Snickers bar, and pretended not to notice.

"What's happening with your case, Dad?" I asked.

"We're filing another appeal. Remember, the wheels of justice turn slowly, Bambina, but a leading professor of securities law and a summa graduate of Harvard Law School recently submitted an affidavit to the court arguing that not only did I not commit a criminal offense, but I did not commit a civil offense." He took a bite of his Snickers bar.

"Well, that sounds good," Josh said.

"Yeah, that's great, Dad."

"Yeah, I'm feeling good about it. Real good about it." He popped the rest of the Snickers into his mouth.

I tried to stay present, but I couldn't stop staring at the concrete walls surrounding us, and the razor wire fence that looked like jagged V-shaped knives looping around the top ready to slice through soft flesh even if grazed slightly. And I couldn't stop thinking about the fact that I didn't recognize my father, and it scared me. And there was a gash on his arm. I saw it, and I know Josh did too, and neither one of us addressed it. I didn't want to be there anymore. My perception of the truth was seesawing, and all I wanted to do was run for the past.

"I want this bird, I want this bird!" Chloe cried, jumping up and down in her green Jelly sandals. She was pointing to the white parrot perched at the top of the cage. Mara was holding her parrot, green and black; she was puckering her lips and pecking his beak. The kind man reached his arm deep inside the cage and grabbed the white parrot for Chloe.

"He reminds me of Sammy," I said.

"He does look like Sammy!" my father exclaimed. Sammy was the parrot who'd lived at the bottom of the pink hotel in Boca Raton, Florida, where we lived for a few months while our house in Virginia was being built. My father had been doing business down there at the time.

"Look, girls!" my mother said. The blue parrot was standing on her head as she tiptoed around in a small circle showing off for us with her arms spread like wings. Suddenly the blue parrot jumped from her head, flapping his wings as he tried to fly away, but his feathers were no longer shaped for the direction of the sky, and the force of gravity pulled him to the ground as he landed and tumbled over his feet.

Josh placed his hand on my back to get my attention. I noticed the energy shift. Family members started saying good-bye as a guard stepped outside to notify us we had only a few more minutes left together.

"That's our time; we better head inside now," my father said, getting up from the table. It rattled me to see him so quick to obey. Never had I seen him report to anyone before.

"Do you know much about the stories of the guys in here?" I asked as he stood up.

"That guy over there." My father averted his eyes, but nodded imperceptibly in the direction of the inmate sitting one bench over from us. "Doing ten years for setting back the odometer of a car."

"Ten years?"

"Oh, you bet. There are many, many sad stories here. I'll have to save them for another day." When my father spoke seriously, he squinted his eyes and nodded his head. "You know, in 1985, the year you were born, Christina, there were 450,000 incarcerated Americans. Today there are 2.1 million. I'm telling you, the mullahs and fundamentalists are running this country now, and it's only going to get worse."

My father led us back inside to the chairs where we'd originally waited for him. "You two must wait here. Inmates have to line up and exit first," he explained. Guards began calling out numbers and names as inmates lined up at the front of the room again. My world was spinning, and I didn't know what to say—how to say good-bye, what to make of any of it. Had I said enough? It didn't feel like enough.

"Sir"—my father extended his hand to Josh—"always a pleasure."

"It was great to see you, Tom."

"And Josh . . . thank you for being there for the girls—my family—when I haven't been able to be. Your kindness and support have been much appreciated."

"It's my pleasure. I love your daughter very much." Hearing Josh say those words to my father twisted my heart even more.

"I'll try and give you a call tomorrow, Bambina. I love you, and what a great time I had with you today."

"I love you too, Dad." We hugged good-bye, and the lump in my throat grew bigger.

The guard shouted a number. "That's me," Dad said. He kissed me on the cheek, and that was it. I didn't know when I would see him again. I watched him get in line, his arms stiffly at his sides like a soldier's. I studied him once more. The look on his face seemed brighter than before—almost childlike as his eyes held steady on the guard.

Josh put the key in the ignition but didn't start the car. A moment of silence between us.

"Are you . . . are you going to say something?" he asked cautiously.

"I don't really know what to say, Josh. I just saw my dad in prison." I gazed at the bare horizon in front of me, affectless.

"You know, it's okay to cry, Christina."

I had hated this about Josh, so welcoming of intimacy and vulnerability, and I felt repulsed by it. And I felt guilty for feeling repulsed by it. And then I felt defective because he loved me, and it wasn't his fault. But I couldn't help feeling physically ill from it, like I would be admitting to some sort of defeat; that it would make me weak.

I was so confused about what exactly it was that Josh thought it was okay to cry about. With specks of doubt circling my conscience, I felt numb, and the tears wouldn't come. Because wasn't my father supposed to be an innocent man sitting behind bars at the hands of the American government? Wasn't he supposed to be the rule maker? The disciplinarian? The authoritarian? The lawyer! Lawyers, police officers, and politicians—they didn't go to prison, right? How could someone of the law and for the law break the law? How could this be? I was naive.

I turned to Josh and looked at him doe-eyed. He looked back at me, ready and waiting to catch the emotion—any emotion. And so I did what I did best: I faked it. I assumed my role—the victim—and then I focused. I replayed the tape of what I had just seen: my father in his khaki jumpsuit, his gray hair, his bowed head and calloused hands, the concrete bench and barbed wire fence. And then I remembered: I remembered how he once put a pumpkin over his head on Halloween, and peas up his nose at dinner, and I remembered his Eskimo kisses, and the tickle monster, and when he first taught me how to ride a bike without training wheels. I pushed—*pushed*—as hard as I could for those tears, because they were expected of me, and because if I didn't cry, it would mean I wasn't human and that I didn't love my own father.

As the perfect tears rolled down my cheeks, I was suddenly Holly Golightly from *Breakfast at Tiffany's*, Scarlett O'Hara from *Gone with the Wind*. An amazing actress! And Josh, he reached over, like the hero, and he held me, and he wiped away my tears. And all I wanted to do was scream "This is fake! It's the moments when I'm alone at night, naked, with my hands and knees on the porcelain shower floor while the water smashes my back, with my mouth gaping wide, and my stomach muscles clenched, because my *real* tears are so heavy they silence the gushing gasps of my breath, because if you really knew the truth—if you really knew who I was—you would leave me. You would leave me and break my heart.

"Just like my father did."

Mom, Dad, Mara, Chloe, and I stood clumped together underneath the coconut tree, giggling with our arms around one another as we finally each got a parrot on our shoulders, squirming, wings flapping, whacking us as we tried our best to pose for what would be our perfect family Christmas card.

"Say cheese!"

"Cheese!"

Christmas 2007

"I'll give you a hint." My father, wearing a Santa hat, leaned back in his leopard-covered chair. Bing Crosby's "It's Beginning to Look a Lot Like Christmas" played on the surround sound. He crossed his legs, twisted his black mustache, and made his eyes big and wide like a cartoon character, striking a flamboyant pose.

My father was always teaching us fun facts about history, art, film, or Greek mythology—the gods and goddesses—quizzing us later and bribing us with money. A $10 bill if you could spell Mary Poppins's *supercalifragilisticexpialidocious*! Or a $20 bill if you could say the entire Greek alphabet or name the Greek goddess of wisdom. "Athena!"

"Salvador Dali! Salvador Dali! Salvador Dali!" Mara screamed, jumping up and down in front of the warm fireplace. My older sister and I had been in his study playing Uno and Go Fish while he worked at his desk until he took a break to quiz us on his art. Chloe was helping Mom decorate the front hall banister with Christmas garlands. Little red bows, candy canes, and glitter covered the floor in the foyer. And mounds of presents in red-and-white wrapping paper surrounded the Christmas tree in the loggia.

My father arched one of his bushy eyebrows so that it was higher than the other, a trick he'd do at the dinner table to make us laugh. He looked at Mara. "Affirmative!" he replied in his military voice while smoothing out the ends of his mustache. He dangled a $20 bill in front of her. She yanked it from him and did a little victory dance around his mahogany desk.

"Oh, man!" I huffed, feeling defeated.

"Now," he continued, "Salvador Dali is the artist, but what is the *name* of the piece?" Mara and I gazed up at the painting, which hung above the fireplace as we sucked on swirly green, red, and white candy canes.

It was the image of an owl. The owl's eyes were black and twisted like the epicenter of two tornadoes, but its wings were folded toward its chest like lungs filled with tar. The sky, blue and black, and below the owl was the sketch of a man in a state of enthralling passion, his arm raised, suggesting an argument. He stood before a murderer, a thief, or maybe an innocent man, or a jury, and they were splattered in red paint, and it looked like blood.

"*The Lawyer!*" my mother yelled from the hallway. My father threw his hands up in the air. "Babe! You just ruined it for the girls!" He always called my mother "Babe," even in the most serious of moments.

Chloe came running in wearing one of her Disney's *Aladdin* costumes, biting off pieces of her candy necklace and yelling, "The lawyer! The lawyer! The lawyer!" Then Mara chased her out of the study, and they went shrieking and galloping into the kitchen for more hot chocolate.

"What, I'm not allowed to play too?" my mother said, playfully.

My father handed me the $20 anyway. "Don't tell your sisters," he said with a wink. I stuffed the bill into my pocket. "But wait: Dad, what is that hanging from the owl's forehead?" I asked.

"Those are the scales of justice, Bambina."

"What does that mean?"

"It's the symbol for truth and fairness."

"Well, it looks silly."

I thought about the painting, how much my father loved it, and what it stood for. And I wondered how much the things we held on to represented our most truthful selves—if at all—depending on the motive behind buying it.

It was almost Christmas. My mother and Richard were away in San Francisco again, and I was driving to their house. The city of Los Angeles, covered with white lights on palm trees, fake snow in windows, frantic and buzzing with holiday angst as people scurried around town panicked to find their perfect gifts.

I pulled into the driveway of Richard's newly renovated house near the top of Mulholland Drive. Brown boxes sat on the doorstep, my name written on each side in black Sharpie.

"You'd better come pick your things up, or Richard is going to throw them away," my mother had warned me. "He doesn't want them in the house; there's no room for them." I had resisted picking them up for a while because I didn't want to have to carry them with me the next time I moved—which I knew would be soon because Mara and Brian were discussing getting engaged.

I stepped out of the car and went to open one of the boxes filled with memories of my childhood. My pink box of love letters from old boyfriends, my ballet pointe shoes, my mother's collection of Nancy Drew books from the 1960s, which she'd passed down to me on my tenth birthday. And more books: *The Napping House, The Giving Tree, Oh, the Places You'll Go!*

I dumped the heavy boxes into the backseat. Before I got back in, I looked through the front window and noticed their Christmas tree, decorated intricately with all of the ornaments from years of our family Christmases. Now, I had bit my tongue at the discomfort of being in Richard's home filled with the furniture from my childhood, and how he slept in my parents' old bed—the thought of which made me queasy. Still, the child in me, not wanting to accept the divorce, held it all in, all of the things I wanted to say, sucked up in me like a vacuum. I had managed to remain as polite as possible whenever I visited. But now I lost it, wounded that they hadn't included me in their tree decorating. Standing there with the scraps of my childhood dumped in brown boxes from Ralphs grocery store because there "was no room for them." To me it meant that Richard didn't want the baggage that came with my mother. He didn't want three daughters. He had said to Chloe once, "I'm done raising children. I'm not planning on raising more." He had two grown sons, whom I'd never met.

I pressed my nose a little harder against the window, and I could see our angel and the ornaments we had made as a family displayed on someone else's tree, locked in someone else's home, and I didn't have a key.

Adrenaline shot through my veins as I got back in the car. I would send my mother an email, that's what I would do, and tell her how I really felt.

I weaved down the canyon as the sun began to set. The glittering colors and twinkling lights dangling from trees and houses, my father's voice playing on a loop in my head. "Soon we'll have a King Air and we'll be able to go where we want to when we want to. San Francisco for lunch! Aspen for dinner! And we'll go shopping in Dad's 1962 Aston Martin DB-4! And our martinis will be shaken not stirred."

I decided then that I hated Christmas; everyone shopping, happy, cheerful, benevolent—not me. I stormed into the apartment, opened my computer, and hammered out an angry email to my mother.

"I am tired of being polite, tired of biting my tongue, tired of bowing down to your needs, and tired of 'accepting' your new life, Mom."

She was moving on too quickly, and I wanted to press the Pause button. I wanted everyone to stand still and just wait a minute so I could regain my balance, but I kept falling farther and farther behind.

My mother wrote me back doing the best she could to comfort me from afar, letting me know that my feelings of anger were a normal part of the process of learning to accept the things we could not change. "What is done is done," she said. Having been the daughter of divorced parents herself, she understood that it was doubly hard during the holidays. Of course, I felt her response was preposterous. She didn't have a father in prison! I was consumed with self-righteous indignation; she couldn't possibly understand the depths of my pain!

As with my mother, I sensed Mara slipping from me too. She had found refuge in Brian. And Chloe got harder and harder to reach in Santa Barbara; most of the time, she wouldn't call back at all. I had expectations—a fantasy—that living with Mara would somehow resemble our past despite how everything around us had changed. I was terrified I was losing my sister to a life that excluded me. I was stuck, fixating on our past, and unwilling to embrace any kind of a future. I couldn't bear watching everyone else move on, because it implied that the family we were had been merely a facade.

A few days before Christmas, I was sitting alone on the balcony of our apartment, smoking a pipeful of marijuana to distance myself further from reality. Doing so was becoming more and more of a habit, along with my drinking for free at the bar. I plucked a fur coat from Mara's closet and sat with it wrapped around me while I blew smoke rings into the cool air as if I were actress Edie Sedgwick from the Andy Warhol film *Poor Little Rich Girl*.

I heard the front door slam shut, and knew Mara and Brian wouldn't be happy with me for breaking their no-smoking rule. But I continued anyway, not knowing how to express what I was experiencing. The bond between us was interrupted by how far I could run from my own grief. I was so afraid of the things I could not say. Instead they were erupting and unfolding in outer rage.

Mara thrust open the glass door to the balcony. "Are you smoking pot in my coat?" she demanded.

I didn't look at her; I took the lighter, lit the bowl, and continued to smoke.

"You are becoming such a pothead, Christina. Just because you're unhappy with your life does not mean you can take other people's things and disrespect our rules."

"*I'm* such a pothead? Do you even *remember* the six-foot bong you smoked out of in college? Stop pretending to be so perfect," I shot back.

"Take off my coat."

"No."

"Take it off."

"No."

"Take it off now, or I'm taking your drugs away." She eyed my Ziploc bag of weed on the table. I sat there, refusing to listen, daring her. Suddenly Mara lunged for the bag, grabbed it, and then ran into the kitchen and dumped it down the garbage disposal.

I gasped, grabbed my lighter, and ran for her Nantucket purse, a gift my father had given her on her eighteenth birthday.

The Nantucket purse is technically a basket. It is a symbol of high status on the island, hand woven with carved scrimshaw (whale bone) in the shape of a whale on top. If you want, and most do, it comes with a mini plaque inside bearing your name and the date the purse was made, engraved in cursive. The basket costs between $2,000 and $10,000, and, depending on how much money you have, one is often put on a wait list.

I held the basket hostage and threatened to light it on fire.

I wanted her to think the same, to feel the same—to survive in the same way that I was. And in that moment, I wanted to see how far she was from believing the possibility that it was all a lie; that maybe our childhood wasn't what it had seemed. The drugs, the basket—the things we clung to. We were two opposite extremes in fight-or-flight mode, and there was so much that went unsaid between us. We could never admit, not even to each other, the confusion and the embarrassment we felt after losing our home, after our father's conviction, after leaving Washington, DC, abruptly for fear of how we would continue to be ostracized.

She lunged at me, and I threw the basket as hard as I could so it broke against the wall.

After Christmas, I'd be moving out.

•   •   •

It was cold and bleak on the quiet Sunset Strip. On Christmas, bars are a place for the lonely, the rebellious, and those whose fears and failures are too painful to face. It was this Christmas that I found myself driving through neighborhoods after the sun had set to peer through yellow-lit windows and watch all the families gathered around the kitchen, where they were safe and warm. In my memory, I kept hearing the sound of John Palmer's voice reporting from the White House lawn for NBC News, the garage door rumbling open, letting us know that Dad was home, the smells of my mother's famous banana nut bread and southern-style green beans. The nostalgia pulled me into a euphoric state of mania where I became obsessed, studying each home I drove by and wondering if the families were happy and if everything on the inside was as beautiful as it looked on the outside. I hoped that someday the answer would come to me, or some other force of nature would pull me back to the reality I wanted instead of the one I had been given. There were some nights where I couldn't even bring myself to drive away—to drive away from some stranger's life that I wished I could be a part of—to the point where I would make myself late for work. All because I longed to be a part of something other than what I had, and to be anywhere but inside myself.

It was just Jimmy and me working on Christmas. All the other girls had requested the night off, but I didn't bother. It would be lousy either way. There were only a few customers sitting at tables, sipping on Coronas and eating prepackaged Christmas dinners that left the taste of lingering plastic on your tongue. Slow nights like Christmas were easy, and I could steal things that I needed, like toilet paper. Single rolls of the cheap kind: thin, rough, and wrapped up in tissue tucked in the center. The kind they sell at gas stations. I used to shove a few into the bottom of my purse and cover them with a sweatshirt. I justified it because I needed money for tampons; they were expensive, and it was easy to steal toilet paper as long as the extra rolls were stacked behind the toilet in the bathroom.

I stood sipping a hot toddy in front of Jimmy as "Feliz Navidad" repeated for the fifteenth time. Every so often, Jimmy's hand would appear clutching a shot of Patrón. "Merry Christmas, baby," he'd say. I'd shoot it each time. But Christmas was quiet that year, and at around eleven o'clock there were only a few customers left when a man in a New York Giants jersey stumbled over to me. He was about to order something when suddenly yellow liquid and chunks of meat spewed from his mouth, splattering to the dusty floor. He caught part of it with his hands as he lurched toward the bathroom. I jumped back, covering my mouth, and spun around gagging from the sour stench of chewed-up cheap turkey and too much whiskey. I started feeling nauseous from all the Patrón, whiskey, and spices I'd been drinking on an empty stomach. I tried to walk away, assuring myself that I was not responsible for cleaning up the reeking vomit, when Jimmy threw a mop and a bucket at me. "No bussers tonight," he said.

Before I could shoot him an *"are you fucking kidding me?"* face, I was conscious of how I would respond, not wanting him to think I was too good to clean up the mess. I closed my eyes, as one does when praying to God, took the mop in my hands, and catatonically dumped it in the orange bucket of soapy water. I mopped the meaty chunks and yellow liquid poured from someone else's pain, focusing on anything but what was right in front of me.

"On Christmas eve many years ago, I lay quietly in my bed. I did not rustle the sheets. I breathed slowly and silently. I was listening for a sound—a sound a friend had told me I'd never hear—the ringing bells of Santa's sleigh . . ." My mother's voice was soft as she read to us from our favorite Christmas story, *The Polar Express*. Flames popped behind the fireplace screen at the other end of the master bedroom, and the warm glow extended toward us as Mara, Chloe, and I snuggled between Mom and Dad in their king-size bed. Our bellies were full of honey-baked ham, mashed potatoes, cranberry sauce, and apple pie. Our hand-knit stockings hung from the fireplace downstairs in the family room next to the Oreo cookies, milk, and carrots we left out for Santa and Rudolph.

On Christmas morning, I awoke in Chloe's other twin bed. Before we moved into the estate in Virginia when I was five, I had been used to sharing a room with Mara. I became easily frightened in my new queen-size bed, so I'd tiptoe into Chloe's room in the middle of the night to curl up beside her.

I sat up with tousled hair in my white nightgown, looked to the foot of my bed, and gasped. A black Labrador puppy with a red bow tied around her neck was fast asleep.

Trying to restrain my excitement, I whispered, "Chloe!" She was drooling on her pillow in the bed across from me.

"What?" she mumbled, cracking open her eyes.

"Look!"

Chloe lifted her head to look down at the foot of my bed and then shot up. "Oh my God!" she shrieked. "A puppy!"

The little black Lab rolled over stretching her hind legs as she yawned. Then she leapt into my lap and began licking my face. Chloe giggled and jumped from her bed to my bed so she could pet our new furry friend.

Through her lace curtains, I could see the bare trees and white sky preparing for the snowstorm that was coming our way.

"Mara! Wake up!" Chloe cried.

A note dangled from the puppy's red ribbon: "To Mara, Christina, and Chloe—Take care of her for me. Merry Christmas. Love, Santa."

We ran downstairs as our new puppy tumbled after us. We skipped through the dining room, through the loggia, and into the family room, where the cookies and carrots had been eaten and the milk had been drunk. Dozens of presents swallowed the tree, and our stockings were stuffed to the brim. Like clockwork, Dad would make us his famous pancakes before we opened presents.

"Dad, it's going to hit the ceiling!" we cried.

"One more time, one more time," he insisted. He expertly flipped the pancake high in the air, shuffled his feet while concentrating on the airborne pancake, and then, falling to his knees, caught it in the pan before it hit the floor.

"Perfecto!" Dad yelled.

Once the video camera was recording and my mother had her cup of coffee, we ravaged through presents like three Tasmanian devils, "Nintendo 64!" "Look at my dollhouse!" "Life-size Barbie!" "Mom, look! It's Addy! The new American Girl doll!" My parents would laugh and look at each other, knowing they had done their job well.

With snowflakes falling from the sky, we stayed in our pajamas all day by the fire in the family room, playing with our new toys. But what I remember the most was my father sitting by the fire with his reading glasses on, a cup of hot tea in front of him. He was reading *The Count of Monte Cristo* by Alexandre Dumas. The 1844 classic novel tells the story of a young Frenchman who is wrongfully incarcerated, escapes from prison, and obtains a fortune while plotting his revenge.

It was his favorite book.

I washed my hands over and over again with the pink soap that made the skin of my fingers crack, and I missed Josh. Since we'd visited my father in prison, we hadn't seen each other often. It had been the longest we were apart from each other. He had meant it in Sheryl's office when he said that his going with me to see my father didn't mean we were getting back together. But I didn't want to be alone on Christmas.

Josh opened the front door, surprised to see me. He wiped his eyes, bloodshot and sleepy. It was three in the morning by the time I showed up.

"Christina," he sighed, looking at me shivering on his doorstep in my black hoodie.

My mother had heard from Madeline that Josh was trying to move on and was dating other people. At the time, I said I didn't care, even when I did. I knew he wouldn't turn me away, because it was Christmas. It didn't matter to me how anyone loved me that night. Just as long as I didn't have to listen to the stillness inside me for fear of what it might say.

I bent over the bathroom sink and lifted my skirt, as if Josh taking me in were a favor he'd done, and this was how I wanted to return it. I remember looking into the bathroom mirror and seeing his reflection behind me. It was as though we were trying to will ourselves back to love, back to the days of *The Partridge Family* where we still felt innocent, where my heart beat fast at the thought of sitting next to him at the lunch table, before the affairs, before the divorces, before the lying and the stealing and the cheating—before prison.

"What's wrong with you?" one of us had said, both of us sweating and shocked that neither one could come.

"Nothing."

It was everything. Josh walked away, wiping the sweat off his face. I knew that the kind of love we'd had for each other wasn't sustainable anymore and that running back there had been a mistake. But I followed him into the bedroom, where we crawled into bed without saying a word. I would hold on to him for one more night, hoping that I would wake up and feel something different.

The next morning, I woke up hungover, my hair reeking of cigarette smoke. I put on my Corona belly shirt that smelled of Patrón and was sticky with specks of salt, when Josh sat up in bed and looked at me. "So what does this mean? Do you want to get back together?" Finally, the words I wanted to hear, but just as they became real, I looked at him and couldn't give him an answer. Afraid to say no—afraid of who I'd be without him. And afraid to say yes—afraid of who I'd become if I stayed with him. Wishing ambiguity could be our answer.

"*You* broke up with *me*, Christina. Why are you doing this? Why do you do this to me? You come over here to be with me, and now you're just leaving without a word."

Josh's lips were quivering. He tried hard not to cry in front of me, because one time I'd told him it made him less of a man. I never saw my father cry. A part of me actually believed that men didn't have feelings. And vulnerability meant that Josh would have to know the truth about me; it would mean admitting the ugliness I felt growing inside of me, and I wouldn't dare do that. I was devoid of any courage, seeping in half-truths. It was easier to trample on somebody else's heart than risk my own.

"Are you seeing someone else?" I asked accusatorily. Wanting a reason to resent him, to push me over the edge, to grab one more moment between us and obliterate it because I needed love proved to me infinitely; because the love we had wouldn't ever be enough. Even when it was. It was over, sabotaged successfully. Josh hung his head. "I have nothing left to say to you, Christina. You got what you wanted. You always do. You should leave now."

I grabbed my purse, its bottom bulging from the hidden rolls of toilet paper. I stepped into my black boots and wrapped myself up in my hoodie. I looked at Josh one last time. I wouldn't let him see me cry, refusing to swallow my pride. I walked out of that apartment building for the last time. I walked along the dewy grass in the cold morning air at the bottom of the canyon. Up above me, glass houses stirred with families and lovers and gifts from Santa. But I kept my eyes steady on the cracks in the sidewalk, knowing I had pushed him away. Josh was gone. As was everyone else.

During the summer, fall, and into the new year of 2008, I never spoke to anyone about the $300,000 my father said would be wired into my bank account. After Father's Day he sent me a letter explaining that his early release date wasn't going to happen like he had hoped, but that I shouldn't worry because I had money coming my way. "Next week, you should receive wire transfers from two of my clients of $150,000. And at the end of August, you should receive an additional $150,000 for a total of $300,000. Keep this information <u>confidential</u> until I tell you otherwise. And *do not* speak about it to me on the telephone except in very general terms . . . Instead of a 911 Turbo Porsche, maybe I'll get an Aston Martin. XOXO, Dad."

I never told anyone. The money never came. And maybe I couldn't tell anyone for fear that the truth would eventually come from someone else's reasoning other than my own—because I didn't want to see it or believe it. I was tethered to the debt in my name, and I was tethered to the hope that once my father got out of prison, the money would come. But the difference between the two was that I chose to tether myself to my father's hopes and promises because had it not been true, who would I have left? What would I have left? I would have nothing left to hold on to.

A few weeks before I moved out of Mara and Brian's place, I came home from work one night and heard my sister on the phone in her bedroom, the crack of light underneath the door peering out into the hallway. It was four in the morning, and she was never up that late. I listened but couldn't make out what she was saying. A few minutes later, she knocked on my door. I knew it was bad because we hadn't said a word to each other since the night of the Nantucket basket incident.

"Chloe's been arrested for a DUI. The police pulled her over after she was swerving on the 101 Freeway with a broken taillight."

"Is she okay?"

"Yeah, no one got hurt. But she's wasted; the police won't let me talk to her. She's refusing to talk to Mom and Richard, and wants us to go get her."

Mara and I flew into sister autopilot. No matter how much we fought, we would be there for one another, wearing the other's pain on top of our own.

Mara threw me her keys. "You drive," she said. "I'm tired." I was so concerned about Chloe that I didn't pause to think it might not be such a good idea for me to drive after having had several shots at work.

We drove up the Pacific Coast Highway, windows down, our hair blowing in the wind as I chugged a cup of coffee. It was like nothing had happened between us.

When we were about twenty minutes from the police station, Chloe called Mara's cell phone.

"Isn't she in jail? How does she have her cell phone?"

"Pick it up," I said.

Chloe was laughing through the speakerphone. "They let me go!" she cried as if she were the freest bird in the world.

"What?" Mara asked, confused. "What do you mean, they let you go?" The police officer apparently thought Chloe was "too cute" to spend the night in jail, and though she had been charged with a DUI and would have to appear in court, they allowed her best friend to come and pick her up from the police station to take her home.

"Fine," Mara said. "We're coming to your house, then." Chloe had been living in Isla Vista, known for its excessive partying, with a bunch of students who went to Santa Barbara City College, while she worked a hostessing job in town.

We pulled up to the house. Beer cans were flung about in the street, and red party cups were wedged in the bushes. Chloe stumbled out of the front door, clapping and waving to us as if we were there to continue the party with her, completely unaware of the fact that she had just been arrested.

"Sisters!" she cried, and did a little twirl on the front walkway. I got out of the car and ran to her. I hugged her as tightly as I could. She reeked of vodka. "You are in so much fucking trouble!" I scolded. "You could have killed someone or killed yourself." Here was I, having just driven up the 101 Freeway after multiple shots at work, telling Chloe the hard truth as if I were talking to myself.

"Where's my ID?" Mara asked. She had given Chloe her old ID as a gift, since they looked alike. "You've lost your privileges," she said, also trying to act the parent. "Hand it over."

"Oh, please, I lost your ID a *looooong* time ago," Chloe slurred. Her eyes were glassy, and I knew she wouldn't remember any of this the next morning. And it wouldn't matter even if she did, because I wasn't any better. I wasn't Mom, and I wasn't Dad—the way we remembered them and wanted them to be. And neither was Mara. The three of us just stood there, a triangle of hypocrisy under the streetlamps as the sun began to rise without any answers. Driving up had been pointless. We couldn't help one another even if we had convinced ourselves we could.

2008: The Year of Fantasy Thinking

"You don't have to sign a lease," Dave told me. He had called me a few weeks before the new year to let me know he'd just moved into a McMansion with a few friends, and they were looking for a fifth roommate. The McMansion was on Melrose Hill Street, in a neighborhood east of Western Avenue between Sunset Boulevard and Melrose Avenue. A neighborhood notorious for its drug busts, burglaries, shootings, and prostitution—a poverty-ridden pocket between the wealthy neighborhoods of Los Feliz and Hancock Park. Brisas Beauty Salon sat on the corner, with white bars and tinted windows. Across the street, the auto body shop fixed vehicles with platinum- and chrome-rimmed wheels while it bumped rap music throughout the day. Next door was Winchell's Donut House, where the prostitutes, the drug dealers, and the occasional police officer hung out. When I drove home from work at night, I had to keep my windows rolled up and my eyes on the red light, so that I wouldn't be propositioned for sex. I learned to ignore it; I never got involved; I just kept driving by with my blinders on and prayed that no one would pull out a gun. The McMansion was two blocks behind Winchell's, past the dilapidated bungalows with chain-link fences, the street filled with abandoned cars and shopping carts full of garbage. Rent was cheap. There was only one problem: "You don't have to sign a lease, *but* you have to put down a two-thousand-dollar deposit," Dave said. I never had more than five hundred dollars in my bank account at a time, except for the few days leading up to when I had to pay rent.

I'd have to come up with the money somehow, as Mara and Brian had already found a new apartment in Beverly Hills. I phoned my mother and begged her to lend me the money. "I'll pay you back," I promised. She would have to ask Richard for the money, and she was not willing to do that. "I'm not asking Richard for the money," she said firmly. "He's already done enough for me."

I remember sitting in my car as Mara and Brian packed up the apartment, not knowing what I was going to do. My last resort: I would call my godparents in Washington, DC. I felt so ashamed to ask them for help. They had no idea what was happening all the way out west, because we had kept in touch only minimally. They were dealing with their own set of crises and losses. My godmother's best friend had passed away from cancer. She had a schizophrenic son who was acting out, his father estranged, and so they were consumed daily by trying to raise him. But I was desperate. I never told them about the credit cards, and the debt. Everything had remained a secret. Finally, I called them, and tried not to cry when I asked if I could borrow $2,000. I was ready to be rejected, ready to be sleeping in the backseat of my car and on friends' couches, when my godfather said, "Yes, no problem," and I started to cry. "Thank you. Thank you. Thank you." A few days later, I had a place to live.

Jessica, a costume designer, owned a Brussels griffon named Chewbacca, whom we nicknamed Chewie for short. Chewie was the house mascot. Jessica hated me because she lived in the room below mine, and night after night, I would stumble home drunk in my high-heeled boots, clip-clopping around my bedroom, waking her up. Noah, who ran the house and was in charge of collecting rent, was a Republican from Arizona. He was also Mexican and gay and had chic blond hair parted to the side. He worked as an assistant to a celebrity publicist and was always coming home with gift bags of free junk from red-carpet events.

Then there was Atticus, who'd grown up with Emily Stone in Arizona. I'd met him one day at her apartment at Park La Brea. Atticus had moved back to Los Angeles after starring in a successful Broadway show. Technically, he didn't live with us—he lived in a studio apartment down the street—but he was always hanging out in Dave's room, playing guitar and singing the latest song he'd written. We called each other "darling," and he occasionally brushed my hair and picked out my outfits.

Rob was a simple guy from Wisconsin who drove a red truck and owned a gun. He didn't like salad or condiments—not even ketchup on his french fries. Simple. Noah and Atticus were the first gay friends he'd ever had, so it took some adjusting. The day I moved in, Rob helped me carry all of my furniture into my new bedroom. It was the fifth time my cocoon of memories had been rearranged into a different room; I couldn't afford anything else, and, besides, I wasn't willing to let them go. I spent hours painting the walls of my new room powder blue and setting up everything the way it had looked back home in Virginia so that it felt calm and innocent—even if it was no longer the truth.

Before I moved in, Noah had said that, for the most part, our neighbors were friendly. There was even a hot dad that lived across the street, whom the boys later forbade me from talking to after they saw me flirting with him in the street a little too enthusiastically. The neighborhood was an up-and-coming vision of Los Angeles gentrification. So despite a few run-ins with prostitutes and pimps, we were safe.

Or so I thought.

"Nine-one-one. What is your emergency?"

"Gun shots. Gun shots went off in my backyard. There's a baby screaming." I hadn't realized how scared I was until I opened my mouth.

"Ma'am, where are you? What is the home address?"

"I'm in my room, in my house." I had been blow-drying my hair topless, getting ready for work, when the gunshots went off.

Pow! Pow! Pow!

"Did you hear that? Now someone's running. I hear running."

"Ma'am, I need the address. What is the address and cross street?"

"Um, it's . . . oh God, I can't remember. I have to check my phone." I had just moved in. I started crying as I scrolled to find Dave's name.

"4957 Melrose Hill Street. The cross street is Oxford, near Western."

"Did you get a visual of the shooter? What race? Any article of clothing?

"No. I didn't see anything! I'm lying on the floor!"

"Would you like to leave your name or remain anonymous?"

"Christina Grace, I mean, Prousalis. I mean—it's Christina Prousalis." Flustered, I didn't know which name to give.

"Stay on the ground. LAPD is on the way. Do not move until the LAPD are at your door, okay?"

The dispatcher hung up. I didn't move. I was lying naked on the floor, waiting for the police, and praying to God the doors were locked. The boys kept leaving the front door unlocked, as if we lived in the middle of nowhere, and I kept yelling at them each night I'd come home from the bar to find it ajar at three o'clock in the morning.

A helicopter circled the house, its spotlight moving back and forth across the backyard. Otherwise known as a "ghetto bird" in Los Angeles. It circled for about forty-five minutes as I listened to sirens and police shouting in the street. I texted Jimmy: "Tell Fiona I'm running late. Gunshots in backyard. Can't leave house until LAPD gets here." He texted back: "Normal."

I spent the next forty-five minutes with my head on the ground, having never been more terrified. When the doorbell rang, I called the police department to make sure it was okay to answer. The dispatcher assured me it was safe. I got up and wrapped myself in my old terrycloth bathrobe and went to open the front door. Two police officers stood in front of me.

"Are you Christina Prousalis?"

"Yes, sir."

"Are you okay?"

"Yes, officer. I have to go to work. Is it safe to leave?"

"Yes, you can leave now."

When I asked them what had happened, they either refused to tell me or claimed they weren't allowed to.

"Okay, thank you, officer." I closed the door and ran to collect my things for work as fast as possible.

A few days later, a neighbor said that the gunshots didn't come from any drug dealer, pimp, or crazy rapist on the loose, which was what I'd assumed. They were *LAPD* gunshots. A SWAT team had raided one of the houses behind us for some drug offense, which explained the baby crying. The helicopter was just backup.

Barack Obama was officially running for president. Artist Shepard Fairey's iconic red, white, and blue image of the Illinois senator covered street corners, storefronts, and billboards. Everyone was suddenly under the belief that change was possible. The word *hope* had reinvigorated us.

For a while, it was a thrilling time at the McMansion, home to a bunch of misfits dying to leave our mark on this world. It was always buzzing with young artists and starlets like Jessica Szohr, Dianna Agron, Amanda Bynes, Nikki Reed, and Lindsay Lohan. Jessica was filming the new hit show *Gossip Girl*. Dianna would soon be auditioning for a television musical that was circulating around Hollywood called *Glee*. Emily (now officially Emma) was dating musician Teddy Geiger, whom we also knew from *In Search of the Partridge Family*, and they would come over when Emma wasn't filming one of her latest movies. It was a house burning with reckless creativity, a place where we could be chameleons in a world that would never make sense yet we were determined to grab it by the reins. It became what I thought was a safe haven away from my crumbling family, while I remained beholden subconsciously to my father and his promises. *Hope!* Locked in a prison where, if I had any sense of reality, I might try to set myself free. But the search for anything outside of myself to numb me, to save me from the pain, would only get worse. Living in a mansion that looked good on the outside but was largely empty on the inside, nestled in the ghetto, was the truth.

I can't remember which happened first: being rejected for financial aid after I discovered I was still on a leave of absence and had one last chance to go back to LMU *or* blowing through $13,000 in eight weeks for a signed Roy Lichtenstein print I'd sold at auction at Bonhams and Butterfields. I can't remember because I smoked pot multiple times a day for almost the entire two years I lived on Melrose Hill. After a talent manager told me I needed a nose job so I could "look more like Megan Fox," I decided to stop acting for a while.

I thought about going back to school to become a writer. There was a budding part of me that felt I had something to say, even if I didn't know what it was yet. And my father kept bringing up the idea of going back to school in his letters. USC, UCLA, Yale University School of Drama. The university needed to be well known. For my father, it needed a label, like designer clothing (Versace is to Brown as Prada is to Cornell)—a degree to prove my status in this world. Much to my parents' disappointment, I had been wait-listed or rejected from USC. (I can't remember which; probably rejected.) My SAT scores were terrible. I never studied for them. On Facebook, I watched as all of my high school friends graduated college, and started submitting their applications to business schools, law schools, and medical schools.

I decided to call LMU one day and ask if I could reapply. I wanted to go back and study screenwriting. To my surprise, an administrator told me, "You're still a student here. Your leave of absence isn't up until after this semester. If you can come up with fifteen thousand dollars by the due date, you can register for classes." *Fifteen thousand dollars?* I didn't even own a credit card. I hadn't told any of my roommates about my current financial situation, not yet. It took me a few months to open up to them about my father being in prison. But the boys were intrigued by the story once I told them. They teased me and said, "Darling, get ready. When Daddy comes home, he's whipping out the gold shovels!" They were convinced he had money hidden in Swiss bank accounts, because it's where Mara was sent to boarding school. It only fueled my desire to believe it more.

I downloaded the FAFSA (Free Application for Federal Student Aid) form and spent an entire afternoon filling it out, excited about the possibility of finishing school. But when I got to the part asking for my parents' financial information, I didn't know what to put down. I couldn't contact my father to ask him certain questions about income, and I don't remember a box to check for having a parent in prison. I was still considered dependent even though I had been managing to make ends meet on my own. I called LMU, and a woman there told me that because I was born in 1985, I was still considered dependent. If there were extenuating circumstances as to why I should be considered independent, I'd have to write a letter of explanation. This was impossible for me to do because I never took Ralph Adler's advice and sued my father. My financial history looked like an out-of-control eighteen-year-old had gone on a rampant shopping spree with a half dozen credit cards. It was hopeless. But I submitted the application anyway.

My mother and I weren't speaking much since she moved in with Richard, but one afternoon she called to tell me she found a pair of signed Roy Lichtenstein prints. She said she forgot she still had them, rolled up in plastic tubes that had been shuffled around in the move. (Because of course one just forgets she has signed Roy Lichtenstein prints.) "They were a gift from one of your father's clients. I never liked his work. You can have them."

I picked up the prints with dollar signs in my eyes and took them back to the house. I remember pulling the prints out of plastic tubes, sitting on my floor, and staring at them for a good five minutes. It was Roy Lichtenstein's *Whaam!*, consisting of two separate prints that went together. One iconic image was of a fighter pilot and his words trapped in a cartoon bubble above him: "I pressed the fire control . . . and ahead of me rockets blazed through the sky . . ." And the other was the image of a crashing jet that had been hit by a rocket, with big block letters sprawled across the red-and-white explosive fire that read "Whaam!" The jets didn't look like enemies. They matched, each drawn in the same colors: red, white, blue, and yellow.

As I studied the airplane and pilot spiraling downward to his inevitable and fatal crash, I felt sick to my stomach. The colors of the prints were the same colors in the photograph of my father standing in between his red Porsche and his red, white, and yellow Porsche Mooney airplane, smiling in his aviator sunglasses. The pair I still wore everywhere for hours at a time. I wouldn't take them off until they'd left two indentations on the bridge of my nose. Men in Ferraris and Lamborghinis would honk and stare at me with my top down in traffic, and I'd smile, rev my engine, and then shift into first, second, third, fourth, fifth gears—blazing through the Wilshire corridor, hoping I was driving them wild like my father said I would. But my car was always breaking down because I never had the money to fix it. Someone told me that in exchange for discounted parts and service, I should just bring my car mechanic weed brownies, and he would hook it up. It worked! I did it three times, and nobody knew.

As much as I missed my father and was doing as he'd asked, I didn't want to keep the Lichtenstein prints—and not just because of how much they were worth but because I didn't want to look at what they symbolized. So strange, how the images remained tucked away in our basement in Virginia all those years, like some deep, dark secret waiting to be found. I wanted them out of my house, my room, my life as quickly as possible. I put the prints back in between the two pieces

of cardboard and called Sotheby's, Christie's, and Bonhams and Butterfields letting them know I had Lichtenstein's *Whaam!* signed by the
artist himself at the bottom in pencil. Bonhams and Butterfields was the
first to respond. A woman told me over the phone that it had an open
house for evaluations and appraisals once a month and that there would
be one the following week.

I sat in an open conference room with about fifty other people. Some
had large pieces of art by their side like me. Others held jewelry, manu-
scripts, cultural artifacts, and sculptures. I wondered what everyone's
story was and why they wanted to sell their possessions. Did they bring
about a bad memory? Or did they simply need the money?

An older woman in a conservative dress and glasses called my name.
She led me over to her table across the room. She thought I was there
to waste her time, as I was by far the youngest person in the room. But
when I pulled out the prints, her demeanor shifted. She took off her
glasses and looked at me. "Were these a gift?" she asked, wondering,
no doubt, what on earth a young girl like me was doing with signed
Lichtenstein prints.

"Yes, from my father," I said with confidence. "I want to sell them
as soon as possible."

"Okay, give me a few minutes, please. I need to verify their authen-
ticity."

She disappeared with the prints for about ten to fifteen minutes. I
sat looking around the room. I felt like I was waiting for medical test
results to come back, and took little comfort at the sight of the other
people around me, sitting nervously at the tables with other art dealers
and appraisers, unsure if what they possessed was worthy of the amount
of money they needed.

The woman came back, took a seat in front of me, and slid a piece of
paper across the table with the estimate: $15,000 to $20,000. I couldn't
believe my eyes.

"We can't guarantee that's what it will sell for, but this is the estimate," she said. I didn't even think about it. "Sell them."

It's pretty hard to get fired from a dive bar where it's normal for customers (mostly men) to vomit in paper cups during football season, but I managed to do it. Just another night at work, and I was late again. Fiona had already left, and Jimmy was taking orders. The bar was a mess, napkins floated about the floor, dishes piled up on tables that needed to be cleared. Before I could get settled, Jerry, the owner, walked in with a date. I cleaned up as fast as I could and took his and her orders, hoping he wouldn't notice that I'd just arrived. At the end of the night, he pulled Jimmy aside, whispered something to him, didn't look at me, and then left. When I turned in my money and credit card slips at the end of the night, Jimmy sat me down and told me I was fired. "I'm just the messenger. Sorry, baby. You've had more than three write-ups, and you know how nightlife goes in LA: girls are always comin' and goin'."

It wasn't long before I received the letter that I had been denied any financial aid from Loyola Marymount University. But three days after I was fired, I received my check in the mail from Bonhams and Butterfields. The Lichtenstein prints had sold for $13,000. I shook with relief. It felt so *good*, like I could breathe again without a man's hands on me demanding drink orders with cigarette breath.

Although the money wasn't technically mine, I'd never had that much money before. It felt like someone had just handed me a million dollars. I was reckless with it. Irresponsible. Underneath it all, I knew that I didn't deserve it; and with all the seeds of doubt and confusion emerging around my father, a part of me felt dirty from it. I certainly didn't appreciate it or use it to take care of myself—like, see a doctor or a dentist, which I hadn't done in years and desperately needed to do. I bought food with it, but mostly I ate out. I met Rob and some friends up in Lake Tahoe to go skiing. I bought memoirs and psychology books like *The Glass Castle, A Heartbreaking Work of Staggering Genius, The Myth of Sanity*. I discovered the cable TV series *Six Feet Under* and locked myself in my room for a few months, consumed by death and stories of survival.

I was blinded by this vain pain, as well as the feeling that because I was going through hardship, I could look down upon anyone who hadn't experienced something similar. You just think they're a waste of your time because they'll never understand you, on top of this feeling of "I am *owed* this; can't you see how hard I've been working? Hustling without the help of a man!" (Was this true?) It was the perspective of the privileged, entitled, and impressionable girl still in me, the only difference being that she was just hanging upside down, not taking responsibility for any of it.

As my bank account decreased from $10,000, to $7,000, to $5,000, to $2,000, to $1,000, I was slipping into a defiant rebellion of sloth and pain, waiting for my father to come home and save me. I wasn't looking for a job. I didn't clean my room. My tub was layered with scum; my sink, toothpaste-splattered; and my floors, covered in dust. I woke up at three o'clock each day. My hair was so long, it hung nearly down to my waist. I hadn't bothered to cut it. I'd never suffered from depression as a young girl. I was always happy, running after things. *I'm going to be a movie star!* The lead in all the school plays: Wendy in *Peter Pan*, Cinderella in *Into the Woods*. I wanted to be seen! But now I wanted nothing but to hide; to walk through the world invisible and voiceless.

I was turning into the roommate everyone hates: who doesn't clean up, who strolls in late at night from God knows where with my latest "Josh rebound." There was the guy in law school I met at a nightclub and ran down thirty flights of stairs to get away from. (He lived in a high-rise.) Then there was the guy who owned a clothing store and gave me free designer jeans. And the Mormon: "*Soooo* . . . you're a virgin who doesn't drink?" Baffled when he kept calling and asking me out again before I finally texted him back, "*So sorry*, this isn't going to work out." I would leave trails of shoes and articles of clothing in the house's common area. And I started stealing food.

Mostly Dave's, because it was always healthy and fresh. I would tiptoe into the kitchen like a burglar, making sure no one could hear me downstairs, holding my breath as I opened the refrigerator door. Then quietly removing the turkey, the salami, the sugar snap peas, and the hummus, eating as much as I could all at once like a starving hyena scavenging through the African wild. For a while, I thought I was getting away with it, stealing shampoo when I needed it, hoping no one would notice. And when I ran into Noah or Dave in the hall, it was that look you give when you know you've wronged somebody; that gaze that bores into the other person's eyes and that speaks only denial. And he or she knows what you've done. It is called incomprehensible demoralization.

I started getting sick a lot. At least every two months, shivering in self-depravation, snotty tissues below the bedside table, dry mouth from Nyquil, and the sour nausea from an empty stomach with only the slight swish of cheap orange juice at its bottom.

"Hi, you've reached Gayle Prousalis. Please leave a message . . ."

I wish I could remember which came first: wanting to go back to school and applying for financial aid and getting rejected, or receiving the money from the Lichtenstein prints. I can't assume one or the other because the explanation of how I acted might reveal something different, although it is ugly either way. And the truth behind both possibilities remains the same.

It's possible that I had sold the Lichtenstein prints first. I blew through the money and then decided to try going back to school. And once I discovered I was still technically a student there, and could have gone back had I not blown through that money, I fell down a dark black hole of shame. Meanwhile, I was still paralyzed financially and ineligible for any monetary aid, because I believed my father was sure to rescue me from this godforsaken mess and any skepticism growing inside my head would lead me back to the water well of a deep depression.

But there was also another possibility: that I had tried to go back to school first, was denied financial aid, and by the time the money arrived from the sale of the Lichtenstein prints, it was too late. So I gave up. I felt nothing mattered anymore while some invisible tattoo artist continued inking the word *shame* across my heart. And I blew through that money, perpetuating the oncoming self-fulfilling prophecy of self-defeat while I continued stealing, speeding, cheating, and spending money that wasn't earned—I was becoming just like my father.

It was cold outside. I stood looking at Josh's furrowed brow under the willow tree. He was staring down at my right leg. There was a metal wire sticking out of my thigh. I yanked on it, tugging at my muscle tissue, and pulled it out as though it were a thread unraveling the seam of something intangible. I turned around. The ivy of our estate was alive and stirring around each shutter. I became lightheaded and my thigh turned black and blue, as blood began to pour out of me. When I turned back around, Josh was looking at my chest. Another wire was stuck in between my ribs. I looked down calmly and pulled on it. As it grazed each hollow rib, a sound and feeling like the crescendo of a xylophone passed through me. I felt dizzy and collapsed onto the grass. Josh rushed over. He wanted to take me to the hospital. "I'm fine, Josh, stop." Then I sat up, and there was another wire poking out of my chest, and another wire and another, and I pulled out each one as it passed through my empty torso, and more blood gushed out of me until I couldn't breathe.

I woke up wailing, drenched in sweat, with my hands clutching my chest. Dave and Atticus ran into my room as I cried for Josh. "Here, baby girl." They handed me a pipe full of weed and instructed, "Suck on this." I inhaled before I could regain consciousness of where I was, in this strange room, in this strange house. When I turned on the light, I thought I would see my bulletin board with my prom corsages and bumper stickers, and the door to my bedroom (*It's on the right, not the left!*) and the yellow chandelier (*It should be hanging above my bed*). But there was nothing, just a blue wall and a spinning ceiling fan.

People say that when you lose a limb, you experience something called phantom pain, where after the limb is removed, you still sense it there. You still think it is attached and part of you. As if your brain is wired over and over again to believe something to be a certain way, waiting for it to arrive at its wanted destination. But when it's gone— the wires, severed, don't know where to go, lost in the illusion of something tangible that makes you feel insane.

On January 24, 2008, I received my father's last letter from prison. He would be departing his "Chateau" on February 11, and would call from his cell phone when he was free. Literally.

- 2 0 -

Dad's Back

BILLIONS LOST AS STOCKS CRASH!
NIGHTMARE ON WALL STREET BRINGS MORE BIG LOSSES!
LEHMAN COLLAPSE SENDS SHOCKWAVE ROUND WORLD!
WHO CAN RESCUE THE ECONOMY?

The world was stricken with panic. Millions lost jobs, lost their homes, lost their life savings as white-collar fraud made international headlines.

I remember exactly where I was when I read about Bernie Madoff's arrest in December 2008. I was sitting alone at my desk, the boys were swinging on the rope swing in the backyard below me and smoking under the umbrella tree, while I obsessively read and Googled articles about the mastermind of the multibillion-dollar Ponzi scheme and his family, fixating closely—my nose just inches from the computer screen—on the images of FBI agents escorting this sophisticated businessman up the same steps that I had walked along at 500 Pearl Street in New York City four and a half years earlier. And when I read about his two grown sons—they were the ones who called the federal authorities, claiming they didn't know about the massive fraud. The feeling I got was unsettling. *Something's wrong. Something's very, very wrong.* Did they know? I didn't want to admit it to myself; it was invoking an investigation inside of me, and I squashed it as best I could because the fleeting thoughts were unbearable. Besides, Senator Barack Obama had won the presidential election and I was leaning on a glimmer of *hope*! I wanted to be done with crashes, losing homes, and debt. I wanted the chance to recover. I believed that the crash I had experienced personally would be it for me. Done! Finito! Oh, but it wasn't even close to the slow-burning wreck about to wreak havoc in my life and take me down farther than I'd ever gone.

My father was back.

In 2003, before he was arrested, my father filed a malpractice suit against a law firm he'd hired to sue a stockbroker that had lost him millions of dollars. The law firm was Cohen, Milstein, Hausfeld & Toll. He was seeking $25 million in compensatory damages and $100 million in punitive damages. I don't know specifically what it was about. I was around thirteen or fourteen. It had something to do with the dot-com crash, and the case had been pending ever since his incarceration. In August, after my father's release, when he was living in a halfway house in Anacostia (a Washington, DC, neighborhood formerly known as "the murder capital of the world"), my divorced parents were forced to appear in court together as a "married" couple for the trial.

My father was convinced that he could win my mother back. They would come face-to-face for the first time since he had visited us during his surprise "furlough" two years earlier. But a few weeks before the trial, Richard proposed to my mother while they were on safari in Africa. I was sure Richard had done it on purpose; calculated, a strike for the win! The dates were too close together for him not to have known. I'm not sure if my father knew my mother was engaged when they showed up together for the trial, but many years later, my mother would tell me that my father had, in a desperate bid to win her back, leaned into her and said, "Babe, what if I can get all your jewelry back?"

My father was keeping my sisters and me updated on the progress of the trial via email each day. "Hi Girls, Mom finished her testimony this morning in court today and she performed beautifully . . . and she held up well. I think the jury likes her sincerity and her pretty Escada outfit. This afternoon I was called to the stand, and I testified all afternoon. Dad was asked to state your birth dates (silly question) . . . and of course, he knew them all by heart. Of course, Dad wowed all the women jurors with his Brioni suit and Hermès tie . . . Stay tuned for more! Dad."

He stood by the curb of American Airlines in a Burberry trench coat, popped collar, and brand-new aviator sunglasses. His hair and mustache back to black. He had gained a little weight after being released from the halfway house. He had moved into a house in Virginia that belonged to the parents of an old friend from law school; in exchange for free living, he would take care of her ailing father in the retirement home down the street while she lived in San Francisco with her husband.

It was Christmas again. An unusually chilly afternoon for the typically 72-degrees-and-sunny California, and Los Angeles International Airport was jammed with angst-ridden drivers. I stepped out of the car to greet my father.

"Bambina!"

He swung me around like I was his Olive again, and he was my Popeye. Sweating underneath my coat, I was coming down from an Adderall binge, anticipating his arrival. Adderall is a stimulant prescribed for Attention Deficit Disorder—and I was using it to get high. The closer my father got to reentering my life, the higher my drug intake became. I hadn't eaten in days. I'd spent the last seventy-two hours manically cleaning the house, scrubbing the floors, toilets, sinks, and tubs so that everything looked perfect for his arrival. Noah had come home early from work and found me on my knees in prayer position in front of the opened refrigerator. "Are you cleaning out the fridge?" he asked, dumbfounded. "Yes," I quipped, dumping ancient jars of mayonnaise and pickles into a garbage can next to me. "There is a God!" Noah cheered, jumping for joy. "I can't wait to meet this mystery man called Daddy you speak of!"

The boys were excited to meet him, after all the stories I'd told them of my enchanting childhood and subsequent fall from grace.

As we made our way down Melrose Avenue, my father examined the interior of my car. "Your car looks good, Bambina. The outside could use a wax. We'll go tomorrow."

"Sounds good, Dad."

"Do you need groceries?" He pointed to the Pavilions grocery store on the corner of Vine Street in Hollywood. "You're lookin' skinny minny," he said.

"Yes, but I don't have a lot of money." Before the holidays, I landed a job as a bottle-service girl at one of Hollywood's hottest nightclubs where regulars included Jessica Simpson, Nicole Richie, Jay Z, and other major celebrities. DJ AM spun every week before his tragic overdose the following summer. I was numb to it all. No celebrity fazed me anymore. Plus, they never tipped well. (Surprisingly, it was the Wall Street guys, business types, who tipped well.) Not even Slash from Guns N' Roses fazed me. In fact, one of his "groupies," a brunette in her late forties, yelled at me for spilling vodka on her suede shoes as I made them watermelon shots at their table. "Do you have any idea how much these cost me?" she screamed. I blinked at her and just walked away, remembering the time my ninth-grade boyfriend spilled chocolate milk on my cashmere sweater at the lunch table. I stood up in front of the entire class like the queen bee, looked down at the dribbled milk, and screamed, "This is cashmere!" It was pink and soft and beautiful, and made me feel special—a gift from my mother on my fifteenth birthday. While I observed and waited on the young privileged girls who trickled in with their Chanel handbags and Jimmy Choos, I began to analyze them instead of myself because it was easier and less painful. *They're not happy, trapped under the financial prison of their parents. They're living in a box, getting ready to take over Mommy and Daddy's company. They're not free!*

I was jealous and repulsed thinking about it all at the same time. I was breaking down inside—the war between two different girls—holding on tightly to the one from my past; so scared to see what would happen and who I'd be if I let her go.

Despite living in worldwide economic crisis, clubgoers continued spending thousands of dollars on bottles of Grey Goose just to be seen in all the right places. Most were 1 percenters, so I suppose it didn't matter to them how much money they pissed away. I still wasn't making enough to cover my expenses, as I was given only two shifts a week. You couldn't hustle at a place like this one. Cameras and security guards were everywhere, tips were monitored strictly, and rarely was anything paid for with cash. I learned that hustling was common in the service industry, and only the bigger nightclubs run by corporations could keep it under control. I was so tired of ping-ponging and bargaining with myself on how I'd spend my money each week. Gas, cell phone bill, food, living under constant stress—at the rate my heart was always racing, I figured I'd die by age thirty.

"Bambina." My father looked at me, his chin down, eyes up over his aviators. "Don't worry about it. Your dad's back."

My father and I loaded our grocery cart with bananas, apples, kiwis, avocados, sugar snap peas, arugula, plastic containers of cashews and pistachios, and fancy cheeses. We bought pancake mix and bacon, and organic chicken, and wild salmon, and honey-baked ham. And potatoes and green beans, cranberry sauce, and cases of Corona and red wine. *And* garlic bread, Entenmann's buttermilk donuts, Nantucket cookies, Diet Coke, Perrier, Carr's crackers, caviar. In the last three years, I don't think I'd spent so much time inside a grocery store. And my father hadn't either.

When the cashier announced the total—more than $300—I looked nervously at my father. He didn't blink. He removed a platinum Capital One card from his wallet. *Huh? How did he get a credit card so fast?*

As we loaded the bags into my trunk, I mustered up the courage to ask him about my credit. He had promised that once he got out, he would work on fixing it. I still hadn't figured out that it was impossible to repair your credit without obtaining a new card and suffering through timely payments at high interest rates. He made me believe that I could simply transfer my debt into his name when he got out. *Can't he just make a quick phone call?*

"Dad?"

"Yeah, Bambina," he said, setting down the last grocery bag and closing the trunk.

"When can we go over my credit?"

"I've been meaning to do that. Why don't you give me a copy of your credit report this week, and I will go over it as soon as possible?"

"Okay." I was proud that I'd addressed it and relieved it would be taken care of soon. My father managed to minimize everything, making it seem so easy. My problems? Not worth the stress. So I continued ignoring the way I felt: the anxiety, the voice that was trying to tell me "This is *not* okay."

When we arrived back at the house, the boys were in the garage playing Ping-Pong. We unloaded the groceries and then carried the cases of Corona into the garage. My father, without having introduced himself, announced, "Whoever beats me in a round of Ping-Pong wins a free case of Corona and a hundred bucks!" Rob and Noah looked at each other and then set down their paddles. "All right! Game on!"

Noah tossed my father a paddle. In that moment, it felt so good to have him back. All my friends in high school always loved him. *Jolly* was the word they used to describe him walking around the house on a Saturday in his Sebago boat shoes and Tommy Bahama T-shirt.

Atticus and Dave watched from atop the washer and dryer, scarfing down In-N-Out burgers, waiting their turns. A hundred bucks? He couldn't have been serious. He was. Dad didn't expect Rob to be so good. *"Goddamn it!"* he kept yelling and throwing down his paddle. Rob beat him, so my father was forced to pull a crisp Benjamin from his wallet. He glared at Rob and said, "Good game," adding, "I was undefeated in the pen, you know." Rob laughed a little uneasily and gently took the money.

My father rubbed his hands together. "All right, who's next? Atticus, you want to play?"

Atticus looked frightened. "No, no. I'm good, thanks."

Later that night, after everyone was asleep, I remembered that I'd forgotten to put clean towels in the bathroom for my father. I tiptoed down the stairs and was passing through the living room when I saw him asleep on the couch, his toes hanging off the edge and a blanket pulled up to his chin. We didn't have a spare bedroom in the house, but I invited him to stay with us anyway, assuming that he couldn't afford a hotel. Mara and Brian didn't have room for him in their one-bedroom apartment. As I had predicted, things weren't going well for them. Brian had called my cell phone one night while I was working. I hid in one of the bathroom stalls to take his call while Journey's "Don't Stop Believin'" blared in the background. "Christina, I came home, and Mara was passed out on the couch. An empty bottle of Grey Goose was on the floor next to her," he said. "She left the stove on, Christina. I'm worried about her, and I don't know what to do." I couldn't believe that Brian was calling *me* for help. I don't remember giving him any advice because I didn't have any to give except that I knew the truth was unraveling, and Mara's semblance of a perfect life wasn't so perfect after all. I remember only that my intrusive thoughts came roaring back, the ones I had about my mother and all the different ways I imagined her trying to kill herself in the early days of my father's imprisonment. Accidentally lighting the house on fire while passed out drunk on the couch had not been one of them. I shook my head and got off the phone. I knew it was the end for them. I knew Mara would leave Brian; maybe that's why I didn't have anything left to say. And I felt a perverse satisfaction when I hung up—comforted, really—in knowing that I wasn't the only one falling completely apart.

My father's shoes and a few articles of clothing were folded on top of the coffee table next to him, his toiletries placed on the other side.

I wondered if this is what he looked like sleeping in prison.

"Bambina?" He startled me. One eye opened as he lifted his head an inch off the pillow.

"Sorry, Dad, I was just putting clean towels in the bathroom for you."

"Oh. Thanks," he said, resting his head back down on the pillow. Earlier, when I had walked downstairs to say good night, he was taking off his pants. I spun around, embarrassed; he appeared so vulnerable: no bedroom, no place to change. I suppose he could have used the bathroom, but everyone else had gone on up to bed; he probably wasn't expecting me to come back down to say good night. And he was used to changing in front of other people—for years he had been forced to do it. I tried to shake the thought out of my head while my guts felt like critters crawling around inside of me.

"Good night, Dad."

"Good night, Bambina. Don't let the bedbugs bite."

The Ivy is an iconic Beverly Hills restaurant known for exclusivity and high-status celebrity customers, with a mob of paparazzi always waiting out front. You go there to be looked at, and anyone who says otherwise is a liar.

The next day, my father and I pulled up to the valet under the white umbrellas in my newly waxed BMW, top down, aviators on—me in my father's vintage pair, he in his new pair—like father, like daughter, ready to take on the world together.

We sat at a corner table in the main dining room next to the grand fireplace. I was staring at the two famed American flags hanging on the wall above my father's head, when he leaned forward and handed me $1,000—cash—underneath the table. I gasped, but before I could say anything, a handsome waiter approached to take our order.

"How are you two doing this fine afternoon?"

My father smiled at me. "Fantastic, sir," he said.

"What can I get for you today?"

"I'll have the famous grilled shrimp salad," my father said.

"Make that two," I said with a smile.

I looked at my father, leaned over the table, and whispered, with a mix of confusion and excitement in my voice, "Dad, where did you get this money?"

"I told you, don't worry about it, Bambina. Your dad's making money again. You just tell me what you need, and I'll take care of it." I began wondering how it was possible to have spent nearly five years in prison, and then to be out and acting as if nothing had happened. As if he'd never gone away. As if we hadn't just spent all that time apart, our lives completely upended. He was so coy, so sure, so calm. And I started thinking about the email he had sent me before he arrived in Los Angeles. It was a summary packet. It said above the heading: "Initial Public Offering." The amount, "$500,000,000," and underneath it: Legends, Americana Library: A Library of 20th Century American and Classical Music. It was his latest IPO. I remember reading an extraordinary number of famous American musicians: Billie Holiday, Bing Crosby, Louis Armstrong, Cab Calloway, and Willie Nelson. In addition to a list of famous classical rock musicians: the Who, the Doors, the Rolling Stones, Pink Floyd, John Lennon, and Yoko Ono. And then below that a list of famous conductors and orchestras of the twentieth century such as Arthur Rubinstein, George Gershwin, Arturo Toscanini, the Hamburg Symphony Orchestra, the Munich Symphony Orchestra, and the London Philharmonic Orchestra. It said something about a musical library and selling it to Apple or Google.

I wondered if the people he was working with were skeptical. To be working on such a huge business deal with someone who'd just been released from prison, wouldn't it raise questions? Wouldn't they want to know things? Why was it so easy for him? And wasn't he disbarred? He couldn't practice law anymore. So what was he doing?

While we waited for our salads, I decided to ask him about the IPO.

"So, I don't really understand what you're doing with the music library, Dad. Are you, like, the agent for it?"

"Sort of," he said, aloof, fixing the handkerchief in his sports jacket. Then he sipped his iced tea and looked up at me.

"This stays between you and me. I'll tell your sisters on Christmas. Everything I'm doing now is being set up under a trust in your names. So what this means, Bambina, is that the money is yours. We'll be able to buy a mansion in Beverly Hills before you know it."

It was so seductive. It sounded so good. The energy between us felt the same way it did the morning I was eating Cinnamon Toast Crunch cereal at the breakfast table, and my father walked in and handed me a black American Express card.

"Check this out, Bambina." I was fourteen. "It's the most exclusive credit card in the world, and your dad has one." I remember how heavy and sharp it was as I traced my index finger along its edge. I looked at the center logo, its classic centurion; the profile of a Roman military leader. To me, he looked like some kind of gladiator, exiled from society to be left bloodied and dead for entertainment. "You could really hurt someone with this thing," I said.

"Only the wealthiest in the world have one, Bambina."

It was this feeling of electricity, of adrenaline, of infinite possibilities and superiority, knowing you had made it.

I looked outside at cameras flashing, as a small crowd of paparazzi swarmed around some celebrity. Our waiter returned. "Two grilled shrimp salads," and he set them on the table. "Can I get you anything else?"

"We're all set," my father said, smiling.

His business deals, his promises: they felt so real, the way he talked about them; the way he described them with intricate knowledge and detail; the energy, electric and alive. *How could he just make up something like this? He wouldn't just lie to me.*

But then I thought about the $300,000 that never came. I thought about the Matron Tequila Company. I wondered what had happened to them; they seemed to have vanished.

I picked at my salad. "Awesome, Dad, I can't wait," I replied.

· · ·

It was our first Christmas together as a family despite my mother not being there. She and Richard were off in Costa Rica. After the trial, my father stopped asking about my mother and *"Le Asshole."* I blamed money for the cause of the divorce. I didn't know yet that the truth was much deeper, and I wasn't ready to understand its dangerous nuances. Chloe was reluctant at first, but she started communicating with my father regularly after he began sending her small amounts of money. She was struggling to make ends meet while working as a receptionist at 24 Hour Fitness and wanted to take classes at the community college. In the weeks before his arrival, the four of us emailed one another our Christmas wish lists under the pretense that he would someday hit it big again. Each of us participated willingly in the fantasy.

Hi Girls,

The following is Dad's Christmas list. In case you have been won-dering.

1. Gulfstream V, white with navy blue stripes and a light grey leather interior

2. Villa on Lake Geneva

3. Apartment in Paris

4. Porsche 911 Turbo Cabriolet, triple black

5. Wilson Pro Staff Leather Tennis Shoes, 8.5 M

Love,

Dad

Dear Dad,

As long as we're sharing, my wish list is as follows:

1. A 20,000,000 picture deal with Universal

2. A Spanish villa above the Hollywood sign

3. A villa on Lake Geneva (preferably the late Audrey Hepburn's)

4. A vintage Porsche like James Dean's

5. *Last but not least, a gift certificate to the grocery store.*
Love,
Christina Bambina

Dear Dad,
Hmm . . . this is easy . . .
1. *A DBS Aston Martin in gunmetal*
2. *A ten-carat diamond eternity band for my right hand . . . so I look like a ballleeerrr*
3. *A house in Santa Barbara (with my own vineyard), Brentwood, and Paris*
4. *All the Jimmy Choos in the world*
5. *Also a gift certificate to the grocery store*
Love,
Chlo-burger

Dear Dad,
Oh yay! My turn!
1. *A compound in Santa Barbara, complete with a vineyard and swarm of papillons*
2. *A flat in Paris, down the street from Dad's*
3. *A new boyfriend for my boss, so she starts acting nice again*
4. *Dangly diamond earrings for New Year's! Not too heavy*
5. *A gift certificate to Bed Bath & Beyond*
Love,
Marsie

A few days later, on Christmas morning, I was sitting on the couch in our empty living room in the middle of East Los Angeles, staring at his gift in my lap.

The color was blue jean, the leather, clemence—made from the tanned cured skins of baby calves—but never mind that. Four gold feet were on the bottom; white stitching, thirty-five centimeters long, twenty-eight centimeters high, and eighteen centimeters deep; gold lock and keys; a dust bag; an orange cloth bag; a square box; and a receipt from Paris. To own a Hermès Birkin bag, one of the most coveted and desired bags in the world, serves as one of the highest symbols of status. Not just in America but also around the globe. They range anywhere from $7,400 to $150,000 each. All are handmade in Paris—and unless you have a connection, or you are a celebrity, be prepared to wait for up to seven years to get one. My father bought Chloe one too, in orange, and he bought Mara a classic black Chanel.

It didn't make sense. He was sleeping on my couch in a gang-ridden neighborhood and yet giving me a purse worth $20,000. I looked it up online before bed, and I had that unsettling feeling again, the feeling that I was splitting in two. *Something's wrong.* I had been making ends meet on my own to bridge the gap until my father got back. Had I experienced anything of value during that time that maybe I couldn't see yet? I was good at not communicating or asking many questions, because the answer was always the same: "Not to worry. I'll take care of it." Money, possessions, and things had always appeared magically growing up; I was never privy to the process—the journey or the struggle of how one gets from A to B. It was: *Poof!* Here's a puppy at the foot of your bed! But that other side of me loved the thought of being taken care of again; it was what I longed for, what I fantasized about while cleaning up puke at the bar and waiting on needy celebrities, wanting to be a part of this, not that. Whatever "this" was. And the splitting feeling wasn't just about me; it was about my father too. So, were the boys right? Did he have money hidden in Europe? Or was he lying? Or was he innocent? Or was he guilty?

"Dad, how did you get this?" I asked.

"Behar's connections in Paris," he said. *Wait, Behar? The Albanian businessman?* I felt my blood pressure drop at the reminder of the email and the stabbing I'd read about all those years ago, like maybe I might pass out. But instead, I was possessed by some automatic lying reflex implanted somewhere within my subconscious and replied, "It's beautiful!"

I wasn't ready. I couldn't think about the "But what if?" Mara, Chloe, and I acted ecstatic. It brought back an association with all of the old feelings I had waking up on Christmas morning to extravagant presents underneath the tree. I was ashamed to admit it too: a part of me felt *safe*—my father's having money again was going to help me get back on track. I could act again. I could be everything he wanted me to be. I could be a *star*! I buried all of my fears in the back of my mind and jumped for joy, thanking him and forgetting all that I had learned—if I had learned anything at all.

This purse would fill my wounds twofold with how much attention I received from it. "Oh my God, is this a Birkin bag? I've always wanted one. Victoria Beckham has, like, a hundred!" Later that week, I spent a lot of time staring at myself in the mirror with it. Holding it, deciding whether it looked cooler if the clasp was loose and undone, or giving it a more bohemian look, or a more A-line look, all buckled and crisp looking. I often rubbed the bag and inhaled its smell of fine leather. And I never put anything dirty in it, like pennies or receipts. I made sure the bottom was always clean and visible. Each time I got into the car with it, I had the urge to strap a seat belt over it, like it was my baby, so it wouldn't go flying forward and get scratched if I slammed on my breaks. It was so expensive; it was worth more than anything I owned, including my BMW. But, really, I felt ashamed because I knew I could barely pay my rent. Still, at the same time, in those moments with my father, I felt we were inching closer to going back to the way things used to be—how they remained in my memory.

The day before my father left to go back to Virginia, we went to see *The Curious Case of Benjamin Button*. As we stood in line at the Grove theater, Mara, Chloe, and I clad in our most fashionable articles of clothing and clutching our new designer bags (making sure each label faced outward), a kind gentleman in a white polo walked up to us and said to my father, "What a beautiful family you have, sir."

"Why, thank you," he replied.

It had been a long time since I had heard anyone say those words: *what a beautiful family*. No one had to know anything about us, or that my father was just released from prison. It was just more fuel for the belief that everything would be okay now. And even though my mother wasn't around for Christmas, I actually had hope that maybe she'd be around for the next. These were the kinds of gifts my father had showered my mother with: Chanel, Hermès, the $1,000 under the table—they were explosive time bombs hiding under the guise of love, a love I believed to be real, just waiting to explode. Mara, Chloe, and I, we were becoming triplet substitutes for my father's need to hook us, fish to bait, because our mother had disappeared, and maybe my father was afraid he would lose us too.

On the morning I took him back to the airport, we were walking out the front door, the Birkin dangling from my arm. "I love it, Dad!" I said, petting it again. He asked me if I had been dating anyone since Josh and I had broken up. "No one worth mentioning," I said. I threw him my keys and hopped into the passenger seat. My father revved the engine, placed his hand on the stick shift, put on his aviators, and said, "You're never going to find a man as cool as your dad, Bambina."

I kissed him good-bye and merged onto the exit ramp of LAX when it suddenly occurred to me: we never went over my credit.

- 2 1 -

Denial

"I need another one." I looked at Atticus, begging him, my eyes like fire, mascara smeared, and beads of sweat forming along my forehead, underneath my arms, my back, in between my legs. Atticus's head flung down, and then up, and then shook from side to side as his fingers fluttered and melted into the keyboard in front of him. He was writing a song, a beautiful love song called "The Sweetest Love Song Ever Written," and I wanted more of his Adderall.

I had just impulsively bought a plane ticket to New York City in a moment of overwhelming drug-fueled joy to be with Atticus while he auditioned for a new Broadway musical. My father had just wired a few hundred dollars into my bank account. It was the first time he had done this since he returned from prison, and I was happy to let him. Instead of getting a second job, I went ahead and let my father begin to take care of me again. On some self-inflicting, vengeful level, I felt he owed this to me. I knew my credit score wasn't going anywhere— he wasn't "fixing it" even when I reminded him—and I wanted to continue cutting corners and blaming him for my lack of financial responsibility while my drug intake escalated. I should have known better by then, but I continued walking through my life with my head turned the other way, and so I did it anyway. I also believed that on some level, the money, along with the Birkin bag and the way our lives were reweaving into each other, was bringing my father and me closer together.

Finally, I told Atticus about the credit cards in my name, and the debt. And then I told him about the email my father had recently sent asking my sisters and me to apply for dual citizenship in Greece. "Girls, as the great-grandchildren of Greek immigrants with a Greek surname, you are eligible under Greek law to become a Greek citizen and have a Greek passport . . . I have retained Jennie Giannakopoulou, Esq., a lawyer in Athens, Greece, to manage our entire application for Greek citizenship . . . I have attached a PDF (open with Adobe) of the legal services agreement that we all need to sign . . . XOXO Dad."

Atticus listened without saying a word except that he loved me. "Tini, I love you," he said. I thought it was a strange time to say this, and in hindsight, he knew that deep down I didn't believe I was loveable. I had expected Atticus to express some kind of an opinion about my father; maybe a part of me was hoping he would, but he didn't. And then my drug-induced narcissistic self thought that maybe he was falling in love with me, or I was falling in love with him. It was the drugs; I couldn't tell. Until he saw that it scared me, and then he grabbed my shoulders, sober and abrupt. "I'm gay, Christina. I love you, but I'm gay, and I'll *never* hurt you. I'm gay." And I remember shaking my head and thinking, *Right, yeah. I* know. My ability to decipher reality from fantasy, right from wrong, fact from fiction was becoming increasingly distorted and disturbed.

"That's the last one I'm giving you," Atticus said, handing me one of his prescribed pills. "You're too little." Adderall had replaced pot smoking for me because I didn't want to sleep anymore, because my nightmares were getting worse. My father kept dying in front of me. I would find him lying on the ground, bleeding to death over and over again, and all I could do was stand there and watch it happen, paralyzed, unable to move my legs or cry for help. Then I'd wake up—this time with the lights on, because I'd known it would come and had been prepared—crying, clutching my chest. I'd take off my nightgown and stumble to the bathroom sink to run cold water over my arms and face to remind myself that I was alive. My subconscious was thundering with truth, and in those waking moments, the closer I got to it, the more intensely I wanted to annihilate it with drugs.

We hopped off the L train at Bedford Avenue in Williamsburg, Brooklyn, when I started talking again about Dad's wanting me to get dual citizenship. I'd taken almost twenty milligrams of Adderall by noon that day. Since Atticus had stopped giving me his pills, I picked them up from a girlfriend I'd met at the nightclub.

"He says you don't have to be fluent in Greek," I rambled. "He told me over the phone; he's been in touch with a lawyer over there. I'll be able to travel anywhere I want—all over Europe—buy property some-day, if I want to. He's going to take us all on a family vacation there to apply in person at the US Consulate in Greece because it's easier and faster than applying here in America. It's so exciting, and I can invite you and the boys someday! Can you imagine all of us in our bathing suits and sun hats riding bikes along the Mediterranean Sea?!"

I looked like a strung-out Margot Tenenbaum, in a vintage fur coat I found at a thrift store for $30 and with my Birkin bag as we strolled beneath naked trees down the edge of McCarren Park across from old button and glove factories, now converted into chic, unaffordable apartments. Atticus, in his green skinny jeans and black director glasses, kept walking, ignoring me. Then he stopped in front of a park bench.

"Right here," he said. Atticus sat down and pulled out a joint.

"Atticus," I whispered, "not in public!" Drug-induced paranoia awakened my senses to all that was around me: coffee shops, vegan restaurants, hipsters riding their bikes in bow ties and skinny jeans.

"Oh, *okay*," he replied with scathing sarcasm. "You'd rather have dual citizenship in Greece like a *criminal*, but you won't smoke a joint on the street in *Brooklyn*?"

Atticus jumped up from the bench. His usual comedic facial expressions melted into serious concern and annoyance. "Christina."

He never called me that. He put his hands on my shoulders, the move indicating I needed some sobering up, and swept his hair to the side.

"You are *not* signing that dual citizen contract, or whatever you're claiming it is," he said adamantly.

"Why?"

"You have to stop."

"Stop what?"

"Thinking that this is normal and okay."

Atticus was rarely ever serious, so this was serious.

"Normal? You want to smoke an *illegal* joint on the street!"

"Your dad took credit cards out in your name. He *used* you!"

"Why can't you just be happy for me?" My adrenaline was rising, my heart about to implode. "He's back and taking care of it."

Atticus threw his hands up in the air and shot back, "He is a *criminal*, Christina! *Wake. Up.* He was in *prison!*"

This wasn't some revelation Atticus was having in the moment. I knew the words had been boiling up inside of him for a long time, ever since I'd told him. But I wasn't ready to hear them.

"You don't even know my dad!" I shouted back. "I was lucky to have a dad like him; he gave me everything! I had a fairy-tale childhood. It wasn't his fault; you don't even know the whole story!" I huffed in utter defiance. I didn't realize it, but I was speaking about my father as though he were dead.

"He loves me," I said.

"Well, your definition of love is fucked. Look at that ridiculous purse," Atticus said with disgust.

I held back my tears over all the debt I'd managed to forget about, knowing it was still lingering in the databases of banks and credit agencies. "This purse was a gift!" I didn't have any words left as I paced the sidewalk, feeling attacked for no reason until the truth spewed from Atticus's mouth like daggers: "You are in so much denial, Christina."

Speechless before my explosive rage rolled through me, I screamed, *"Fuck you!"* at the top of my lungs, flinging the Birkin bag in the air.

Atticus turned around and started walking back to the L train, dismiss-
ing my outburst with a calm sense of power, his boots steady on the
sidewalk.

I panicked. "Where are you going?"

Atticus shook his head down at the sidewalk and kept walking. "I
can't talk to you right now."

Where are you going?" I stood there, panting in the cold air next
to the open park, my heart palpitating, my warm breath like smoke.
I didn't know where I was or where to go as I watched New York-
ers whisk by me with determined direction. I felt dizzy, a panic attack
coming. I hadn't eaten anything in almost two days. I flinched as more
human beings raced by me while I shuffled in circles, unsure of what to
do, whom to call, or whom to trust.

That summer, I met Liam, tall, dark, handsome, at a party in the Hollywood Hills. I told him I was a writer. I had started writing late at night
to sort out my thoughts, searching for the things I couldn't see. Though
I wasn't a writer in any professional sense of the word, which was how
I had implied it, I said it because I wanted to appear smarter than I felt I
was and because every time I said "actress," I felt like a failure. Only
later did I tell him I used to be an actress, and that's when he asked me
if I wanted to audition to star in a horror film he was producing about
biker gangs and exorcism. He said I would be perfect.

"She's an innocent college graduate who survives at the end, and
you don't have to take your clothes off." I gave him my number. I didn't
believe he was serious. But a few days after the party, he called, insisting
that he take me out to dinner and that I audition for the part.

Soon I was coming home to find care packages on my front doorstep. Books like *The Illustrated Woody Allen Reader*, with little notes tucked
inside: "Christina, this is my version of a dozen roses. Love, Liam." Or
Six Feet Under: The Official Companion, with another note: "Christina,
I'm sure you're thinking, this guy's romantic."

Eight weeks later, we were filming in a little town outside of San Francisco called Petaluma. I quit my job at the nightclub to make $100 a day on an ultra-low-budget horror film. And before I left, I had been so excited about my father's release from prison that I even changed my name back from Christina Grace to Christina Prousalis—*to honor him.* The opening credits of the film would read "Introducing Christina Prousalis." As if the movie star had arrived!

Most days I was tied to a chair, bound in Saran Wrap, being tormented by rockabilly aliens with pompadours and sideburns, screaming lines like "You're a monster!" while the stunt coordinator kept trying to look up my skirt. I should have caught on when he kept using me to demonstrate certain moves for other cast members. "Christina, come here." He'd pick me up and throw me down on the mattress. "Good girl, Christina."

I sent out mass emails to family and friends letting everyone know what a fabulous time I was having; how much I was learning about my "craft."

But my week of fantasy stardom fell into a dark reality when I awoke one morning to a phone call from a high school friend of mine. One of our best friends, Stone, and his brother, Holt, had been killed in a car accident the previous night somewhere in the Shenandoah Valley. A summer thunderstorm hit, it was pouring rain, and a tractor-trailer couldn't stop, slamming into their car and pushing them underneath the truck in front of them. An explosion. Everyone went up in flames. I read later that they had to mill and repave the road the next day.

I sobbed, rocking back and forth on my bed with the phone pressed to my ear in my bleak motel room, thinking about our childhoods together, thinking about his parents. It was an unfathomable loss for the entire Washington, DC, community. Stone and his brother, they were doing something of substance with their lives. They were going to change the world. They were heading back to DC from Texas to attend a book party for historian Douglas Brinkley's new biography, *The Wil-*

derness Warrior: Theodore Roosevelt and the Crusade for America. Stone had
been his research assistant while at Rice University.

And here was I, sitting in a makeup chair later that morning, watching the makeup artist splatter fake blood across my face, my arms, my
legs, surrounded by fake cars, fake knives, fake aliens, fake people. This
violent depiction we call entertainment—yes, it was so *entertaining*.
What was I doing here? Playing make-believe. Was this what I wanted?
Was this the "dream"? Drained and swollen eyed, the thought of such a
violent way to die permeated a deafening silence in me. The AD called
my name to set, my body sick with violent visions and grief as she led
me out into the empty field where for the final shot, we had to pretend
that life as we knew it was ending.

After we wrapped, I hopped out of the white van. It was dark
outside, and I walked toward the motel room of one of the support-
ing actors, who I knew had drugs. He handed me a prerolled joint,
"Are you going to be okay?" he asked, after I told him what had happened.

"Fine," I replied, the fake blood dry and cracking and flaking off
my skin.

Suspended from the universe, I don't remember the walk back to
my room before I opened the door, sparked the joint, and inhaled as
much as I could to obliterate my feelings, sliding to the floor with my
back against the door. Stone had been my first crush; the first person to
say hi to me when I was new in the seventh grade and didn't have any
friends yet. I sat behind him in Ms. Bowen's history class. I forced him
to listen to Mariah Carey's hit single "Emotions" in the tutorial room
when we were supposed to be doing our history homework. Instead,
we danced on the tables while lip-syncing the lyrics. I taught him how
to freak dance in his driveway. We could talk for hours over the phone.
Why couldn't I have told Stone the truth when he'd messaged me on
Facebook and asked how I was doing?

I exhaled as the smoke billowed toward the blue Birkin bag sitting
on the motel desk. Where had all of my friendships gone? I had pushed

everyone away. Hiding in shame, the depth of my pain, reaching for the sky, my heart numb and high.

That bag: it looked so fucking stupid.

I held on to the red string, wobbling inside the bar the next night, my entire body aching, but I was drunk enough to the point where I stopped feeling the pain. I walked up to Liam and the cast, who were taking shots of whiskey. I had ripped the red string off the end of a balloon outside on the back patio and watched as it soared up into the sky before meeting its fatal pop. I grabbed Liam's wrist and began wrapping the red string around it. Then I took my wrist and tied the other end of the string around it. I wanted him attached to me, so close that we could breathe only each other's air.

We stumbled up to my motel room, attached at the wrists, the string nearly cutting off our circulation, trying to take off our shirts every which way, leaving them loose and hanging in the middle of the string, our pants and underwear strewn about the floor. I shoved him onto the bed as we thrust forward together. "You can never leave me," I said, abandoned, scared, closer to the truth. I slammed our wrists against the headboard. Liam grabbed the back of my head, so it bobbled back, meeting my unconscious, masochistic, spellbinding need to feel everything and nothing, enraptured in self-denial.

"I'm not going to abandon you," Liam whispered as we fucked each other for the first time so I could bind myself to him with nothing but misplaced gratification of trauma and pain.

When the film ended, Liam took me wine tasting in Sonoma Valley. He showered me with lavish dinners and lied to the concierge of a quaint inn in Glen Ellen so that we could stay in the honeymoon suite. I knew it wasn't right. I knew deep down that I should have never gotten myself into that relationship, that my motives were all screwed up and selfish and wrapped up in pain, and maybe his were too. It was at dinner one night that I told Liam about my father. He listened intently and

then confided that he had taken his father to court over money. After Liam was accepted to Brown University, the only school he ever wanted to go to, his dream was shattered when a few months before first semester, the money in his account was gone. His father, a prominent brain surgeon, blew through the money on drugs and, shortly afterward, tried to kill himself. As a result, Liam couldn't afford to enroll. "I sued my father," he said, his resentment palpable. "That bastard stole my college tuition. I wasn't going to let him get away with it." He was communicating the truth to me through his own story. But it was like listening with a thin, invisible blanket over my brain, the denial preventing the dots from connecting.

A few days into our trip, Liam wanted to take me canoeing down the Russian River to clear my head.

We pulled up to the wooden house along the dirt road to pick up our canoe paddles and life vests when my father called me. "My client sent a bad check, Bambina. It'll be just a few more weeks before I can send you money."

The next day was August 1. I'd have to tell my roommates I couldn't pay rent. It was the first time that I knew I wouldn't be able to pay my share. I sat paralyzed, staring at my cell phone. It was a mistake to make the film with no job waiting for me back in Los Angeles. I couldn't see beyond the fantasy of "stardom," of making my father proud, of wanting to prove to everyone "I've made it." And after the loss of Stone, and all that it represented—the loss of friendships and a life that was no longer mine—none of it mattered, and I ran to what I thought was safety when I knew that it wasn't the truth.

"Okay, Dad. Thanks for letting me know."

It suddenly occurred to me that every time I spoke to my father over the phone, each time I tried to ask him a question about something, I hung up feeling more confused than when I had initially called trying to sort things out or understand exactly what was going on with him and his "work." I was perpetually lost in a circular loop of ambiguity, making me feel unable to understand anything.

Liam turned off the car and turned to face me.

"Everything okay?" he asked, tapping the brim of his yellow LA Lakers cap so he could see me.

Liam had been skeptical all along, far from fooled by the man my father was. Here was his chance to serve me with the truth, and because of my recent fight with Atticus, a small window had already been cracked.

"He told me his client sent a bad check." I couldn't look at him when I said it.

Liam's brow furrowed, and he gazed out the windshield.

I wanted to read his thoughts, hoping they were anything but what I knew deep down they were.

Liam took off his seat belt, put his elbow on the console, suddenly present for everything. Then he sighed, unsure of how to say it, and looked up at me, his lips pursed together.

"What?" I asked.

"Do you want the boyfriend answer? Or the real answer?"

"Just be honest with me."

"Look, your father went to prison—"

Quick to react, almost compulsively, I blurted out, "Yeah, but he took a plea deal! We don't know for sure if he was actually guilty."

"Christina, let me finish . . ." he said gently. He spoke slowly, clearly, concisely. "Your father went to prison."

How many times was someone going to have to say it to me? It was clear that I had disassociated myself from this fact, even though I was there, even though I had stood inside the confines of his imprisonment. I could intellectualize it all I wanted, but I was still going to ignore my gut.

"Whether your father actually committed the crime or if it was someone else who committed the crime, it doesn't matter. You have to understand that, regardless, he was doing business with people who broke the law. He made the choice to associate with those people. There is something to be said for that. Something to be said about the fact that an investigation was warranted."

"Okay, then, where's the *proof*? I need *proof*," I demanded.

Liam scoffed at the absurdity of my statement. As if prison wasn't proof. As if a bad check wasn't proof. As if all of the business deals of Matron Tequila and the $300,000 weren't proof.

"I don't want to talk about this anymore." I turned to look out the window.

"Okay," Liam replied, backing off as if to say, "Fine. Go for it. Keep believing. See where it gets you."

We got out of the car, and walked over to rent our gear. A friendly old man came around the side of the house and led us to our canoe. I stepped foot inside it as it rocked back and forth, rippling the stillness of the Russian River and sat at the far end. Liam hopped in after me. He carried two paddles and handed me one.

"Have you ever canoed before?"

I shook my head.

"It's hard work. I hope you're ready."

Bailout

I wanted a bailout. I read all the news headlines: $29 billion for Bear Stearns, $350 billion for Citigroup, as the Fed printed fake money for corporations it felt needed it. And where was all that money coming from? Why were they so concerned with bailing *them* out when the majority of the people who needed it had already lost their homes, their jobs? Whom were they trying to protect? Because, frankly, I didn't care about any of them: A-listers, cave dwellers, whatever.

The money from my father never came. When I arrived back in Los Angeles with no job and no money, I called him again.

"Bambina, why don't you ask Mom for money?" he said.

"Mom doesn't have any money."

"Mom didn't give you and your sisters any money?"

"Dad, what are you talking about?"

"Your mom was awarded five hundred thousand dollars in our lawsuit against Cohen Milstein."

I nearly fell out of my chair. "No, I didn't know that."

"Jesus Christ," my father said under his breath. "What on earth has been going on over there?" As if he weren't a part of it.

I had been so distraught over my mother's engagement to Richard that I forgot to ask about the outcome of the trial. I got off the phone with my father and Googled my mother's name to see if I could find anything written up about it. "The jury awarded $500,000 to Gayle Prousalis but did not find in favor of Thomas Prousalis. Thomas Prousalis, a former Washington lawyer, found himself in trouble with the law shortly after filing the complaint against Cohen Milstein."

I called my mother immediately, blood boiling. She picked up. She seemed distracted. In fact, every time I called, she seemed distracted, floating farther away from me each time we spoke.

"Hi, honey," she said.

"Dad just told me you won five hundred thousand dollars in the Cohen Milstein lawsuit."

There was a long pause.

"Yes, I did."

"I need money for rent. Can you loan me some money for rent? Just this month? *Please*, Mom? I'm going to have to move out of my house."

"I gave what was left of the money—after taxes and the attorney's fees—to Richard. I don't have any money to give you, Christina."

"How could you give all of that money over to a man you've barely known two years?"

"The money has been invested in a furniture business for Richard and me to build a financially stable life together."

"With a furniture business?"

Furniture stores along Melrose and La Cienega Avenues sat vacant with foreclosure signs in windows. Each week it seemed as though another went under.

"The money is not yours. I gave you the Lichtenstein, remember? You are twenty-four years old. I feel like the fucking Giving Tree. I'm a stump! I'm a fucking stump!"

She was right. I was blaming everyone but myself as I continued to make bad choices, crippled by the illusion from my childhood that money and things could appear out of thin air.

She hung up on me after I pleaded once more. I sat cross-legged on my bed, panicking, thinking about what I was going to do. Then I looked to my left, where the Birkin bag was perched on the end of my blue-and-white-striped chair, the gold lock shining in the reflective light, the keys looking beautiful and glorious. Had I been on mushrooms, I might have seen a halo above it.

My saving grace, I said to myself. *I'm gonna sell that goddamn Birkin bag.*

I had fifty cents in my bank account, was driving around in a bank-owned black BMW with a lien against it, carrying a Hermès Birkin bag worth $20,000 and looking like an asshole. Mara had mentioned that her boss's wife owned an eBay consignment business that sold high-end clothing, shoes, purses, and other women's accessories. When I told Mara I wanted to sell the bag, she said she'd look into it for me. After she got back to me to say that her boss's wife would see the bag, I called my father to let him know. He'd been so excited when he gave me the gift, I would have felt guilty selling it without telling him first.

"Dad, I have no job, no money. I can't pay my rent. The bag is beautiful, but it doesn't make sense for me to keep it. I love you, and I hope you understand, but I have to sell it," I said nervously over the phone, hoping I wasn't hurting his feelings.

"All right, Bambina, I understand," he replied. I was expecting him to try to talk me out of it, to tell me he had another deal coming in, but that was it. No further discussion.

I stood in a little waiting area by the front door and clutched the Birkin wrapped in its orange dust bag, wondering if it would be beautiful enough to pass the test and worthy of sale. I probably looked eerily similar to a stage mother who brings her baby to an audition.

"Come in, come in," Carrie said, opening the door of her office. She was a petite brunette with long, silky hair, and looked every ounce a fashionista. Dresses with tags from Yves Saint Laurent, Gucci, Oscar de la Renta, and Vera Wang hung on racks along her wall, and boxes filled with Jimmy Choos and Stuart Weitzman heels were stacked below.

"You said this was a gift?" Carrie asked. She had removed the Birkin from the dust bag and was examining it.

"Yes, from my father," I said.

"Wow, lucky girl. You don't hear that every day."

Carrie set the bag on the carpet and began snapping photographs. "Six pics ain't gonna cut it for a twenty-thousand-dollar item." Her voice was quick and direct, like a Hollywood agent's. She snapped a few more photographs of the receipt from Paris, the keys, and the dust bags, and told me we would start the bidding at $17,000.

"I'll contact you as soon as we get a bidder."

"Wonderful."

Seventeen thousand dollars. It was my chance to get it right. To make up for all the dumb mistakes I'd made. The money from the Lichtenstein, quitting my job to make the movie, not getting a second job, doing too many drugs, depending on both Liam and my parents.

I walked out of the consignment shop fantasizing about what I could do with all that money: pay my rent, find a job, stop eating Dave's food, save, save, save. Determined now to turn around my life once and for all, prove to myself and the world that I could do it on my own and start behaving like an adult.

A few days later I received an email on my phone from Carrie:

"Hi Christina, I'm sorry to share this with you but the Hermès Trademark Infringement Team has ended my listing for your Birkin under the pretense that it is a replica. My apologies that I will not be able to sell it for you. Best, Carrie."

After I read it ten times, I had that feeling of immediate hyperawareness of only what was around me. The way I moved my hands, the sound of my breath, Rob editing in his bedroom, the sound of a broken record, voices scratching, music stopping, replaying, over and again, over and again, Carrie's words, over and again.

I ran toward Rob's room and burst through the door. I stood in front of him. Breathing. Starting to sweat.

Rob, startled, swiveled around in his chair.

"What, Christina?" He seemed annoyed. I was always interrupting him, mad about something. Panting now, in and out.

"Christina, are you okay? What happened?"

"It's fake."

"What?" I could see that he was trying not to laugh. I could hear Rhett Butler's voice from *Gone with the Wind* in my head: "I've always thought a good lashing with a buggy whip would benefit you immensely."

I'm sure I appeared unhinged.

"The Birkin—" I began to hyperventilate, the words coming out of me like the sound of a fading whistle. "My life . . . My father—" Collapsing into a dramatic heap on the floor before the ugly tears and snot came out. Poor Rob didn't know what to do with me. He kneeled down beside me to rub my back while I gasped into his hardwood floor.

"What's going on in here?" Dave walked in, looking concerned.

Rob whispered, "That blue bag she has? It's fake." He shrugged his shoulders like he wasn't sure if what he had said made any sense.

"Oh boy," Dave replied.

I called my mother first, before I did anything, hoping she would sympathize, hoping she would understand that I understood *now* why she had left my father. I wanted this fact to bring us closer. I wanted to talk about all of those times she called me asking questions about him: "What's your father up to? What's he doing for work?"

Which is why I was so shocked when she replied impatiently, "I don't have time to listen to you have a meltdown, Christina." She and Richard were on their way to Palm Springs to plan their wedding. I wanted her to tell me that it would be okay, that she understood. I wanted her to say "Welcome, dear," like being initiated into some secret club of mutual understanding, but she was not interested.

Then I called my father. I would confront him, get him to admit all that he had lied about, get him to tell me the truth.

"You've reached the voice mailbox of Tom—" I didn't hear from him until three days later, after I'd sent him an email.

September 25, 2009

Dad—I am beyond heartbroken and disappointed to find that the Hermès bag you gave me is, in fact, a fake. I almost caused the poor woman's business to be shut down because the Hermès Infringement Team contacted her. Not to mention embarrassing Mara at work, as this is her boss's wife's business. Knowing this was not my fault, she let it go, and no one is in trouble. Just like the bag, you have been trying to create some replica of our old life, which does not exist anymore, nor do I believe it existed in a pure, open, and honest way from the beginning. You have not fixed my credit like you said you would. Now I am left without a home, or a car, because you lied to me and said you had the money when you did not. I am sad because you have the inability to be truthful. All I needed was for you to fix my credit, tell me you're sorry that you don't have the money (because had I had enough time, I would have been prepared; over the last 5 years, I have never missed a rent check), and that you love me. And I would forgive you. But you have not. I see you as a man who has emotionally abused his children and taken credit cards out in their names for the sake of yourself and has lied. I am angry.

Three days later I received his response. The boys called Liam to come over to the house because I was so distraught over it. "Christina, I have been in Eastern Europe since Friday and I have not had the opportunity to respond to your e-mail . . . You have every right to be angry at our present circumstances because, quite frankly, they have been crummy. Your Hermès bag and Chloe's were purchased in Paris by a friend's wife from a boutique in Paris as a favor to me . . . I have never in my life purchased a fake anything. Secondly, the American Express Cards and Visa cards that were opened for you and Mara were done so for your personal benefit. However, when the family experienced a financial emergency as a result of the government's unwarranted case against me . . . we used the cards to benefit you and our family. I did not use the cards to benefit myself."

The boys and Liam were watching me like three babysitters while I read it aloud to them, unsure of what I would do next. I was going down the rabbit hole with every passing sentence. ". . . You seem to have given up on your old Dad. That is a mistake. Because everything I am doing now is for the benefit of you and your sisters through a trust . . . I remain very optimistic and that is why I am here in Europe . . . I have always acted in good faith in the matters of our family. I have always been loyal. I have always loved you. . . . Stop being angry . . . you are not lying on a gurney in an oncology ward. We will overcome all of this but we must remain proactive despite having temporarily been dealt a poor hand of cards. Never, ever, give up. I love you very much, Dad."

When I started Googling, the boys and Liam couldn't stop me— my internet search fed an obsessive downward spiral of suspicion and anger: My father had said that he didn't intentionally purchase a fake Birkin, so what if he was telling the truth? Why would he ever put me at risk of being sent to prison? I looked up counterfeiting laws, and you can go to prison for up to five years for such a crime. I was devastated, and I didn't want to believe that he would put me in jeopardy, unless he actually believed that I'd be able to get away with selling the bag at full price—proud of his daughter for pocketing $17,000 for a bag really worth a few hundred. So he must have known the bag was fake, right?

Then I came across a *New York Times* article written by journalist Dana Thomas, "Terror's Purse Strings," which said that counterfeiting can be linked to terrorism, human trafficking, and child prostitution. Someone once told me that the Albanian government was infiltrated by the Mafia. I didn't know anything about it, but if my father was telling the truth—that he didn't intentionally purchase a fake; a fake purchased by the Albanian businessman—should I be worried for his life? Why was he entering into business with these people? I knew the only way I would survive this would be to cut him off until I discovered the truth. I would have no choice. In retrospect, the only fully rational part of my thought process was its conclusion: Something inside me was telling me to not give up on him yet—but *run*.

Couch Surfing

I was homeless.

No cash. No credit.

I watched Rob lift my MacKenzie-Childs desk out of my empty bedroom. Each drawer hand painted with green ivy and pink roses, and each knob had a different design: criss-crosses, polka dots, and stripes painted in different colors—lavender, yellow, and blue. It was the last piece to go. He would load it into the back of his pickup truck with the rest of my furniture and take it to the public storage unit near Pasadena that I was able to rent for $45 a month. I would not sell anything. I would not let it go. I had called the nightclub several times to see if I could get my job back, but they never returned my calls. Forced to move out, I couldn't make my rent or afford to pay bills, and I couldn't leave the boys in a bind. Finally, at the end of the month, I had a little over $100 for food and gas to get me through the week after the small amount of money that came in from the film. I was able to pay my rent the following month for the previous month, and the rest I'd have to figure out.

Mara had lost her job at the online shopping company after massive layoffs began occurring all over the country. Her instincts had been right. Shortly after she left Brian, she moved into my mother and Richard's house because she didn't have any income. So that was not an option for me. Things between my mother and me were still tense. I had gone as far as threatening not to show up on her wedding day. Chloe was still hostessing. She moved into a house and shared a room with her best friend as she continued trying to make ends meet. I called both of them and broke the news that the bags were counterfeit. If they were as hurt as I was by the dishonesty—that, like our life, the bag was just another knockoff—they didn't show it. And as the weeks went by, we would casually bring up our father.

"Have you heard from Dad?"

"No. Have you?"

"Nope."

Rob and I unloaded everything into the dark storage unit, a location that was becoming all too familiar. I looked at the possessions I had left: my dresser, two nightstands, my desk and chair, bed frame, lamp, and a few boxes of my childhood books and family photographs. We dumped my mattress in the back alley. It wouldn't last in the storage unit, so it was better off being given to the homeless man behind the building. But I had my car, I had a few friends left, and I had Liam.

I flip-flopped between Liam's apartment and my friend Audra's living room couch for the first few months. I'd met Audra when I worked at the nightclub. A Lithuanian-born Jew who was raised in Michigan by her immigrant parents, she had the best work ethic of anyone our age I'd ever seen. She worked full-time at a talent agency while putting herself through UCLA and before that always had multiple jobs. Her parents brought her to America when she was a toddler. They instilled in her at a very young age the value of hard work. When her mother came to town, she would yell things at me in her thick Russian accent, like, *"Vhen you get real job?"* Then she would hold me captive in the kitchen to help her cook some kind of sausage medley or teach me how to fold sheets properly.

I drove Audra crazy, stealing her Adderall, eating out of her fridge. She used to come home and ask me, "Are you sober today? Have you eaten? Yes or no?" She would pester me but never judge me about looking for more work, which I had been doing every day on Craigslist, going on restaurant interviews, and reaching out to some of the girls I'd worked with. But nothing was panning out; competition was steep. I filed for unemployment as soon as I moved out of the McMansion, hoping that my check would arrive quickly so I could continue paying my bills and pay Audra a little rent. I was attracted to her for all the things that I lacked, watching her in awe. My nickname for her was Little Phenomenon. She would go on to become one of the youngest talent agents in Hollywood.

When November rolled around, I let guilt get the best of me and went to my mother's wedding. My feelings for her ran the spectrum. There were days I loathed her and days I was filled with endless compassion. She had married my father so young, without any father of her own. My mother's father had emancipated her when she was seventeen to start a new family. He didn't want to be held financially responsible for her anymore. My mother worked her way through college and then met my father, who promised to take care of her. It felt as though I were watching her in her midfifties make the same choice all over again, just with a different man, wondering if I could trust Richard at all.

I held myself together with a combination of Adderall, marijuana, whiskey, and allergy medication that had me seeing only what I wanted to see, throwing up and blacking out each night. The things I remember: Tripping as I walked my mother down the aisle. The baby voice she used as she read her vows. It was startling because, standing there in front of her, I remembered it as the voice she used when she read to me as a little girl, and it used to make me anxious. I would yell at her, "Mommy, use your real voice!" because I thought she was pretending. She was acting out the characters, and I wanted her to be *her*.

The wedding was an eclectic mix of old friends from my mother's upbringing in Long Beach, a few Washington, DC, couples who hadn't abandoned her, and Richard's motorcycle friends. Michele was my mother's maid of honor. She came with her investment-banker husband and by the end of the night had to be carried off to bed. Poor thing beat me to it. Passed out from all the booze when suddenly her patent leather Chanel heels went whisking by me in the air while I danced with my sunglasses on, wondering if she wore her nine-carat yellow diamond to work. She was a psychologist. And then there was Richard's friend, the one who kept grabbing my waist all night, handing me whiskey gingers while trying to take selfies of me with his cell phone. Madeline was there with a man she had started dating. On the dance floor, she came over and wrapped her arms around me, and for that moment, I missed Josh. I couldn't believe that after all we had gone through together, he wasn't by my side when I walked my mother down the aisle. But he was moving on. He had already found the woman he would spend the rest of his life with, while I was a walking catastrophe.

The morning after the wedding, I woke up facedown on top of a bare mattress in my bridesmaid dress, with fifty-six missed calls from Liam. I don't remember why the sheets were crumpled in a pile in the corner. Apparently I had called him and told him to drive to Palm Springs so I could have sex with him, but blacked out, and locked myself in my hotel room before he could get there. I had invited Liam to the wedding, and then disinvited Liam; and then invited Liam again, and then ultimately disinvited Liam to the wedding. I had confessed to cheating on him the week before with a guy I met at a nightclub. Obliterated by the booze, it could have been anyone.

I told Liam I couldn't be with him; that I was, in fact, defective, and he should stay far, far away from me because I was an F-5 tornado blazing through the fields of other people's hearts, hating my own, destroying any possibility of love. But he was still fighting for me, still trying to make things work between us, while I continued doing what I did best: testing his love, wanting him to prove to me how much he loved me, pushing him farther and farther to see just how hard he would try to love me because I felt my father didn't. And I knew he wouldn't be able to make up for both. The task at hand was impossible for any human being. There were no more superheroes in my story anymore; no more saviors, no more knights, no more Prince Charmings, no more Popeyes—none of it was real. I had built them up in my head and had blown them all to pieces with my own heart.

"It doesn't exist, Liam. It doesn't exist."

What was love? I'd ask. Love didn't have meaning. Love was empty or love was pain, obsession, ambiguity, and rushes of toxic energy spiraling into an endless sea of shit. That was my definition of love.

When I called Liam the next morning, he said he almost broke down the door but decided against it. Instead, he sat out by the swimming pool eating Cheetos and drinking leftover champagne with my cousin Alex before he got into his car and drove back to Los Angeles.

After my mother's wedding, I received the last email I would ever receive from my father. The subject title: Redemption. "Bambina . . . I just returned from a two week trip overseas . . . I know you may be still mad at me (for various and sundry reasons), but give your Dad a chance to redeem himself. Love, Dad."

"For various and sundry reasons." That is all that I saw, that is all that I read. He wanted to silence me; he wanted to minimize all that was brewing inside of me. I could feel him taking me down. And I couldn't risk it. I had taken myself down far enough. I would not respond. I wasn't ready to forgive him when I still didn't know the truth.

Within the span of about a year and a half, I moved five times. Liam and I remained on and off, depending on the week. I didn't want to be at Whole Foods with his credit card, strolling for things like lamb and chicken—things to roast. *To roast.* I'd never cooked in my life and had always wanted to be the kind of woman who didn't spend her time in the kitchen, the kind of woman who dined in leather booths at power lunches. I wanted to be one of those women who could take care of herself, a woman with a career. All my life, I wanted to be an actress. It was the way I received attention growing up, the solution to expressing all of the repressed feelings of uncertainty I'd had as a child, repressed by good manners and expectations, and if I expressed any kind of an opinion other than the one my father agreed to, I was put down for it. I wanted to unleash myself somehow. My being an actress had been inextricably linked to my father's approval, and now I had no sense of who I was or who I wanted to become. And when I was with Liam I found myself looking up recipes online, and setting the dinner table, so unsure of what to do with my life. We fought over things—things I can't remember; mostly just my endless loop of unhappiness. And at the same time, I was so in need of love that I began to stray, looking for the very thing that was killing me to begin with.

After my unemployment check arrived, I moved in with an actor friend named Dillon. His apartment was off of Pico Boulevard near La Brea Avenue. He said I could live there for $600 a month. I didn't have to sign a lease or put down a deposit. We lived above a nice man who loved to smoke crack. He was missing two teeth on the right side of his mouth and liked to pace around the courtyard. Each time I came home, he offered to carry my purse upstairs for me.

"Hi, beautiful, you need any help with your purse?"

I would bolt upstairs and lock the door behind me. He must have had five other people living with him in the studio apartment below us. Long whiffs of crack billowed up through my window screens at night. I would spend my days looking for cocktailing jobs and occasionally going on an audition—sometimes drunk if Dillon had leftover beer in the refrigerator. After a few months went by, my roommate came home one day and announced that he had eloped—drove down to the courthouse on a whim with a girl he'd met at a nightclub—and that I needed to be out of the apartment in three weeks.

After Dillon came the Creative Artists Agency talent agent. I had met him at Audra's friend's birthday party. It was a Hollywood miracle he didn't try to sleep with me. We remained platonic, and I lived in his cottage by the beach for two months while he was housesitting for one of his clients in Nichols Canyon.

It was while I was living at the cottage that my mother ended up at Cedars-Sinai Medical Center. It started with a high fever and then vomiting; she was so weak she couldn't walk. Mara picked her up off the bathroom floor and took her to the hospital while Richard was at work. They diagnosed her with a severe kidney infection. When she called me from the hospital, her voice, soft, fragile, childlike again, and asked if I would visit her, I hesitated. I didn't want to watch Richard stand there cosigning the denial as the replacement patriarch for my withering family when not just my mother but each and every one of us needed help. I knew my mother's lethal combination of antidepressants and bottles of Chardonnay were more than partly to blame, and I was afraid to look at her being even more vulnerable than I knew she already was, because it wasn't just a reflection of her but a reflection of all of us. I was so afraid of losing her, even if it felt like she was already gone.

I went to the hospital for only an hour. I sat in the corner, in a wooden chair below the window overlooking the bleak parking lot, watching the antibiotics drip into her bloodstream. She would need to stay there for two weeks. Her stomach was so swollen that she looked pregnant. Pregnant with untouched grief, all these years trapped inside her. She looked at me, her face opaque yet smiling, her body covered in white sheets, when she told me that she loved me and that my coming to visit her was the best part of her day. I sat there holding back gut-wrenching sobs. I wanted to climb into bed with her, press my cheek to hers. I wanted to say "Please stop drinking, Mom. We need help. We need help from everything we are too afraid to talk about."

A few weeks later, when it was time for me to move out of the cottage, I was in luck. I received a Facebook message from an old family friend, the daughter of billionaire David Rubenstein. Ellie had just graduated from Harvard and moved to Los Angeles. Her father, whom I began referring to as Daddy Warbucks, had leased her a mansion in the Hollywood Hills. Ellie said she had five spare bedrooms, and to come on over and pick one. They were always generous. Always donating millions to charity.

When my father was indicted, they didn't care. The Rubensteins threw a joint birthday party for Chloe and Ellie on a yacht in the middle of the Potomac River. This kind of money—Daddy Warbucks money— trumps cave dwellers, A-listers, celebrities, and even presidents. The Rubensteins have so much money that reputation doesn't matter. But it mattered to me, and I could not tell Ellie the truth when I finally got another job at a nightclub downtown—because of what really went on there. After all, the Rubensteins owned the Magna Carta.

The "urban nightclub," as they called it, was a few blocks west of skid row. I never understood the term "urban nightclub." As in "a nightclub for black people"? I stood in line behind the metal detectors, wearing patent leather thigh-high boots that laced around silver hooks all the way up to the top, a black miniskirt, and a red leather corset that zipped in the front, for the first time making it look like I had cleavage.

The metal detectors were new. A few nights earlier, rapper Rick Ross had showed up with his entourage. Apparently someone put a gun to a security guard's head. All hell broke loose on the second level. People were beaten to a pulp near the deejay booth in the VIP section. I escaped after being groped by a three-hundred-pound man with gold rings on every finger. I ran as fast as I could down the back stairwell, kicking open the back door, and sprinting into the alley toward my car. The club was owned by an Armenian family. Each night, the theme catered to a different race or sexual orientation: Tuesdays could be Asian night, or Fridays could be gay night. Even after all the years working in nightlife, only then did the segregation of nightlife culture occur to me.

It was spring of 2001. I sat wearing my white terrycloth bathrobe at my mother's vanity table with my eyes closed as she swiped her soft makeup brush back and forth along the crease of my eyelid, her sweet breath inches from me. My hands were carefully placed, fingers spread along my thighs, as I let my new Hard Candy nail polish dry. The color was called "Sky." My corsage and Sam's boutonniere were downstairs in the refrigerator, waiting. My heart thumped thinking about him. He was the captain of the varsity soccer team, a straight-A student, and the principal's son. He, a senior, and I, a young sophomore. The day he asked me to the prom, I came home, my stomach filled with soaring butterflies.

With the prom just hours away my mother asked, "Do we need to talk about the birds and the bees?" I could feel her smiling at me.

"Mom!" I cried, humiliated, with my eyes still closed, and wanting to keep them that way.

"I just want to make sure you're safe."

The buzzer went off as I passed through. It must have been the wires in my corset. The security guard, recognizing me, let me in without any frisking. The nightclub covered four levels of what was once the Los Angeles Stock Exchange Building downtown. It looked like an abandoned art deco warehouse with giant clocks covered with projector screens and strobe lights on the middle level known as the "Trading

Room." I imagined West Coast Wall Street men in their Brioni suits and Hermès ties up at three thirty in the morning yelling over phones and watching growing numbers as the giant clocks ticked by above them—only now it was a place to come to exude money and power over alcohol and women.

And in thinking about it, not a lot had changed.

I convened in the women's bathroom with the other girls as we applied our red lipstick and curled the ends of our hair before we took our designated places at the VIP tables around the dance floor. The girl standing next to me in an identical uniform was one of the most aesthetically pleasing women I had ever seen. My eyes kept flicking back to her perfect bone structure, dark wavy hair, elegant nose and jawline, and glowing skin. I asked what her ethnicity was. Ethiopian, she said. We started talking, and I asked her if she had another job. The nightclub was open only on weekends. I was still collecting unemployment checks and not reporting the money I made at the club each week. I didn't think I'd get caught. Any corners I could cut to save money for my own apartment someday, I would. I heard my father's voice in the back of my head: *"Bambina, what you want to do is the least amount of work for the most amount of money."* But I knew I'd have to find a second job soon.

She looked straight at me. *"Girl,"* she said, *"you* need to come to Miami with me." Then she whispered, "You're hot enough. I know these basketball players. They'll fly you out on a private jet, pay you five thousand dollars, take you shopping. All you gotta do is dance with them at the club and sleep over. Plus they're cute. How do you think I bought these?" She pulled back her hair to reveal sparkling diamond studs. "Think about it," she said and then strutted back to her table.

I stood at the top of the staircase in my sky blue, floor-length gown, soft curls, and clear lip gloss, my sterling silver Tiffany charm bracelet with its dangling heart loose around my wrist. My father pointed his Nikon camera at me. "Movie star! Smile!" I struck a pose at the top of the stair-case, when the doorbell rang.

Sam stood tall: tousled dark, blond hair, black suit, shiny silver vest, and gray silk tie. He looked up at me, and his clear blue eyes made my heart beat fast. I walked down to face him.

"You're so beautiful," he said.

I stood there thinking about the night I lost my virginity. About where I was and the darkness that has the power to encapsulate one's outer beauty, forcing me to believe this was all I had. It was all I was worth. Staggering beneath the spinning strobe lights, swaying side to side in my platform boots, the eyes of cocky men with pockets full of cash, howling on tabletops, fists pumping aggressively to the illusions of power, of money, of drugs, of sex, while their eyes burned through me like I was there just to be to be fed upon, to be touched and served like a bloody little lamb spinning on a spit.

I'd be walking into Ellie's house later, staring at photographs of the family with President George H. W. Bush, and here I was pondering the idea of becoming a prostitute inside of an old stock exchange build-ing downtown because I felt I had run out of choices.

I had never felt more ugly.

Red Porsche

He drove a red Porsche—like my father.

His words of multimillion-dollar film deals were like dominoes tumbling out of his mouth, and all I wanted him to do was shut up and drive faster. He was in film finance. Only later would I see in him the striking resemblance to Christian Bale's character in *American Psycho*.

Weaving up Laurel Canyon, passing shrubs of old trees and abandoned cars with each curve, I watched my mother's Chanel purse tip from side to side at my feet. Mara had taken the purse first from Mom and Richard's house, and then I took it from Mara. My mother didn't even notice it was gone.

We were heading to his mansion up Mulholland Drive. His name was Paul, and we met through a friend of a friend—I don't remember—at a bar one night. An exclusive bar. One with a red velvet rope. He had gone to an Ivy League college, and his brother was famous, and it turned me on. He was older and loved to play Eric Clapton's single "Change the World" on repeat while we snorted cocaine off the side of his pool table with lucky $2 bills.

Tap, tap, tap went the American Express card. His was metal too. Black like my father's. So sharp a terrorist could slice someone's throat with it. I watched him roll the $2 bill, lean over, and snort. Quick. Then exhale. Then sniff again as he passed me the dirty bill. I didn't ask him how to do it. I thought about Michelle Pfeiffer in *Scarface* and Julianne Moore in *Boogie Nights*. I leaned over, plugged my left nostril with my left hand, took the rolled-up bill in my right, and sniffed. Slowly. Moving to the left, watching as the white line disappeared. Like a pro, I handed Paul back the $2 bill.

"Keep it," he said. I tucked the bill into my purse, and I remember all I wanted to do after that was look at myself in the mirror. I wanted to see what I looked like high from cocaine for the first time. I walked up the staircase along the glass windows overlooking the city of Los Angeles and swallowed hard as I felt the drip trickle from the back of my nose down my throat. Paul watched me climb the stairs with his hand beating on his heart as Clapton's "Change the World" kept cycling through: "If I can reach the stars / pull one down for you . . ." My parents loved Eric Clapton. Paul continued singing to himself as I walked into the bathroom. My stomach felt like bunches of heavy butterflies tangled around one another trying to get out. I looked at my gold hoops, curled hair, red lips. People always told me I looked like my mother, but I never felt as beautiful. I thought about her in her strapless velvet dress, her red lips. The way she and my father looked together as they drove down the driveway in his red Porsche after a charity event. The smell of Chanel No. 5 on her neck as she tucked me in under the covers, her breath familiar, like rosé and chocolate. I missed her butterfly kisses and my father's Eskimo kisses when I would fall asleep to the sound of descending airplanes along the Potomac River.

I set down her Chanel bag on the counter. That's when I noticed the needle, the tinfoil, and the silver spoon. I had never seen heroin before.

A few months later, I would see Paul in the news: he had dragged a girl thirty feet, hanging by the side of his Porsche, after a fight. She was trying to grab her purse at the foot of the passenger seat when he revved his engine and took off.

· · ·

Sex for power, for freedom—liberation. I ran farther in the direction of an opposite extreme under the guise that it would set me free, when the simple need for love remained the same.

I remember taking off my clothes in the dressing room, putting on the white bathrobe, and dropping half an Adderall in my pocket. My hair was tied up in a loose ponytail, with a black ribbon around the rubber band to make me look sweet—innocent, maybe—except it didn't. It was my fuck-you to the world.

I opened the door, and a couple, also in white bathrobes, smiled at me but didn't say a word. I could hear techno music coming from the pool area. I walked over to meet Jason, who was also in a white bathrobe, sipping on a piña colada next to the bar and holding another one for me.

The hotel was hidden down a private road, way out in the empty desert. It felt intimate as soon as you walked in, as though it were family owned. Jason and I were by far many years younger than everyone else. It appeared to be filled with middle-aged couples trying to save their marriages. I met Jason in an acting class I took back when my father was sending me money. It became a place to brag about one's pain, to continually receive validation from the people around me while I was up on that stage. Jason and I had done a scene together. A breakup scene, and that's when we started sleeping together. He told me about this place, and he wanted to bring me.

Jason handed me the piña colada. He was still wearing his sunglasses. He reminded me of Channing Tatum. He took my hand, and I followed him over to one of the lounge chairs next to the pool.

He dropped his bathrobe first and stood stark naked, flexing his six-pack and unafraid, like he had been there before. With someone else. I chugged my piña colada, swallowed the half Adderall, and then dropped my bathrobe with confidence despite feeling insecure about my small breasts and bigger bottom. If I was going to do this, I'd have to fake it.

"You're not allowed to touch anyone but me. I have rules," I said, as if I were in control.

"Of course." Jason laughed as if this were no big deal. "Same goes for you."

It was startling to see the woman's head bobbing up and down in her husband's lap on the steps of the swimming pool. The sun was down, and everyone suddenly felt uninhibited in vulnerable skin—a little looser, a little freer despite what no one could see. Trapped in unrequited love that no matter how we fucked in front of one another no one could seem to feel or understand. My black ribbon had fallen off. It was pushing and pulling in the filter of the swimming pool. I saw it and left it there.

Jason led me into the open bedroom and placed me on the bed. Candles were lit in all corners of the room; three bodies were entangled below us that looked like a sprouting lotus flower on the dirty floor. The room spun, tipping sideways when Jason climbed on top of me. A couple stood close to the side of the bed. They were plain-looking and stroked each other as they watched Jason slide into me. It was too late to ask him to put on a condom. I had never desired or been turned on by any kind of exhibitionism before, but I used curiosity and freedom as justification. When I performed, in those moments, I remember looking past Jason's sweaty shoulder and seeing the faces trying, as I was, to reach climax, to reach some kind of Nirvana, but instead I felt numb. Had I not been so drunk and high, I might have felt the pain. I didn't want to let anyone down, as if I had some sick responsibility to entertain, so I did what I did best: I acted. I threw Jason over and arched my back in that room that smelled of sweat, chlorine, and tequila; a room filled with hopeless love and people whose hearts were just as broken as mine.

When I got up from the bed, the husband from the couple standing watching us said to me as I passed by naked, "You are so beautiful.

Thank you. It's our three-year anniversary," as though I had been a gift. And then it occurred to me: I wouldn't go on a private jet for $5,000 and have sex with a basketball player, but I would do it with someone else, in front of other people. For free.

I don't remember what happened after that. I don't remember driving back to the hotel where we stayed. I don't remember if I had broken the "no touching anyone else" rule. I don't remember falling asleep.

When I woke the next day, Jason suggested we grab a bite at the sports bar, Hamburger Mary's, before we drove back through the desert. I sat there staring at my undercooked cheeseburger. I wasn't very hungry. Jason mauled his like a lion across the table.

"So do you come here often?" I asked.

Jason swallowed, and then looked at his burger. "I mean, I would never take my future wife here," he chuckled.

I suppose it was a silly question.

I picked up my burger. I set it back down. And I looked out toward the sun.

It was fall. The leaves were yellow, orange, and red as we sped down Georgetown Pike. My father accelerated, reaching forty-five miles an hour, and Mara sat next to him with her hand on top of his as he shifted his red Porsche Carrera into third gear. Chloe and I sat in the leather bucket seats behind them.

"*Blowout!*" Mara cried. That was our code word for rolling down all the windows. He'd let us stand up and poke our heads out the sun roof, our hair whipping across our eyes.

"Faster, Dad! Faster!" we screamed, and before each shift in gears, my father yelled, "Hold on to your hats, girls!" jerking us forward as we belly laughed. And I remember watching the car's hood, bearing the Porsche emblem of a black horse on a gold, black, and red crest, swerve back and forth across the yellow lines, letting the world know we didn't need to live by any such rules.

• • •

When I woke up, everything was white as I opened my eyes and squinted at the bright fluorescent ceiling lights. My mother was sitting in the chair by my side, and Liam stood behind her. I was in the emergency room at Cedars-Sinai, just as my mother had been. An IV needle protruded from the back of my right hand, dripping fluids. I had told the doctor earlier that my head felt like thunder. All I remembered was Liam coming over and picking me up off the floor of Ellie's mansion and carrying me out to the car because I couldn't walk. I must have called him. He must have called my mother. I was throwing up violently and couldn't stop. It felt like my guts were unraveling.

The doctor didn't have a diagnosis. Maybe a bug, he said, but it didn't seem like it. I knew I was having a nervous breakdown. It had been a year and a half. It was the longest I'd gone without speaking to my father, without a letter, an email, or a phone call. It was 2010 now. I kept waiting for him to show up on my doorstep one day; to call on my twenty-fifth birthday. I would replay conversations over and over in my head of how it could go. But there was nothing. No card. No email. No phone call. He had vanished. Why couldn't I let him go? I had told myself I wasn't worth fighting for. Mara and Chloe never heard from him either. I blamed myself for it, that he didn't call on their birthdays because I had written the email to him about the Hermès Birkin bag. I didn't understand why he wouldn't at least fight for their love, when they hadn't confronted him like I did.

The debt was still mine to handle, with creditors still calling my cell phone. I didn't know how I would pay for the hospital visit. My driver's license was about to get suspended for failure to appear in court. I was flipping off officers, being pulled over for reckless left-hand turns, and speeding on a regular basis. I received a notice in the mail that my bail amount was $849, and if I didn't pay it, I was at risk of getting arrested.

It was hard coming home each night to Ellie's mansion. I couldn't relate to her on any level. I could see that money couldn't buy happiness, love, or freedom. Her father was always disappearing somewhere in the Middle East and couldn't be reached. People kept trying to take advantage of her. Everyone wanted to get to know her: Be a producer on my film! Start a production company with me! It was all bullshit. Damned if you have money, damned if you don't. Watching it, I was paralyzed by both ends, the juxtaposition of each where the solution was neither here nor there. I could see how money changes you, molds you and folds you, and when you have it, you still can't see any more truth than when you don't have it. And whether you're trying to attain it, or just trying to keep it, there still doesn't seem to be any understanding of what is real and what is not. So whom and what are you supposed to trust when you can't even trust the very thing that's dictating how you're supposed to survive? I couldn't think about it anymore—poverty and wealth—it was making me sick.

Mom and Jordan Belfort

My mother saw how sick I was. Lost on the edge of defiance. After Mara had been hired by another tech company and moved in with a friend of hers, my mother spoke to Richard, and he agreed to let me stay in their guest bedroom until I could get back on my feet. The thought of living with my mother and Richard was horrifying—it was humiliating having to move back in with a parent—but it was either that or go to the homeless shelter downtown. I'd exhausted the only friends I had and was determined not to depend on any man I dated for money.

A few days into my stay, Richard offered me a job at his furniture factory filing paperwork and drafting up orders from clients. As I'd predicted, though, the company was on the verge of going under, struggling to make payroll, pay vendors, barely breaking even each month. It was a sinking ship I willingly jumped onto. On every block in West Hollywood, furniture and other retail stores continued going out of business. The Blockbuster across the street: gone. More homes with foreclosure signs and For Sale signs planted in grassy front lawns. The world as I knew it, like my past, was ending. Facebook and Apple were exploding, and Occupy Wall Street was all over the news. And all of the wreckage from my past was catching up to me.

I stuck out the job for a year despite feeling like I was in purgatory. Richard resented my upbringing, always reminding me of my poor work ethic and financial irresponsibility. I began to think he thought of me as a mere extension of my father. But I kept my mouth shut. I needed that paycheck; it was my only way out. I saved as much as I could. And I was grateful for the opportunity and was willing to withstand his comments about my father and me until I had enough money. I did nothing but eat, sleep, and work. I eventually got fired from the nightclub downtown for not being a "team player." Then I got another job cocktail waitressing at the Roosevelt Hotel in Hollywood part-time while I babysat friends of friends' kids when I could.

When 2011 rolled around, I could finally remove my bad credit history. It had been more than seven years since I'd discovered the debt in my name. As long as seven years have passed from the time of the delinquency date—the date that my father had defaulted on payments—I could remove it. There were still two credit card debts that would remain on my report for another year and a half, but at least I could start cleaning up the mess. And compared with the rest of America at the time, my financial situation didn't look so bad. I finally qualified for my very first studio apartment in Hollywood. I collected my furniture out of the storage unit, cocooned once again by my childhood bedroom, yet I still wasn't happy. As I kept working at the factory, which continued to struggle and cause tension between my mother and Richard, I had no direction in life.

Most days it was painful to watch my mother in the role of Richard's wife, struggling to run the business with him. Not long after she'd left the hospital for her kidney infection, she developed a syndrome called fibromyalgia. Most doctors relate it to depression, anxiety, and post-traumatic stress disorder, where your body has chronic, widespread pain. I knew it was because of all the untouched grief inside of her—the same reason that I had ended up in the hospital. On the days when she wasn't at the factory, she'd be lying on the couch or sleeping in bed. I tried hard on a daily basis to forgive her for the choices she'd made, because even though I couldn't feel it yet, I knew that someday I would have more understanding of the truth. Of her truth. So I started by asking questions.

My mother and I sat across from each other at the cheap sushi place on Larchmont Boulevard.

"Mom, I need to ask you about Dad," I said, pouring more sake into her glass.

She looked uneasy. "What do you want to know?"

"I want to know if there were signs. There had to have been signs, Mom."

She paused and looked down at her plate of sashimi. "You know," she began, "your father and I created a beautiful life. It really was a fairy tale . . ."

"I know," I replied, even when now I suspected it wasn't true.

My mother took a deep breath. "Are you sure you want to talk about this?"

"Yes."

"Okay." She took another sip of saki. "Well, there were little signs here and there that I . . . looking back . . . I think I chose to ignore or didn't think much of—red flags, I guess you would say. Like when we'd go to a dinner party, and he would tell people he went to Harvard, when he had only gone for a summer program one year. He went to Howard, the all-black university. But he would phrase it in such an ambiguous way that if you were to catch him in the lie, he could spin it and tell you something making you believe that *you* were the one who was mistaken.

"And there were other times I'd catch him in little lies. Nothing big, but things like, I'd ask him if he had paid the gardener, and he would tell me that he did, but then I'd find out later that he didn't. Or that we were late paying this bill or that bill. We were always late on our payments for things. He was always pushing the envelope, always want-ing more even when we couldn't afford it. And I felt I was always trying to keep up, always trying to keep everyone in the community happy who may have been upset with him, usually over money that we owed. I always felt I had to be perfect. But he never let me look at our finances. He never let me see the money. He treated me like one of you girls.

"And, you know . . . I was happy with that. I was happy to be Mom and organize ballet lessons, and pack your lunches, and plan benefits, and raise money for charity without having to worry about our own money, because I trusted him. I loved him. We married very young, and I always had believed that he would be a good husband and father in providing for me and for you girls. He always promised me that. And he did. But then things just seemed to get bigger and bigger, our balloon of wealth . . . it just felt, to me . . . it began to feel so out of control. But I had no control. You know, sweetie, I'm just a small-town girl from Long Beach. I would have been happy with a little house and white picket fence, but your dad, his dreams were bigger."

When she said these things to me, I remembered that it was around the year 2000—right before the dot-com crash—when my father upgraded from a Beechcraft Barron twin-engine prop plane to the King Air, swapped his Porsche for the 911 Turbo, bought another Range Rover, and traded my mother's BMW for a Jaguar. And the year before that, he'd taken my mother to Paris, along with Joan and Bernie Carl. It must have been at the same time as the French Grand Prix, where my father and Bernie drove their vintage Ferraris, racing across the country while Mom and Joan followed in a limousine behind them. My parents were sitting at the top of the Eiffel Tower when my father handed my mother the jewelry box, the same jewelry box that held her ring all those years ago. Inside was a gold Baldwin key to the Nantucket house at 44 Liberty Street. A Victorian house that sat on an acre of land right near Main Street. We had always rented, but now, we owned. It was also around that time that my mother got her upgraded nine-carat dia-mond from Tiffany.

"So why didn't you leave him?" I asked.

"Why are you asking me all of this?"

"Because I want to know the truth."

"Well"—she looked at me, treading lightly—"I did think about leaving him. But I was afraid to."

"What happened?" I felt I was getting closer to something.

"Do you remember the summer in Nantucket? It must have been around '94 or '95, when we took you girls down to the docks and showed you that enormous yacht that came to town? The one everyone on the island was in a tizzy over because of how big it was?"

In the nineties, new money started rolling in on the island. Forget the old modest Victorians and cottages owned by local fishermen; compounds were being built for the families of bankers and tech executives. Flying into town on their Gulfstreams and Learjets. I remembered that trip down to the docks well. I was around nine years old when I stood next to my father, staring up at the *Naomi*.

"Girls, over here!" he yelled. The 167-foot yacht glistened in the afternoon sun as Mara, Chloe, and I carried bags of fudge from Aunt Leah's, the local candy store. As we walked down the dock to get a closer look, my mother explained how everyone on the island was gossiping about how tacky they thought it was and not representative of the island's humble beginnings. But my father loved it. "This is where Mom and I are going to party tonight," he said, and then, "I'm going to buy one for Mom, and we're going to call it *Gayle Winds*—get it?" My mother whacked him playfully in the chest. He never did get the chance to buy her the yacht.

"I remember that," I said.

"Well, a man named Jordan Belfort owned it. He had a party there that night, and I had never seen more cocaine, diamonds, and drugs in my entire life, and it scared me. Something felt off. And later that night, your father and I got into a huge fight about it. I told him I didn't want that man anywhere near you girls. Ever. I mean, this was a man who took us to dinner at the Chanticleer and threw twenty thousand dollars

at the maître d' because he had forgotten to make a reservation. Everyone was high on quaaludes or something."

"Were you?" I asked.

"No, I'm way too much of a prude for that. You know I like my
Chardonnay. The guys were ordering Jerry Bombs all night. The total
bill was around forty thousand dollars."

"Jesus," I said and shot the rest of my sake.

"It felt sleazy to me. And then a few years later, all those guys ended
up in prison, and it was shortly after that that the government started
investigating your dad."

"So Jordan Belfort was the guy they flew out to testify against Dad?
The reason Dad took the plea deal?"

"Yep."

"Do you think Dad knew he was a bad guy? I mean, what if Dad
was conned by this guy?" I was still willing to justify and defend Dad. I
still wanted to believe there was a possibility I'd be proved wrong.

"Honey, I'm tired. My fibromyalgia is flaring up. I need to talk
about something else now." My mother looked deflated. She had never
talked about this before, and I got more out of her than I thought I
would. It was as if she had handed me a Norman Rockwell painting of
my childhood. Yet behind it, an X-ray of hairline fractures could finally
be seen—fractures that had been there all along, hidden beneath the
perfect family portrait.

A Wedding and
the New York Federal Courthouse

It was 2012. The cherry blossoms were in full bloom around the tidal basin below the memorials of Dr. Martin Luther King Jr. and Abraham Lincoln. It was still cold for April in Washington, DC. I quit the factory before I left. Richard and I had gotten into an argument over pieces of furniture. He blamed me for being behind schedule again. He called screaming on the other end of the phone. "Bloody hell, Christina, you can't do anything right!" I hung up. This was no different than depending on Josh or Liam. I was done living anybody else's life but my own. This was not my calling. This was not going to be my life. I had to stop depending on everyone and anyone but myself to create any semblance of a stable anything. Not to mention the fact that I was a terrible factory worker.

I left everything on my desk. And I walked out.

I went back to Washington, DC, for the wedding of Molly Palmer, the daughter of Nancy and John Palmer. I had decided that after the wedding, I would take the bus to New York City and once and for all figure out the truth.

Alan Greenspan's frail frame made me nervous, like he could collapse at any moment. I stared at him and his wife, journalist Andrea Mitchell, at the table across from me—the perfect Washingtonian couple. We were in the ballroom of the Chevy Chase Club overlooking the golf course, and I tried not to feel uncomfortable inside the old cave dweller, A-lister stomping grounds. It was my first time back in the social whirl of Washington, DC, and I was awestruck by it all. As I had been living with Ellie, I felt so far away from it even though the guests were gracious and kind. So many years had gone by that the faces I did recognize—those who'd once mingled at parties with my parents—looked aged. And though it had been a part of my childhood, and I had to accept that, I knew I didn't belong there, and there was a reason I felt I never did.

After the father-daughter dance, Nancy pulled me aside to ask how I was doing. She must have known those moments were the most painful. It didn't matter where I was—I could be in line at the Coffee Bean, watching a father and daughter chatting together, and I'd burst into tears once I got back in the car. I knew that Nancy and my father had kept in touch through letters while he was in prison, but I didn't know whether she had spoken to him since he had dropped out of my life completely.

"Have you spoken to your father, honey?" she asked, never one to shy away from the truth, which is why I liked her so much. I told Nancy that I hadn't spoken to or heard from my father in three years. I could see from the look she gave me that she hadn't spoken to him either.

"I'm so proud of you, honey. You're so strong, you know," she said. The wind might as well have blown me off my feet. Proud? Strong? For what? For abusing drugs? For losing friends? For not holding down a job? For being incapable of loving anyone? I didn't feel proud, and I didn't feel strong, but Nancy's kindness was the only reason I still felt as though I belonged. Nancy didn't know the things I had done to survive.

She didn't have an opinion of my father either; whether she believed he was innocent or guilty. She and John, as journalists, made me feel welcome. They never judged me or judged our family. I think those who were close to my father felt just as confused as I did about how all of this could have happened, what a tragedy it was, and how strange it was that he had been MIA since 2009.

The day after the wedding, I bought a cheap bus ticket to New York City, where I would retrace my father's steps at the very beginning.

I hopped off the J train at Chambers Street and headed to the federal courthouse. It wasn't the way I remembered it eight years ago. The entrance, the steps—everything—seemed mixed around, as though I were trapped inside a Picasso painting. The Occupy Wall Street protestors had been silenced, the barricades surrounding the steps of the US Southern District Court of New York now vacant and lonely. I wore a black blouse, black skirt, and brown boots, my hair was wild and long, and I carried a journal in one hand and my purse in the other.

The security line was empty at eleven in the morning. I walked up to the metal detectors, ready to pass through, when the security guard stopped me. "You have to walk through the zigzagged ropes to pass through," he said. I looked around me. No one was waiting. He was on a power trip, and it made my chest feel tight, but I did as he asked. He was wearing a bulletproof vest. When I placed my purse on the conveyor belt, a hefty middle-aged woman sitting behind the security monitor asked, "You have a cell phone or anything electronic on you?"

"I have a cell phone," I said.

"You don't have an iPod?" I took this to mean she was dumbfounded by the fact that someone like me didn't own an iPod or think to bring one.

"Nope. Don't own an iPod."

"Really?" she asked.

"Really."

Another large security guard with dark hair and a Brooklyn accent asked me to take off my boots.

"Oh, it's like the airport now," I said, casually making conversation. He didn't acknowledge me.

"Have to check your cell phone first; no electronics allowed upstairs," said another security guard, standing to my left.

"Okay, I just need to write a few things down from my phone." I sat down in a chair against the wall next to the conveyor belt and whipped out my journal. I jotted down Dad's case number, a few telephone numbers, and the floor and suite number of the records office where I was going.

"Records office is in room 370, right?" I asked, just to be sure.

"Yes," said the security officer.

As I was jotting down the numbers in my journal, a man in a black suit strolled out of the office where you have to check your cell phones, then he casually strolled back inside.

"Hurry that up. Boss isn't happy about whatever you're doing there," the security officer said. Security was irritated that I took the time to sit down and write down numbers and information from my phone before turning it in. It made them nervous, my jotting down things in a journal, observing everything as though I were a ticking time bomb they didn't have the code to disarm.

The room was empty but for a few wooden desks and a copy machine. Behind the counter, a girl in gold hoops and curly black hair pulled back in a messy bun, filed paperwork in a library that looked like it hadn't been touched since the nineties. Stacks of boxes and papers stood everywhere. It was amazing they could keep track of anything.

"Can I help you?" the girl asked.

"Yes, I'm looking for the records of Thomas Prousalis Jr.," I said, not knowing what to ask for or how it worked.

"What's the case number?"

I fumbled through my purse and pulled out my journal.

"It's 03 Cr. 1509."

"Okay, what file do you need?"

"What file?" I had no idea what file I needed. "All of them," I guessed.

"All of them?" She looked down at me like I was insane.

"Yeah. All of them."

"Okay," she sighed. "Driver's license, please."

A few minutes later, she came out pushing a metal cart filled with a half dozen file boxes.

"Return everything when you're done. Copy machine is over there."

"Thanks." I couldn't believe how easy that was. And all for free.

I riffled through Dad's court records for hours. Nothing was organized.

The first document I examined was exhibit 6: the floor plan of our house in Virginia. I looked at the drawing and saw the upstairs level, including my bedroom and the bathroom. Then below that, the family room, and below that, our playroom. The next document listed comparable houses in the neighborhood—houses I remembered, like the Fabianis' across the street from the Kennedys' Hickory Hill estate. Next to each house was its address and appraisals on how much it was worth. In 2004 the homes were worth somewhere between $7 million and $15 million. I wondered what they were worth now.

Then I came to "Community Contacts": a list of things that reminded me how good Dad looked on paper: 1970, College of William & Mary; 1977, Howard Law School; 1975, White House law clerk; 1970, Officer Candidate School, Lackland AFB; 1973 (reserves), US Air Force; 1980, Decorations: Presidential National Defense Expert, honorable discharge; 1977, married to Gayle Lee McDowell by Malcolm L. Lucas, former US district judge and chief justice of CA Supreme Court and family friend.

Did all of these things about him—all of these things that made him a "good man"—matter anymore?

I flipped through documents titled "Octagon" and "Czech Indus-
tries Inc," with the name Stratton Oakmont labeled across the bottom.
The dates on these documents indicated that my father conducted his
first IPO with Stratton Oakmont after Jordan Belfort had already been
barred from the securities industry. Wouldn't this suggest that my
father willingly worked with a man he knew was a crook? I found cop-
ies of Belfort's business calendar from the 1990s and saw my father's
name written in it, as well as reminders such as "helicopter lesson" and
"cancel Rabbi Greenman."

Then I pulled out a document titled "Appearance Bond: United
States District Court Eastern District of Virginia"—when I looked at
it, my father had gone through it and made note of every single gram-
matical error, including dotting the *T* for his middle initial, and adding
commas and semicolons. After having just been arrested—his entire life
and livelihood on the line—he still had time to shame someone's gram-
mar. My father was always trying to be funny in light of all the dark. Or
maybe he was just desperately trying to fix whatever he could.

Then I came across a letter that Bernie Carl had written to Judge
Cote begging her to grant my father leniency during his sentencing:
"I believe I understand the motivation behind Mr. Prousalis's wrong-
doing. It was not, as the government might suggest, a taste for high living or personal greed—rather, it was a desire to shield his family from
all the things going wrong in his life. . . . As a man about to lose even his
family home, he was desperate. He cut corners to get the deal done. He
made fatal mistakes. . . . I am convinced that, while Mr. Prousalis may
have facilitated a criminal scheme, he was neither its primary author
nor its primary beneficiary."

What? I had believed, sitting at the trial at nineteen years old, that
Bernie believed my father to be innocent. But Bernie knew all along
that he had committed a crime. He threw my father under the bus,
and he felt guilty about it. But my father conned him, didn't he? Why
was Bernie so quick to forgive him? As I continued flipping through

documents, I wondered why I could not find anything else written about any other victim. I wanted to know who the rest were. What happened to them? Did they lose their homes like we did? Could they pay their bills? It was frustrating not to know. I wondered if maybe the reason was because they were wealthy like Bernie and still had plenty of money in their bank accounts; maybe they weren't, in fact, left in financial ruin.

It was almost three o'clock. My eyes were tired. I got up to look inside the last box, and there was a document: *United States of America v. Thomas T. Prousalis, Jr., Defendant.* It was a transcript dated April 9, 2010, between my father and Judge Cote.

Dad: First, excuse me, I have a very bad cold. Sorry for my voice . . . I am sorry it has taken so long and my hard head to deal with the realization that if it's cash flow, if it comes into the Bank of America account, then 20 percent is due to the government. Fundamentally what happened here is that I did not timely pay 20 percent of my cash flow until a hammer was held over my head. For that I apologize. Secondly, going overseas on that business trip and even though it involved a serious amount of money, an $187 million contract for which my clients are grateful that I have put it together, and they are very happy, nevertheless I violated a ruling by this court and for which I am profoundly apologetic. That is not something that I would do intentionally. It was inadvertent, nevertheless I did violate it, and I am sorry for that.

Judge Cote: Hardly inadvertent. You knew you didn't have permission to go.

Dad: Ma'am—you are exactly right. My probation officer said that I could go to Los Angeles and instead I went overseas and that was wrong. So I think going forward, Your Honor, I have learned a severe lesson. The MCC is not a happy place, and I am sorry about all of this, being out for 2 years and screwing up like this, it was awful, and I feel very bad about it. My daughters—it's a sad situation, and I am sincerely apologetic.

Judge Cote: Well, I found it tragic. I think the probation department's request that you receive mental health counseling is a good one. I think there is something profoundly, profoundly wrong here. You lavished gifts on your daughters, engaged in travel, took money from your father, did everything to please yourself, misled and lied to the probation department . . . doing everything you could do to evade your obligations. And your submissions to me in connection with this sentence, again, with falsehoods and obfuscation and denial and shifting blame to others. Now, fundamentally you were convicted of a fraud, and fundamentally what has been happening here while you have been on supervision is very similar behavior filled with falsehoods, evading your legal duties, depriving others of funds that they were entitled to receive, and the truth of a lot of what you have had to say is hard to pin down, but when one does enough work, one finds that underneath it all there was no "there" there. So I am not hopeful, Mr. Prousalis, that you truly understand what it would require for you to live a law-abiding life and take responsibility for your actions as opposed to shifting blame on others and taking money, really, from others that doesn't belong to you. It is tragic that your first term of imprisonment did not have any significant change on you whatsoever, just tragic. So I am now going to send you to prison a second time. This will give you a second opportunity to reflect on what course you want your life to lead. And when you come out, I want you to treat your probation officer, whoever that person may be, with respect, to deal with that person honorably, to participate in good faith in mental health counseling to try and understand what is driving you to do these very self-destructive things.

Please stand. I impose a term of imprisonment of 9 months

to be followed by a term of supervised release of 2 years and 3 months.

I got up from the desk, shoving the chair so that it tumbled backward. I left my wallet. My ID. My sanity. I ran into the bathroom down the hallway, flung myself over the toilet, and threw up. As I gasped for air, with my hands gripping the sides of the toilet bowl, my heart heavy from all of the years I defended him, blinded by this life of false evidence—*there were signs*—and I chose to ignore all of them. *I* did that; they were flashing before my eyes:

Stratton Oakmont popping up on the caller ID at the dinner hour, and my father screaming, *"Do not pick up the phone!"* The dinner party for the Albanian government official. The $300,000 he said he would wire into my bank account but never did. Matron Tequila and my two million shares of stock, the Legends, Americana Library: A Library of 20th Century American and Classical Music, and the Gulfstream, and the Porsches, and our future houses in Beverly Hills—wherever and whatever he told me to do, it was coming to me in a vacuum: "Let this remain confidential, Christina Bambina." It was deception, illusion, strategic manipulation filled with lies, allowing my instincts and intuition to be smashed away because the truth was too impossible to swallow. My childhood was just a fractured reality—and now the revelation I had, along with the documents, showed I had been conned by him *over and over* again. His being a repeat offender solidified that for me. It was proof. I had been addicted to his ambiguity, never knowing the whole truth; squashing those voices inside of me with reckless abandon, leaving me capsized on the other end of a battle that would only remain inside myself. My only way out of his insanity—*out of my own insanity*—would be to let those voices scream.

Memorial Day to the End

It wasn't denial. It was the truth that took me down. Lower than I'd ever gone before. It was Memorial Day weekend, and I drank, did drugs, and had sex to stay alive because I thought reality would kill me.

I wasn't sure how much Adderall I had taken. I stopped counting. After every few drinks, I seemed to pop one more each hour to keep me up. Afraid to sleep. Afraid of the nightmares. I sat next to my friend Matty, whom I'd met when I lived with Mara and Brian. He had lived in the unit below us. We swiveled on the bar stools at Jumbo's Clown Room, an exotic "dance bar" in Hollywood where girls who look like Disney princesses pole dance wearing American Apparel hoodies. I had told him what I discovered in New York. "Let's get fucked up," I said.

Matty sipped his Miller Lite as I rested my elbow on the bar and looked at a young girl with silky hair and a perfect body dancing onstage while men threw money at her. "I want to save her," I slurred. There was an innocence to her, and I was obsessed with wanting to know her story. I wondered if it was anything like mine. How easy it was to feel that this was the only choice. I looked around at the red leather chairs, and the men who would leave to go jerk off to her in a booth at the XXX video store down the street. I know because I stumbled past it while trying to hail a cab. I marched inside to yell at the man behind the counter in a drunken rage, when Matty grabbed my arm and pulled me out to the curb. "Are you trying to get yourself killed?" he hissed. I flinched back, left him and my car somewhere on Hollywood Boulevard, hopped into a cab, and told the driver to take me up the canyon to my mother and Richard's house. They were out of town for the weekend, and they'd given me a key to watch their dogs while they were away.

What I remember: The cab fare being $50. Standing at the kitchen island and pulling ice cubes out of the freezer. Dumping the rest of a bottle of Grey Goose into two crystal glasses I knew were a gift from my parents' wedding. Opening the front door for Chad, a man I'd met at the Standard Hotel a month earlier. Chad standing at the kitchen island telling me of the last conversation he had with his father as he lay dying from colon cancer in a sterile hospital bed before he took his last breath. Me trying to listen with my elbow on the table, fingers running through my hair as I floated in and out of consciousness.

I woke up to feel my head banging against the guest bedroom headboard. I was on my back. My legs were bent and spread wide. It was dark. My right arm reaching for anything but air. Chad jackhammering his entire body hard against my lungs. My heart beating fast from all the Adderall. I thought I might not ever breathe again. "I can't breathe," I mumbled. Chad kept going. I never told him no. I never told him yes. I was a wilted leaf blowing in his wind. And when I looked up, he looked angry, and I wanted to cry, but my tears felt stuck in between the palpitations of my heart until he came with my hair bunched in his hand, and the world went black.

"Dad! Dad! Guess what?" I was beaming, wearing my green choir jacket with the St. Patrick's shield my father had sewed onto my pocket the night before. He had learned to sew while in the air force. I was in the sixth grade, and his red Porsche made a rare appearance in the carpool line. He'd left work early to surprise me.

"What? *What?*" When my father knew I was excited, he exuded an equal level of excitement to match mine.

"I won the election!" I exulted. "I'm the president of the upper-school choir!"

"That's my girl! I'm so proud of you," he said.

I was a loser, a failure. I stared into the mirror at my blue eyes, the round tip of my nose, my lips, my dark brown hair. They were his. I didn't recognize myself. I was twenty-seven years old with a death wish, standing under the pale and sober light. And I wanted to die. My childhood—it was only in my imagination, wasn't it?—its perfection, because the truth, no matter how it rippled and roared and escaped through me, would eventually come back around again covered in the echoes of my father. The euphoria that had dealt its own hand in my version of what was and what wasn't penetrated my nervous system so profoundly that I had missed the whole truth. Only now did I realize I would have to kill it if I wanted to cross the threshold into reality.

I called Mara first. She picked up, and I told her where he'd been; why he'd disappeared. "I just spoke to him the other day," she said, nonchalantly. "What?" I asked. "Yeah," she said. "He's doing business in Albania."

"Mara, stop, stop!" I yelled as she continued rambling on as though she were proud of him. Mara didn't want to hear the truth. She argued with me. She wanted to keep my father locked in the light of his glory days—*our* glory days. She had recently become engaged to a local musician and part-time fitness instructor, and I could feel her slipping from me too into the darkness of denial. She and her fiancé couldn't afford an engagement ring, so she wore our mother's. The ring my father had proposed to her with. "Like fate." I couldn't stand looking at it, for all that it represented. I couldn't understand how she could wear it, and as a symbol of what? The conversation would instigate the beginning of a torn relationship between our differences of perception, of reality, and I couldn't change her. I couldn't make her see the truth, just like Atticus and Liam couldn't make me see my truth. We fall when we fall, and it's not up for anyone else to decide when or if it ever happens.

I got off the phone. Disoriented, I had been driving somewhere in a neighborhood in Beverly Hills, and when I hung up, I had no idea where I was. I needed someone to believe me so that I didn't feel insane. I had photocopied the statement that Judge Cote made when resentencing my father. I kept it in a folder in my purse, so I could look at it when I needed to and be reassured that I was right and he was wrong.

Then I called Chloe. My little sister was doing well. She'd begun working for an event planning company and had established herself in the Santa Barbara community, with many friends that were now her family. When I told her where our father had been, she said, "I'm not surprised," as though she had let go of him long before I had. Still, after I read her the judge's sentencing statement, I could hear in her voice the pain that she still carried. It had reopened and solidified old wounds. After my argument with Mara, self-doubt was inevitable, the thought again that maybe I could be wrong; it was hard to shut it out without the help of others. But in that moment with Chloe, I felt safer. I felt connected to her. I felt I wasn't crazy, just hearing a glimpse of the commonality of our pain as sisters, as our father's children, pain that wasn't, for once, hostile, but real. It was all I needed—not to feel so alone so that maybe I had one more chance of reclaiming my life.

When I called my mother, we decided to meet at Mel's Drive-In on Sunset. I pulled into the valet parking lot and saw her standing under the retro-neon sign, waiting for me. She looked like Mom. There were moments when I would catch glimpses of her the way I remembered her to be, and I tried to hold on to them as long as I could before they would disappear again. Her red hair was pulled back in a ponytail. She wore jeans, ballerina flats, and a white blouse. I was surprised at how happy I was to see her. I felt I understood her more for the choices she was forced to make and that she too had been conned. And even if she'd had the slightest intuition to run from him, I understood how difficult it was to do without any real proof. We sat in a booth by the slanted glass windows. It was sunny, and I ordered a Coke and a cheeseburger. She did too, like we used to do on days when I played hooky in elementary school, and she would take me to the McLean Family Restaurant just to talk, like grown-ups do.

When I told her what I had discovered about Dad, she asked warily, "How did you find all of this out?" She asked it as though she were guilty of something; as though I were talking about her.

"I went to the federal courthouse and went through his records," I said. "It was easy." With the look of guilt written across her face, my mother told me she had known about my father's resentencing all along and had kept it a secret from everyone. She knew back when we'd had sushi together. Deborah, the lawyer representing her in the Cohen Milstein case, had called to tell her. It's why her fibromyalgia flared up. It's why she ended up at Cedars-Sinai hospital for what she claimed was a kidney infection. But I knew it was her body's breakdown, her own experience of the truth being forced upon her physically, as it had been for me soon afterward.

"Why didn't you tell me?" I asked.

"Because your dad and I were already divorced, and I didn't want to get involved. I didn't know how your relationship with him would go." She picked at her french fries. "But it seems as though history continues to repeat itself." My mother was referring to her relationship with her own father, the parallels of our stories. How both of our fathers left our lives on the edge of adulthood.

"I'm so sorry," she said. Her pain was my pain; her story, my story. I was only just beginning to see this. How it was up to me to break the family cycle.

I pulled out Judge Cote's remarks from the sentencing and read them to her at the table. She wanted to hear every word. We were putting together the pieces to the puzzle of a man we loved and hated, who'd shattered our moral compass that our only hope for healing would be to detach completely. To let go. But my mother had known this long before me. And though she jumped into the arms of a man who claims to have saved her, I wanted the ending of my story to be different.

I realized the very person I had continually and delusionally thought would save me had just destroyed me. And I had let it happen. I didn't know how I would forgive him or how I would forgive myself. The difference between my mother and me was that I had a great big future ahead—one she could never get back.

"I can't take back all of those years. I gave my life away to him. I gave him my beauty, my youth, all of the love I had inside of me. But you can. Let him go."

The MCC Trust. I had forgotten about the contract my father asked me to sign in order to obtain dual citizenship between the United States and Greece. He'd wanted a Greek passport to open up European bank accounts. I never signed the documents he sent me after the fight I had with Atticus on the streets of Brooklyn. Subconsciously I must have known that my friend was right. The two of us never talked about it again; we just slowly slipped back into our old friendship. After seeing my mother, I went home and frantically searched through my emails, and found the contract. The contract was drawn up by the Law Offices of Jennie Giannakopoulou, Esq., but there was no contact information. I Googled her name, and she popped up. She was real. Her offices were located in Athens, Greece. I found her email address on her website and emailed her that night.

> Hi Jennie,
>   This is an agreement that was sent to me by my father, Thomas
> Prousalis Jr. of Richmond, VA, in 2009. He mentioned that you were

the attorney working with him on obtaining dual citizenship for my
sisters and myself. I am just trying to get clarification on what the final
status is, as I am no longer in communication with my father.

Thank you in advance for your help on this matter. This is a time-
sensitive issue.

Best,

Christina

Dear Christina,

I am in receipt of your email, which has made me thinking. We were
never retained by your father on this or any matter. The name Prousalis
sounds familiar (he may have contacted me for information), but I only
found a George Prousalis informational letter in our files and no client
under the name Prousalis (for this I am certain).

I will be happy to be of further assistance if you need.

Kind regards,

Jennie Giannakopoulou

The next day, I drove to the Social Security office as fast as I could. The
line at the office on Vine Street in Hollywood reminded me of the line
that Josh and I stood in waiting to visit Dad in prison. When I made
it to the front door, I was greeted by two armed security officers who
checked my bag before letting me enter and then asked me why I was
there. I told them I was there to request a new Social Security number,
a new identity, and that I was a victim of identity theft. It was the first
time I said the words out loud. My entire face was quivering, and I
tried not to cry as they directed me to the kiosk ahead. "Sign in there." I
walked over and tapped the electronic screen, indicating the purpose of
my visit, and then sat down in the waiting area. The more I waited, the
more my paranoia grew. How would I know if I had accounts opened
under my name in Europe? My heart raced, and I prayed to God someone here could help me.

They called my number over the loudspeaker, and I walked up to the second window. An old lady with curly gray hair and glasses sat behind the glass wall that separated us, and I spoke to her through an intercom. Calm. Composed. "Hi, I'm here to request a new Social Security number," I said.

She gave me a look. "What is the reason?"

"I have been a victim of identity theft—of fraud," I said, hoping she wouldn't notice that my voice was shaking.

"All right, do you have proof your Social Security card was used?" she asked.

"Um, no. I mean, I could get you a credit report."

"Nope. No, that won't do. Do you have a police report?"

I glanced at the people standing at the window stations on either side of me, hoping they wouldn't hear me. I moved closer to the glass and kept my head down.

"No, I never went to the police. It was my father. My father took my identity. My father used my Social Security number. He left me in one hundred thousand dollars' worth of debt, and there's a chance he's opening accounts under my name in Europe. I don't know."

She took off her glasses to get a good look at me. "I'm so sorry to hear that," the woman said, "but, honey . . . I need proof."

Her compassion broke through me. I couldn't hold back my tears any longer. "But he was my dad. I never went to the police. I didn't know at the time what was happening. I believed him. I believed him for so long." She had no idea what I was talking about. I had completely disassociated from who it was I was talking to, as if she should know my entire story—one that even I couldn't articulate fully.

"Are you in any danger?" She seemed concerned and tried to keep me focused. "Are you the victim of any violence or abuse? Are you being stalked?"

I wanted to scream "How does someone prove abuse when you cannot see it? When it's abuse of one's sanity, of emotions, of one's entire psychological makeup?" And when she asked me if I was in any danger, I thought about the information I found on my father's computer about the stabbing in Albania. What if my name was being used to do business with these people? How could I prove this?

"I don't know," I replied. "I could be in danger. He might be doing business in Albania."

"I'm so sorry; there is nothing I can do to help you," the woman said at last. "I would go to the police station and file a police report. That might help."

"But this happened eight years ago. I never sued him! I never sued him!" I began sobbing harder, begging her to let me change my number.

"I'm really sorry; there is nothing I can do to help. I need to call the next person in line now."

I turned around to see everyone in the waiting area staring at me. I sobbed with my head down and walked out.

I got into my car and sped to the Hollywood police station a few blocks away on Wilcox Avenue, pulling over in the blue loading zone. I ran up the ramp and startled the police officer standing behind the counter.

"How can I help you?" he asked, hands on his belt.

"I need to know what the statute of limitations are for credit card fraud," I said. The officer laughed at my sense of urgency. I was just another lost girl desperate for an answer, desperate to take care of herself, and didn't know how.

"Did the crime take place in the state of California?" he asked. I grunted and doubled over in frustration. "No!" I groaned. I was losing my mind. "My father took my identity. He left me in a hundred thousand dollars' worth of debt, and I never sued him. I never sued him, and the Social Security office won't give me a new number because I never filed a police report, and I can't prove it even though my credit was destroyed. Even though I was homeless once. Even though I've been chased by creditors for seven years. I just want to see if I can file a police report."

"Damn, your own father?" The officer shook his head. "And you never sued him?"

I just looked at him, out of breath, out of answers, out of anything. "It was complicated."

"Okay, where did the crime take place?" he asked.

"Virginia, I guess, where I grew up."

"What you need to do is call the local police department there and ask them to help you."

I sighed. "Okay," and then I left.

I sat in my car and Googled on my cell phone the Fairfax County Police Department's local number. When a female police officer picked up, I explained to her my situation, and that it had been over eight years—although, according to my credit report, I'd had a credit card with my name on it since the age of fourteen, thirteen years earlier. The woman told me that she wasn't entirely sure; that it might be too late. Then she asked, "Would you be willing to file a lawsuit?"

I was exhausted. Exhausted from this life, this story, this nightmare. I wanted it to stop, to be over and behind me. If filing a police report to obtain a new Social Security number would mean going to battle against my father in court, I wasn't up for it. I was still processing my feelings of betrayal, and I couldn't fathom any more years of my life being wasted on a matter of money. He'd served his time in prison, not once, but twice, and it didn't do him any good. A third time certainly wasn't going to make him love me any more, or any less, and it wasn't about the $100,000. I could give two shits about the money. I had wanted a father. I finally—*finally*—was beginning to realize that going to court would not give me a father, my father, a man who had broken so many laws to always get whatever he wanted. He didn't want me. I told the kind officer that I was not up for it, thanked her for her time, and hung up.

But I wouldn't stop there. I would not give up. I would not remain a victim when I was just beginning to feel myself moving in the right direction, even after seven years. I knew this was my chance at regaining control of my life; there was still time to take back my power. I stopped drinking. I quit smoking pot and popping Adderall to numb the pain. If I was going to face the truth, I'd have to live in reality to do it. No matter how painful the feelings, I'd have to feel them—it was the only way to reach the other side of this. It was my only way into the truth.

Funeral, Car Accident, Name Change

I couldn't help but feel that my name was tainted, publicly tarnished, stepped on, and filed away in FBI boxes, shared by estranged family members, his father, his brothers who weren't there for us and a constant reminder of the power my father wielded over me, his name overshadowing mine. I couldn't trust that he wouldn't use it again. I needed to let go of the girl with two happy parents and a perfect life. It was never perfect. The light of my memories seemed dim in the days after I arrived home from New York. I would wake up and wonder if it had ever been real, if we ever were as perfect as we seemed, because, in hindsight, the perfection was exacerbated by the loss, and I couldn't see my past clearly. I didn't want to believe that perhaps my upbringing, all of our happy memories together as a family, was merely a facade, an image to please the surrounding community, something for my father to use only for himself to prove to others how much better we were. It was a historical pain, along with getting sober; a realization that had me in withdrawal, sweating and dry heaving on the bathroom floor for weeks, the pain shooting throughout my entire body, and I thought my feelings were going to kill me. I finally surrendered and asked for help.

I took it upon myself to go back to therapy, to find someone who would hold me accountable for the choices I had made and for the choices I would make moving forward; someone who believed in me and supported me until I could learn to believe in and support myself. I had to turn my life around. No one was going to do it for me, and unless I wanted to remain paralyzed in broken dreams—afraid of the future and tortured by my past—I'd have to do something about it. I continued cocktail waitressing at the Roosevelt Hotel, knowing it was a means to an end, while I began writing during the day; a steady thread to help me heal, to make sense of the world around me, and to understand myself better.

I had no idea what steps to take to legally change my last name. I couldn't afford a lawyer. I'd have to figure it out on my own. One morning I woke up, threw on black slacks and a white blouse, and drove down to the Los Angeles Superior Courthouse.

"How do I legally change my last name?" I asked the woman behind the glass window near the security line. She explained that I would need to pick up paperwork on the fifth floor, fill it out, then file a Petition for Name Change form. I picked up my Name Change Packet, complete with a list of steps to take, took it home, and that afternoon sat at my desk for four hours with dictionary.com and law websites opened up on my computer screen for the definitions of words I didn't understand.

1. Present Name (specify): Christina Grace Prousalis
2. Proposed Name (specify):_____

I had thought long and hard about the last name I wanted to take. Over the course of a few weeks, I had written down a thousand signatures and practiced autographing on endless notepads. I didn't want just any random name. I wanted one that I could feel proud of, that was still rooted in family, a name that kept me tied to the blood that, no matter what I did, I knew I could never change. McDowell is my mother's maiden name, and though that side of the family has its darkness too, Mimi, my mother's mother, was a writer. She wrote the social column for the *Long Beach Independent* newspaper. Her name was Carolyn

McDowell, and my great-grandfather was a pioneer in building and operating local radio stations during Hollywood's golden age, promoting films for Warner Bros. and Fox Studios. His name was Lawrence McDowell. My mother would tell me stories of how he used to go hunting with the likes of Clark Gable on Catalina Island, how elegant and kind he was. I could be proud of those roots. I knew it wasn't perfect, but I was done with perfect.

The next day, I went back to the courthouse, paid the $395 filing fee, and my petition for name change became official. Then I was given a criminal history assessment form to fill out, and after I turned that in, I paid a $95 fee to have my name published in an approved legal newspaper giving those who might oppose my changing my last name an opportunity to deny the petition. Even though it was in an obscure legal newspaper, I feared that someone—anyone—might try to stop me. But there was also a part of me that wished my father would find out, and that he would show up at the courthouse to beg my forgiveness for all of the broken promises and the lies that he told, and that he was sorry. But I knew that was just a fantasy.

A few weeks later, I received a notice in the mail. I had been approved for the name change, passed the criminal background check, and received my official court date. I would need to appear in court before a commissioner on August 12 at nine o'clock in the morning. I had two months left as Christina Prousalis.

White candles lit my apartment, which didn't take many for only four hundred square feet of space. I was lying on top of my coffee table, pretending to be dead. One of my acting headshots was framed on the table against the wall in memoriam, and I'd set out an assortment of chips and dip for my friends. A funeral seemed appropriate. Christina Prousalis needed to die. I wore a long black sundress, and my feet dangled over the edge as Rob, Noah, Dave, Audra, Liam, and Carter, Nancy and John Palmer's daughter, sat in a circle around me. Carter and I had reconnected when she moved out to Los Angeles. I wanted my friends to share their favorite memories of Christina Prousalis.

As each person began to tell his or her story about me, what I heard was not what I had wanted or expected. There was nothing I was proud of, nothing I would miss, nothing I thought was funny or a reflection of the kind of person I wanted to be. And though I knew that girl in me needed to disappear—that she was sad, lost, and didn't know who she was—I had been thinking about the funeral only in terms of letting go of my connection to my father, as opposed to my connection to myself. What I heard was entirely different from what my friends were saying:

The time someone spilled milk on her cashmere sweater. The time she got so drunk at the Beverly Hills Hotel that she walked over to the concierge and demanded a bungalow, exclaiming, "Do you know who my father is?!" The time she walked from West Hollywood to the La Brea police station to file a lawsuit against the bartender who'd thrown her out of the bar because it was after hours. The time she showed up at the courthouse in a sexy pencil skirt and blouse and cut in front of the line of "ordinary Americans" because she told security she was a lawyer, and they believed her!

The time she went to a sex club; did drugs instead of work; the times she cheated on all of her boyfriends and had promiscuous sex with so-and-so because of his last name; the time she believed she was entitled to become a famous movie star because her father told her she was one; the time she believed she owned two million shares of stock in a tequila company and acres of farmland in Puerto Vallarta, and $300,000, and $500 million worth of American music; the time she carried around an Hermès Birkin bag, thinking it was real, and hoping other women would be jealous of her; the time she needed love so badly she invited a stranger home and instead was sexually violated.

I heard once that when you hit bottom, you are really meeting yourself. I was listening to the product of an upbringing that paved the way for a sense of entitlement and narcissistic dreams. Though that is only how I heard it, the stories that my friends shared about me, even if they didn't see it (but I knew that they did), bless them for loving me anyway. They laughed and continued reminiscing, but I could hear only my flaws, all of the things I hated about myself and about where life had taken me, or where I had taken life. Changing my name wouldn't be enough. It wouldn't change *me*. I needed to bury all of those things that defined me from the inside out. My entitlement. My self-righteousness. My fantasy thinking. My judgment. My fear. My being and acting like a victim. And I needed to get rid of all the things—the possessions I had left—that I'd let define me, that represented a history of me that was not grounded in reality, in truth, or in my authentic self. I wanted to get back to the eleven-year-old who had not yet abandoned herself to fashion magazines, material possessions, drugs, stealing, promiscuity, and an obsession with wealth and fame. I wanted to get back to the eleven-year-old girl who didn't give a fuck what she wore to school that day because she had an endless curiosity for life, and for creating and going on adventures with friends rather than projecting an image for attention. I wanted to get back to the girl who felt so free to be her true self that she wasn't even conscious of it because she *lived*.

One of the first things I did was apologize to Liam. I wanted him to know that my inability to love had nothing to do with him, but that it was time to let him go so I could grow into the person I had the potential to become. The person I wanted to be. It wasn't easy. There were some mornings when I didn't even get out of bed because I was so afraid to face the world alone with the knowledge that everything inside of me would have to change; that everything would have to be different if I wanted to create a new life for myself. I would start by taking action.

I had stolen money when I worked at Jerry's bar. I would need to pay him back even if he had illegally denied us breaks and fraudulently sold alcohol. This was about righting my wrong, not his. And the fake Hermès Birkin—I still had it in the back of my trunk. And my mother's Chanel bag, pearl necklaces, gold bracelets, my Tiffany watch, and designer clothes. After my amends, I would have to sell and give away everything.

I had received a check in the mail for a few hundred dollars from a law firm or a corporation—I can't remember. But along with the check came a document that said several cocktail waitresses from the bar I worked at ended up suing the company for not giving us legal breaks and paying us wages owed. It was a sign: justice was on its way. And I could do my part. I sent him a financial amends along with an anonymous letter of apology.

A few days later, I drove with a girlfriend of mine to eat dinner at a Mexican restaurant in Pacific Palisades called Kay 'N Dave's. I told her that I needed to make peace with the neighborhood where it all began. As we drove into the village, I noticed that the Wells Fargo bank on the corner was gone, replaced by Chase Bank. The stationery store, remodeled. The rental house, filled with another family, one that I hoped was happy. It all felt a little more real than the way I had remembered it.

We walked into Kay 'N Dave's and sat down at a little table near the front door. The restaurant was quaint and quiet. As the two of us were talking, in walked an older couple: a short man with white hair, and an elegant woman wearing a pink cashmere sweater with perfect blond hair and makeup.

Ralph Adler.

I leaned over the table and whispered, "Oh my God." My friend looked at me and then at the couple, who stood no more than five feet away. "What?" she asked.

Ralph saw me and looked away quickly.

I could barely speak. I told my girlfriend everything that happened nearly ten years ago, about the porno and what he'd said to me: "because I know you need the money." That he had helped my mother pro bono, and when I confronted his business partner about what Ralph had said to me, he refused to believe it—and then wrote me a letter "firing" me as a client. For so many years, how I fantasized about how I would get my revenge.

"Holy shit! You have to do something!" my girlfriend exclaimed as I watched the Adlers sit down two tables away: Ralph, with his back to me, and his wife looking almost straight at me. "Here, take my plate; dump it on his lap."

"No," I told her. "Look at him. He's so sad, and his poor wife. You have to be in a lot of pain to be living a lie like that."

I would know.

"So what are you going to do?"

Our waitress came over to the table, and in her broken English asked how we were doing.

"Fine," I said, "except can you do me a favor?"

"Sure."

"Take my credit card. I'd like to pay for that man and his wife's dinner," I told her. "He's an old friend of the family's." I winked at my girlfriend. "But don't tell him I paid until I after I've left. I want it to be a surprise."

"Okay. So tell him pretty brunette girl pay for dinner. But after you leave."

"Exactly," I said, grinning.

Ten minutes later, the waitress brought me his check. After paying it, I took the itemized receipt and wrote in red pen at the top: ". . . Because I know you need the money. Xo Christina Prousalis." I folded the receipt, handed it to the waitress, and said, "Give this to him for me, will you? It's a little note."

The waitress thought this was so cute. "Yes, of course." I gave her a $20 tip. "Let's get out of here," my girlfriend said.

"A little bit of forgiveness mixed with a little bit of revenge never hurt anybody, right?" I fantasized about the questions his wife might ask him: "*Who* paid our bill?"

My girlfriend couldn't stop laughing. "You're so crazy." We high-fived each other, and I walked out the door with my head held high and thought, *Eh, Pacific Palisades ain't so bad anymore.*

A few days later, I threw on jeans and a T-shirt and ransacked my closet. Marc Jacobs, Diane von Furstenberg, Stuart Weitzman, Prada, Burberry, and Ralph Lauren went flying into a pile on the floor. I threw my Tiffany watch, Michele watch, pearls, and gold bracelets into a pile on my bed. I grabbed the fake Birkin, the classic Chanel, and the Yves Saint Laurent handbags I had forgotten about, and dumped them in another pile. With each item I discarded it felt like I was peeling away a layer of dead skin. I threw everything into trash bags and lugged them downstairs and out to my car. I had made a deal with myself: I would sell half to pay my bills for the month, and I would donate the rest to Goodwill.

There is no greater feeling than watching all of these expensive name-brand fashions and accessories being dumped into a dirty blue tub at the Goodwill in Hollywood, knowing that they would go to people who actually needed it. And I don't mean they needed a Chanel purse; I mean simply a purse. Or a pair of shoes—no, not Stuart Weitzman shoes. Just shoes. Not because they needed to prove to someone that they were of a certain class or that they were more beautiful or better than other people, but because they needed it for a job interview so they could put food on the table for their three-year-old. The old man who handed me my receipt didn't say "Wow, thank you for these designer labels!" No. That would never even cross his mind. He was grateful for the donation of functional clothing and accessories. I thanked him, and I was off to the next location.

Wasteland is a hip vintage clothing store on Melrose where you can sell used clothing and accessories. I walked up to the counter and dumped the Hermès purse in front of a tall hipster wearing suspend-ers. "It's a fake," I said. "How much is it worth?" He told me to wait a minute, took the bag, and showed it to his boss, who seemed interested. After a minute of looking at it, the hipster came back and said, "We'll mark it at three hundred seventy-five dollars. You get thirty-five percent of that price."

"Sold." I didn't care about selling it myself online or pocketing the full amount; I just wanted it out of my life. Gone! Good-bye! I couldn't believe I had kept it for that long. The hipster wrote me a check for $131.25, and I was out of there. On to the next location. That bag had no emotional significance. I had wept over it long enough.

The pawnshop on the corner of Melrose and Cahuenga Boulevard was a little terrifying on the outside: bright yellow with bars on its blacked-out windows and a doorbell you had to press to be let inside. A young Native American man with a long ponytail opened the door. I had never been inside of a pawnshop before. I imagined it would feel dark and sleazy; maybe gangsters smoking cigars in the back. But I looked around at all the old trinkets and things, guitars and old music equipment displayed on high shelves, and it felt completely the opposite. Shoppers strolled around, and the staff was friendly. I scanned the jewelry cases filled with old watches and silver bracelets as I made my way to the bulletproof glass window to have my Tiffany watch appraised. The man came back through the side door and said, "I can give you a hundred."

"One hundred dollars, that's it?" I replied, dumbfounded at how worthless it was. But given the way I responded, it didn't feel so worthless. "Yeah," he said. "I'll probably only be able to sell it for around a hundred and fifty." I paused.

"If you need cash now, I can always give you the loan with interest, and as long as you give it back by a certain date, the watch is yours again." I felt tears coming on and a lump rising in my throat. "I need a minute to decide," I told him. Was I just doing all of this out of anger, and would I be sorry later? Or was I really ready to let go, and be happy and free from all of these possessions and gifts from my past that I thought meant something? Even if I decided to keep the watch,

it would never feel the same on my wrist. I would feel the shame from the possibility that it was bought with stolen money, and maybe at somebody else's expense. And if it wasn't bought with stolen money, was it really a symbol of my father's love for me? Was this what love meant to me?

I stood there, and I remembered what happened the only time my father ever physically hurt me. I was eight or nine. Mara and I were fighting over a hairbrush in the bathroom. My father was in the other room on a business call. He heard us, threw down the phone, stormed through the door, grabbed me up by my arms, threw me up against the bathroom wall, and screamed at me. When he dropped me, I curled up in a ball on the bath mat, heaving and crying so hard that my mother ran in to see if I was all right, but I was covering my face—I wouldn't let her see my face—and my mother kept yelling, "Let me see your face! Let me see your face!" until she had to pry my fingers away. She was so afraid he had hit me and that I was bleeding and didn't want her to see. My father was gone for a few hours after that. I remember the sound of his engine as he peeled out of the driveway.

And when he came back, he brought me a present. It was wrapped in white paper with a velvet green bow on top. I opened it up while sitting on his lap. It was a Madame Alexander doll of Scarlett O'Hara from *Gone with the Wind*.

I dumped the watch back on the counter. "Take the watch," I said. "I don't want it anymore."

"You sure? You don't want a loan?"

"No. Take it."

The only possession left was my BMW. But I wasn't planning on giving that away. I wanted to keep it. And not just because I thought it made me look cool and sexy. That it got me attention, and made me feel good enough. But because it meant I could still hang on to my father, and to my story. The truth was that my mother had sold the Chagall

painting to pay off the lien a few years earlier but had forgotten to tell me. I was living with my actor friend Dillon above the crack addict's apartment when she told me.

"I sold my Chagall to pay off your car," my mother had said.

"Wait, what? When did you do that?"

"I don't know, Christina." The question made her exhausted just thinking about it.

"So, I've been able to sell my car this whole time?"

"You have to get the title back first."

"What's a title?"

"Proof you own your car. The bank has it."

"Which bank?"

"I don't remember. Whoever we were banking with."

"How am *I* supposed to remember?"

"Washington Mutual?"

"Washington Mutual doesn't even *exist* anymore, Mom!"

"Well, it was over a year ago, because that's when I got the money."

"I was homeless and driving around in a BMW! How could you not tell me this?"

I had to retrace my steps to the Wells Fargo bank in Pacific Palisades where it all began. A banker pulled my credit history, and I was able to get proof that the lien had been paid. After filling out a series of paperwork and going to the DMV, the title was finally mailed to me. But when I got it, I didn't sell the car. My father taught me how to drive stick in that car. It was one of our last moments alone together before he left for prison, and I wasn't ready to let go. I wanted to keep it forever, for as long as I could, until I was an old lady and it would be declared a vintage. But, the universe had a different plan.

A few days before I was to appear in court for my name change, I was driving along the 101 Freeway near Coldwater Canyon. I remember feeling numb. There was so much change happening in me. I was driving the car but I *wasn't* driving the car—someone else was driving

the car, and I remember it was quiet. I wasn't listening to any music, and I wasn't on my cell phone or even looking at my cell phone, which was buried somewhere in my purse. It was clear and sunny, and I was cruising at forty-five miles an hour in light traffic. I put on my right blinker and moved into the right lane. The freeway was splitting ahead and I continued on toward Laurel Canyon Boulevard. I needed to move over into the right lane, so I checked my wing mirrors and put on my blinker again, then looked over my right shoulder. Before I could glance back at the car in front of me, all I remember seeing was the blue, white, and black BMW logo on the steering wheel before my head smashed against it, accompanied by the sound of crunching metal. Breathing hard, I lifted my head. I touched my face, my nose, to see if I was bleeding. There was no blood. I looked at myself in the mirror. I had hit my head. A bump growing on the left side of my forehead. I looked up and could see the hood of my car smashed like a folded accordion. In a daze, I stepped out of the car and into the middle of the freeway, I began walking into the mirage wavering off the asphalt, squinting my eyes, cars whipping past me blowing my skirt and hair all about. No one stopped to see if I was okay. Then I spun around. The person I hit was sitting in his car. It was a Toyota Sierra. There was only a small dent in his bumper, and he never got out of the car.

"Get out of the road!" someone shouted from an ambulance. Before I could respond, a young woman in an EMT uniform had grabbed me by the arm and yanked me over to the shoulder.

"You're going to get hit by a car!" she yelled. I turned and looked at her.

"You're in shock," she said as I touched my head. The air bag hadn't deployed.

I sat in the back of the ambulance as an EMT wrapped a blood pressure cuff around my arm and started pumping to make it tighter. I looked out at my car and realized what I had done. I exploded into sobs, crying as I looked at my totaled BMW. The emergency medical technician kneeled down in front of me. "Breathe," she said. "Breathe. It's going to be okay."

"My car, my car, my car, my car . . ." I started hyperventilating. "It's gone."

I had shut down both lanes of the freeway. Gridlock was emerging. Drivers slowed down and saw my mascara-streaked tears in the back of the ambulance.

"Look at me," the EMT said sharply. Her cheeks were glowing from the heat. "Do you believe in God?"

"What?" I asked, breathing in and out.

"Do you believe in God? You know, something bigger than you? Big breaths now."

I exhaled. "I'm willing to believe in anything at this point," I told her.

"Then repeat after me: God—"

She grasped my hands in hers.

"Repeat. After. Me," she reiterated. "God—"

I looked out at my totaled BMW. A tow truck with flashing yellow lights was pulling up behind it as a police officer paced around it filling out the accident report.

"God—" I said at last.

"I'm giving this to you."

"I'm giving this to you."

"Thy will be done."

I let out one more exasperated sob. "Thy will be done."

I was still sore from the accident as I waited in the security line at the Los Angeles Superior Courthouse once more.

I had never noticed her before, the statue above me. The word *Justice* carved below her feet, a terra-cotta goddess draped in judicial robes, all-powerful, and holding a sword in her right hand. Two men kneeling on either side of her; the scales of justice balancing on her head, while an American eagle perched above, its wings spread.

I don't remember what I was wearing and now, perhaps, it doesn't matter. Raw to the tip, I walked inside of the courtroom. I sat on the wooden bench in the second row. *Humbled*. Across the aisle from me, a Hispanic man sitting next to a young Hispanic woman held a baby girl. An Asian man sat behind me, and a girl of mixed race sat next to me.

"I'm Gloria," the girl whispered. "Are you changing your last name too?"

"Yes," I whispered back.

"To what?"

"McDowell."

"Pretty."

"Thanks. What about you?" I asked.

"Jones. You wouldn't be able to pronounce my birth name. It's hard to find work with it, you know? So this is much better." She smiled.

"Sounds perfect," I said. Gloria tapped her fingers on her folder and waited.

A few minutes later, Commissioner Matthew St. George, a soft-looking man with a white beard, entered. He took a seat and called the first person to the podium. For each person, he stated the reason for the name change. I squirmed in my seat at the thought of him saying for all to hear, "She is estranged from her father, Thomas Prousalis Jr. He is a convicted felon. She does not want any association with him, his family, or his name, as he illegally took advantage of her Social Security number. She wants to protect herself." I panicked. *Oh God, why did I write that? Now everyone will know.* For a minute, I debated leaving as I watched the Hispanic man carry his baby to the podium to be granted a new name. It would be too humiliating.

But it was too late. "Christina Prousalis."

That's my name! That's—was *my name, will not be my name anymore, almost not my name*—oh God, *he just called my name.*

I stood up. My hands were shaking as I squeezed past Gloria, and my purse hit the back of the wooden bench making a banging noise that everyone heard, which was embarrassing, as I made my way to the podium to stand before the commissioner.

There I was standing in front of him. I exhaled slowly.

"Good morning," he said.

"Good morning, sir."

"You have also filed a petition for name change, I see here."

"Yes, sir."

I was ready for him to say the words out loud, in front of everyone, why I had done it. My heart held still—ready for his words to hit me, more painful to hear the truth about my father from someone other than myself.

The commissioner looked down at my file and paused. He looked up at me, and his eyes grew kind, as though he had read my thoughts.

"Congratulations on your new beginning, Ms. McDowell," was all he said.

My eyes flooded. "Thank you, sir."

I was finally safe.

Amalia

The building sat isolated down the street from an abandoned warehouse with bars on its windows. "Jobs Not Jails!" was painted in blue across the side. I stepped out of the used Volkswagen Jetta I bought with the insurance money I got from the accident. I was wearing jeans and a black T-shirt. The building wasn't far from the old nightclub I'd worked at near skid row. Cars whizzed above me toward the bridge over the Los Angeles River. A homeless man, the only person in sight, moped by, pushing a shopping cart filled with blankets, backpacks, and trash. I looked both ways to cross the street. The address was marked inconspicuously on the sidewalk a few feet down. I walked up to the steel door, which was propped open by a giant rock. "Office of Restorative Justice," it said. Afraid to enter unannounced, I rang the intercom button and waited.

A man with a bald head swung open the door. "It's open. See?" he said. He was no people pleaser.

I took a step back. "Yeah, I know. I just wasn't sure. I'm here to see Amalia. Is she here? She told me to come by today."

"Yeah, yeah, Amalia's always here. Come on up. I'm Francisco." He held out his hand.

"I'm Christina," I said. His arm was covered in tattoos. When he turned around, the back of his neck was red and swollen. Gang tattoo removal. He must have just been released from prison.

He led me up a dark cement staircase. Crosses and candles lined the stairwell.

Upstairs was a typical office space. Francisco led me down to Amalia Molina's office at the end of the hallway.

She was more elegant than I had anticipated, sitting behind her desk in a blouse, pearls, and black slacks. Her hair was long and dark, with a few gray streaks. She got up from her seat to shake my hand.

"Hi, I'm Christina McDowell. I called you earlier this week."

"Yes, yes. Hi, Christina, have a seat. Please." She pointed to the chair in front of her desk. A few days earlier, I had Googled "families of the incarcerated, Los Angeles." After all that I had been through, I thought maybe I could be of use and help.

"So what can I do for you?" Amalia exuded a wisdom and serenity that any woman would hope to have in her later years. I noticed stacks of handwritten letters on her desk. I knew they were from prison. No one handwrites letters anymore except people in prison.

"I'd like to help," I said bluntly. "Put me to work. I can come in three days a week to volunteer." Amalia smiled at me, wondering why I'd come all the way down there demanding I be put to work without any pay. I was young, not wealthy, and not doing it to fulfill some social elitist expectation or for my college resume. I was still cocktail waitressing and nannying when I could, wondering what I was supposed to be doing with the rest of my life, wondering if I had any kind of purpose or use on this earth. I was searching for something, and Amalia knew what it was before I did.

Each day that I showed up at her office, I sorted through mail and filed letters from prison inmates while I watched Amalia take meetings with mothers, wives, and homeless children who'd come seeking her help. One woman came in panicking because her electricity had been turned off; she could no longer pay all of the bills because her husband had been the main breadwinner, and he was gone. She didn't know how she would care for her daughter. Amalia held her hand. She listened. She took notes, and she told the woman she would help her look for more work. But I knew there was only so much she could do. I could see the surrounding community drowning in these issues. Ones I related to, yet, because I was white and from a privileged background, I didn't feel right bringing them up. Dare I say I understood, because I didn't. The reality of my childhood was starkly different, because even if it was based on some fantasy of my father's, the things—those material things—I did have, I did touch. I did have an education, and I was privileged. And the shame of it all permeated deep inside of me.

Amalia planned bus trips for families to see loved ones in prison because so often they cannot afford to travel. Many do not own cars or have the money to travel the long distances to isolated locations where many of the prisons are located. She also planned events for the families to gather, as a way to create a supportive community.

"Can you call the number next to each name on that list and check off who is coming and who is not?" Amalia asked. We were planning a trip to the beach. Many of the children going didn't own bathing suits, had never even set foot on sand or seen the ocean. In fact, most had never even ventured beyond a ten-block radius of their neighborhood.

The next morning, we met at the public school nearby, where buses parked out front waited to take us to Malibu for the day. I was one of the chaperones.

"You see?" Amalia said, pointing to what the children were wearing. About fifty Hispanic and black children climbed up onto the bus in their shorts and T-shirts. Most of them were being raised by a single parent, some with no parent at all, and all of them with a parent in prison or facing deportation.

The afternoon was spent on the beach. I watched a young girl touch the ocean for the first time. I watched them learn how to surf and boogie board. They built sand castles and buried one another in the sand. And I spoke with the mothers and grandmothers, who shared their stories.

Back in the office the next day, I was sitting at the computer, drafting the monthly newsletter, when Amalia walked over and asked point-blank what my story was.

I told her everything. She listened, and then jumped up from her seat, excited, rubbing her hands together as if concocting a brilliant plan. I was hoping my sob story would warrant tears, but instead she beamed and said, "You're coming with me to prison next week. You're going to share your story in one of my victims' workshops."

"Um, okay," I said, having no clue what she was talking about. But I trusted her.

The following week, at the crack of dawn, I met Amalia at her home. Another woman was coming with us to share her story too. Norma was the mother of a teenage son who was killed in a drive-by shooting, his body obliterated by an AK-47. He was standing on a street corner in Watts, headed for high school, when a gang member's bullet blew off his elbow, soared through his heart, and blasted his abdomen. A senior, he planned to attend UCLA in the fall. This woman had more faith, courage, and forgiveness inside of her than anyone I had ever met. I didn't understand at first why my story should be told, how it related to any of this, because of my socioeconomic background, because of my race, because of everything I thought made me separate or apart from. But Amalia kept insisting it didn't matter. She'd say with affection, "*Mija*, it's not about the money."

Pleasant Valley State Prison is an all-men's prison about midway between Los Angeles and San Francisco. It sits on a blanket of brown in an empty desert, like most prisons. The air was dry and smelled of cow manure, and the thermometer read 104 degrees. I could see the desolate compound in the distance as we drove through its deadbeat town filled with Jesus-themed clothing stores, frayed American flags, and scattered one-story homes. I was reminded of when I visited my father in prison. I asked myself why was it that faith seemed so prevalent amid such darkness and why, in the light, it's often taken for granted. I didn't tell Mom or Mara or Chloe what I was doing. They were on their own journeys of grief.

"*Amor*, how are you doing back there?" Amalia looked at me in the rearview mirror.

"Great." I smiled back at her. I felt sweat from the heat forming on my forehead and upper lip.

When we arrived, we walked through metal detectors and checked in. The experience was entirely different from when I checked in as a visitor to see my father. Pleasant Valley treated me like a staff member, with more respect. I was a victim to them now, coming to share my story. As if I hadn't been a victim before, being the child of an inmate?

We stood in front of the security booth as the chaplain's hands strapped an alarm to the belt loop of my pants. "If you feel your life is at risk, just press this center button here, and it will sound an alarm for security," he said, pulling down on the device to make sure it was secure. "See those monitors there? We're tracking your every move, so we know exactly where you are at all times." I pressed my hands and nose up to the thick tinted glass to catch a glimpse inside the security booth. Correctional officers sat wearing stab-proof vests in front of monitors, buttons, and gadgets. The chaplain grabbed a brown clipboard off the steel counter behind us and said, "Sign your name here and slide your driver's license under the window." I took the pen and began to write my name—a name I still wasn't used to signing; a name that still didn't feel like mine: *Christina McDowell*.

I handed the chaplain back his pen and clipboard knowing that I'd signed my life away. Knowing that if a riot broke out, this alarm, which resembled our garage clicker from the nineties, wasn't going to save my life.

Nervous adrenaline pumped through my arms and my legs to the tips of my fingers and up through my neck and temples as the three of us followed the Chaplain to the security gate leading out to the yard. Two correctional officers in khaki military-style uniforms sounded the alarm initiating the clicking of metal doors, a sound that was familiar to me. "Clear!" They opened.

You could feel the desert heat rising from the asphalt. See its wavering colors in the distance, brown, blue, and beige. Brown for the desert, blue for the inmates' uniforms, and beige for the run-down cells around us.

We began walking, and all eyes fell on me. It was a vulnerability I'd never felt before, beating out of my chest as I kept my head held high and my eyes focused on what was right in front of me. *These motherfuckers will not intimidate me; it's too late for that.* Basketballs dropped, weights dropped, arms let go of chin-up bars to an unsettling stillness as the three of us passed by, each inmate's daily routine now interrupted by a visit from three women strolling across their yard. I was told they're called lifers—these were men locked up for murder, serving the rest of their lives in prison. I still wasn't sure why the hell I was there, but Amalia said all I had to do was share my story.

As we entered the makeshift chapel, a few inmates known as trustees stood in a receiving line to greet us. They were a mix of black and Hispanic men. I was the only white person (once again) other than one correctional officer who waited outside in the yard. The inmates shook our hands and nodded respectfully. The ones who'd helped set up the room were preparing to go in front of the parole board, the panel of individuals who decide whether an offender should be released from prison, and had been awarded privileges and special work duties for good behavior. They entered and set up rows of chairs facing the front podium, which I would sit behind with Norma, facing everyone while Amalia gathered her papers on the podium. I wasn't sure where to direct my gaze, afraid to inadvertently stare at anyone. I snuck in a few glances to see who trickled in. I saw an old black man with white hair who was having trouble walking; his left leg was limp, so he leaned on a cane as he sat down in the back row. Then I saw a young black kid who looked my age, midtwenties, wearing black-rimmed Ray-Ban glasses and Chuck Taylor sneakers. Others came in with gang tattoos covering necks, faces, and bald heads. The only white inmate I saw had the words "Fuck the Police" tattooed across his forehead.

As the seats filled up, the energy became tense, as though everyone's fear was right on the surface and the only thing keeping us in the moment was trust. A black man sat across from me. He had the darkest eyes I'd ever seen. He was staring at me, his eyes like lasers. I had read in a book about prison that staring is used as a technique for intimidation. Chances are he was the man who called the shots, deciding who needs to be killed, how, and when. I remembered to breathe and then exhaled, with my eyes focused on Amalia. There wasn't a single correctional officer in the room with us, just me, Norma, Amalia, and a hundred lifers. I had no cell phone, no ID. No keys or pepper spray, just the alarm attached to my waist. *Well, if you die, you die.*

My fear dissipated when Amalia began to speak. "Take off your mask," she said. "I don't care where you're from, what gang you're a part of, what race you are, what your crime was. Today, right now, we are human beings sitting together having a dialogue with mutual care and respect."

When Amalia nodded at me, indicating that it was my turn to speak, I looked to Norma in sheer terror. I wanted to run, but it was too late now. Norma placed her hand on my back. "All you have to do is tell them the truth," she said softly.

I didn't plan what I was going to say. Not for any reason other than it was too painful to think about beforehand, and I didn't know what to expect. When I looked up at all of the men in blue and introduced myself, I wanted to know one thing before I began:

"How many of you have a daughter?"

Bodies shuffled in seats before a few hands raised, and then a few more, until almost every single man raised his hand. I looked at all the arms raised in blue uniforms, and for the first time, I felt what I had to say mattered.

When I spoke, the deepest pain I felt about my father's betrayal unraveled before them. Everything I had wanted to say to him over the years but had never expressed, I said to them. I raged at them. I told them about the fraud, the facade, the promises, the lies, and that all I wanted—all I needed—were truth, accountability, vulnerability, and love. Love so badly that, look! It took me to the darkest place in America to find it. And all the drugs, alcohol, and sex I had to numb the pain, the way I abused myself, hated myself, because of the shame I felt for everything I had and everything I didn't have. I told them of the things I wasn't proud of, and that I took responsibility for those things now and that until I know what justice feels like, I will remain broken, wishing I could make sense of him and all that had happened.

I sat down, and the black man who had been staring at me raised his hand. Amalia called on him. He stood up, and his body melted into humility when I found the courage to look him in the eye. "My name is Jerome. I am serving twenty-five to life for gang-related murder, and I have a daughter I have never met. I write to her, but she doesn't respond." He bowed his head, and his lips quivered. "I, um, I just want to apologize on behalf of your father, and was wondering if it would be all right if I shook your hand to thank you."

I extended my hand after Amalia nodded that it was okay to do so.

"Thank you for listening." As our hands met, he then asked, "Are your mom and sisters okay?"

"Yeah, I think so; we're each dealing with our grief in our own ways," I told him. My heart felt depleted, though I hadn't noticed yet—it wasn't as heavy.

The young black kid in his Ray-Bans raised his hand next. "Thank you for sharing your story. My dad was in prison my whole life, so I feel your pain. I understand your abandonment. I didn't want to end up like my father, but here I am." He had tears in his eyes and shook his head. "Drugs, man. You know, I hadn't seen my father in seventeen years until I was incarcerated myself. We ended up at the same prison together." When I heard this, my heart shattered, and I wondered if on some subconscious level the pain he felt of losing his father—the need for love from his father—led him to prison. His father's prison. Although there is no statistic showing that men and women with an incarcerated parent are more likely to land in prison themselves, I couldn't help but relate. As I stood inside that prison, I had been searching for him so I could let him go. I felt my anger dissipating as more inmates stood up and shared their stories, shared about the pain they felt after losing a parent, their struggles with addiction, their own need for love and purpose, recognizing their failures, holding themselves accountable for the crimes they committed. It was remarkable. Unlike anything I had ever witnessed in my life—an unspeakable power.

After I shook a few more inmates' hands, we left. Amalia, Norma, and I stepped out into the yard in the blazing sun. As we walked toward the exit, I looked into the distance and watched two correctional officers in full SWAT gear, wearing protective goggles, walking toward us with an inmate shackled at his hands low to his waist, his head bowed in shame. It felt like I was watching a performance, a play, everything made to appear darker, to keep us trapped and imprisoned in our own perceptions of what we fear, so afraid of a reality that might not be so terrifying if we had the courage to face the root of all our pain. And when I heard "Clear!" one last time, I wasn't so angry anymore.

A few days later, I walked into Amalia's office. She had stepped out, and there was a note on her desk with a letter underneath it: "Christina: this was addressed to you." It was a letter from the prison. I tore it open, sat down at Amalia's desk, and read it.

Dear Christina,

I am writing to thank you for coming to Pleasant Valley to share your story in the Victim Awareness workshop. I must say, it was one of the most meaningful things I have ever done in my life, to hear your testimony; to hear the testimony of a daughter; the testimony of a prisoner's daughter.

Like your father, I am a prisoner; a father of three daughters. I have been incarcerated for 25 years. So with this background review, you can see that I have been practically absent from their lives. And what little time I have been, the memories are more mine than theirs. And I cling to those memories as a man clings to his very breath.

To be honest, I do not feel close to my daughters and I am learning I have myself to blame for that. It is I who abandoned them; it is I who refuses to write when they don't. I should write them regardless if they write back or not.

The best thing you can do for your father is tell him exactly what you told us fathers. Christina—Mija—God used you as a vessel on October 24, 2012. You have set a part of me free, and for that I shall be forever thankful.

Be good to yourself. God Bless You.

Steve

- 30 -

Good-bye, Dad

It was Mara's wedding day. As much as she had denied the truth, I knew it was within her as I watched my sister walk down the aisle in her white veil, being given away by a man that wasn't our father. I held steady up at the altar of St. Alban's Church in Westwood next to Chloe in our lavender gowns, looking at our beautiful, brave sister. Knowing he was gone. It was this image, his absence on a day we had dreamed about as three little girls, that ignited my acceptance, the culmination of everything that made my father's disappearance from my life real.

He wasn't there.

It didn't matter how many times the pain would strike me and attempt to take me down, I refused to set myself up to be hurt by him again. I had heard through my cousin Alex, who had heard through the grapevine at the wedding after-party, that my father was fine. He had remarried, was traveling the world, and was continuing to do business overseas. Of all the truths, it was the most painful to discover. There had been so many nights when I wondered if I should reach out to him because: What if he were homeless? What if he were sick with cancer and living on the streets? He was getting older. Would I be able to forgive myself if he died and I never saw him again? All of the things I never said to him; would I get to say them? The truth is, it doesn't mat-

ter. I'll never know the truth surrounding him. It sounded as though
he had landed perfectly, just as he always did. And I had been the fool
once more for believing it would be any different. My father was doing
fine without me. Without my mother, without Mara, and without
Chloe. How do you reconcile with someone who believes—who really
believes—the lie is the truth? You cannot. Any letter I wrote, any words
I could say, they wouldn't matter, it wouldn't change him. I had created a prison for myself while chasing his love. The letter I would write
wouldn't be for him. It would be for me. And I could do that without
having to see or speak to him ever again. And I could accept that. It was
my only path to freedom.

Dear Dad,

    *I wanted to write you this letter to tell you a little bit about who I am
today and to share some things with you I thought you should know.
My journey hasn't been easy. And I've often battled whether or not I
could or would ever share these things with you because a part of me feels
you don't deserve it and a part of me longs for you to know. All my life,
I wanted nothing more than for you to be proud of me. Over the past
three years, after I decided I could no longer be in communication with
you, those were the darkest days of my life. I turned to alcohol, drugs,
and men to numb my pain. It was more betrayal than I could handle,
and I'm sensitive to the truth. Before I hit rock bottom, I discovered you
went back to prison a second time, and that's when I decided to change
my name. I discovered the truth, you know, and if I could take it all
back—to have a Dad, I would. I'd take it all back. Take back the Tiffany watch you gave me when I was fourteen, the watch I showed off at
school bragging to all of my friends, and instead, I'd rather you teach me
about hard work, teach me about showing up for people, teach me about
humility. Take back the trip to the Plaza Hotel with our toys from FAO
Schwartz and our lobster dinners, and instead, take me on a walk in the
park and teach me how to put one foot in front of the other, and how to
walk through fear. Teach me about kindness and patience. Take back*

those weekend trips in your private plane and instead bang on the door of my bedroom when you hear me crying because the first boy I ever kissed broke my heart. Teach me about friendship. Take back the diamonds and the pearls you gave us—you gave Mom, and tell her she's beautiful without them, tell her she's enough. Tell her you will never abandon her or hurt her, take back all of those broken promises, the bank accounts, the credit cards, and the friends we had because of the last names they carried, the illusions that they would make us feel enough. I want you to tell me that we are enough without a penny to our name.

Dad: I would have loved you anyway, had you told me the truth. You know what I did when I got back to Los Angeles after digging through your court records? I held a funeral for myself. Yes, I still have a sense of humor. I get that from you. And after I changed my name, I let myself grieve. There were days I didn't get out of bed because my body felt so heavy. My throat swelled up. I couldn't eat. I felt so ashamed. And I allowed myself to cry and scream at the top of my lungs. And you know, things are getting better. I started volunteering at the Office of Restorative Justice. I went to prison and spoke to incarcerated fathers and told them my story. I was able to say all the things to them face-to-face that I could never say to you. And it has helped me heal. Sometimes I wonder what life would look like had you never broken the law and gone to prison. I wonder if we would have lived the same, how we would have lived. Would I learn the harsh truths of life another way? Or would I have remained blind? I try not to think about it too, too much. We'll never know. Maybe fate does exist. But I do know the things I want out of life have shifted the more I discover my authentic self. For a long time, I stopped believing in love, and slowly I've regained my faith. It's just that I have never experienced it before, that kind of love. I am looking forward to creating a family of my own someday—possibly even get married. The future for me now looks a lot brighter because I'm laying it down with a foundation of truth. And with that, I can forgive you, Dad. I forgive you. I accept that you will never change, and God, how angry and sad it makes me. But I get it now. I get it. We're different. And I forgive you for all of it. I forgive you for not protecting me, for never telling me the truth. And you know what, Dad? Thank you. Thank you for being my greatest teacher. You have taught me a great deal about love. Because, goddamn it, I love you so much. But it's done nothing but hurt me. And I can't carry that kind of love anymore. So, here—take it. It's all yours.

    Christina

The End

I had to go back, to get away, to experience once more the juxtaposition between Hollywood and politics, Los Angeles and Washington, DC, poverty and wealth. To take that clichéd trip down memory lane. To see from a new perspective how far I'd fallen from where I had come from. Had I missed anything? There is always some other subconscious story unfolding that we don't know yet. And I wondered where it had gone. All that which divided me.

It was America's birthday weekend; the year, 2014. American flags and banners hung from redbrick town houses and mansions along cobblestone streets. It was hot and muggy, and I was staying at the Palmers' elegant home on the edge of Rock Creek Park, a neighborhood where embassies hang foreign flags. Where, back in the day, Nancy's daughters and I would run around the fish ponds and through the gardens of the Hillwood Museum, once home to cereal heiress Marjorie Merriweather Post.

Nancy and her youngest daughter—her name is Hope—were gracious hosts. They were grieving John's death. Husband and father, an American journalist from another time. From the days of Carter and Clinton. As a little girl, I'd see him on the television screen reporting from the White House lawn while my mother cooked macaroni and cheese in the kitchen, and my sisters and I would shriek, "Look, it's Mr. Palmer!"

The old neighborhoods I once roamed felt aged and weathered— eerie almost, as most young Washington families have pushed farther into the city toward Capitol Hill, or farther out into the suburbs of Virginia and Maryland for larger properties. The wealthy home owners of Spring Valley and Wesley Heights are now older, getting ready to retire if they are lucky. Their children grown and thriving somewhere. Maybe. And I wondered about Listrani's, our family's favorite neighborhood Italian place on MacArthur Boulevard, where we'd go every Sunday night for dinner. I had gone back there, and a sign was posted in the window:

Dearest Listrani's Customers,
It is with a sad note we inform you that Listrani's is
permanently closed. On behalf of the staff, we thank each
and every one of you for all of the years you have kept us
in business.
With love, Listrani's Staff.

I wondered if it took a hard hit when the economy fell, or if it was just the natural course in the evolution of time where nothing lasts forever. When I went back there, I was hoping for the angst-ridden feeling of rebellion I'd carried throughout my childhood, eager to move out west, to become a star! To stick my finger up at that town, and leave it all behind. Eager to point the finger at its classism, blame it for the disappearing middle class, and the reality that our country is broken. Divided.

And to think when I lost everything, all I wanted was to get it back. I went searching for it, yet I was rejecting it all at the same time—the definition of insanity. But what I came to realize going back there was that the narrative I'd told myself was only half true. We are all human. No *cave dweller* was out to get me. It was just the shame I had been carrying for far too long, wanting to blame it all on someone else. We're all

just looking out for ourselves, really. It wasn't personal. I might not ever
understand it fully. It's a complicated world. Maybe I'm only supposed
to understand my own mistakes, my own wreckage, to be accountable
for that. To be honest.

I had gone back to our old house. I got a rental car and drove
straight there. I crossed Chain Bridge over the Potomac River and into
Virginia. Passing the mansion belonging to Prince Bandar bin Sultan
of Saudi Arabia, remembering having read a year earlier that the Saudi
compound nearby was being investigated for human trafficking. I
shook my head. *Things are not what they seem.* I continued on down Dolly
Madison Boulevard, where two hundred years ago the First Lady fled
the burning of the White House at the hands of British troops during
the War of 1812. I passed the CIA, just ten minutes outside of DC, on
my right. And I passed what was left of abandoned farmhouses and the
old nineteenth-century church house around the corner from the Kennedys' Hickory Hill estate. What I noticed instead was the bulldozing
of ancient trees and how the humble beginnings of America were being
replaced with enormous megamansions. Ethel Kennedy sold her property a few years back for around $10 million—to a tech entrepreneur.
I drove by. He'd gutted the house and made it bigger. Because the size
it was before, once home to eleven of America's most famous children,
was now not big enough for four.

When I was a little girl, and our house was under construction in the
late eighties, we were one of the first families to build in that old neighborhood. At the time, it felt like the beginning of something extraordinary, a big tale of an American Dream. And that's why it hurt to realize
there is no such thing. Dreams are peaceful. Dreams contain serenity,
not ambition, not greed. Dreams make you feel like you're right where
you're supposed to be: in the middle, close to the pulse of real things
where humility lives. So I don't know what we're striving for anymore
as our so-called dreams have been razed to the ground by money.

Nancy had shared a letter with me that my father had written to
her after he was placed in solitary confinement for ten days. He wrote:

"Nancy . . . I'm sorry if my letter has appeared to be a bit grim, but it's worse than I've presented. I'm the eternal optimist, but the ugliness demonstrated sometimes by the human condition is distressing. America has lost her way, and there's no leadership on the horizon to straighten out these entrenched problems. But, Washington in the springtime is one of the most beautiful places on earth, and let's be hopeful for the November elections. As Bob Dylan said, "You don't need a weatherman to know which way the wind blows.""

My father was right. America has lost her way. If only he could see his part. Why was it so easy to point the finger? Why has it been so hard to look at ourselves?

I pulled up to the house and hopped out of the car. There was a new driveway built in front, covering half of our old front lawn, and fancy posts placed out front with streetlights. New flowers and bushes had been planted. I walked up to the front door and peered in the window. Gold furniture and frilly curtains covered the living room. No one seemed to be home. I sat down in the grass next to the driveway. An airplane was passing overhead. Descending down the Potomac River to Reagan National Airport. I couldn't make out any faces or see what airline it was. But I looked up, shielding my eyes from the sun's glare with my hand, and watched it fly by. And I missed Dad. I missed Mom. I missed Mara, and I missed Chloe. I missed my family. The way we were, or the way we could have been. Ten years had gone by. And for what? For love, my father would say. He did it for love. I said good-bye to my house; it didn't belong to me anymore. It never did to begin with.

That night, I had a strange dream. I dreamt that we had come back. My father was outside watering the boxwood bushes with a green hose. Chloe swung on the yellow swing set, while Mara played in the swimming pool. My mother was playing the piano in the loggia, and I could see them all. I could see my mother swaying back and forth to the music through the lace curtains, and I started running with Coco, our black Labrador. I was eleven years old. And I ran chasing her down the street into the cul-de-sac, and everything was the way I remembered it before the turn of the twenty-first century. And we were happy, the stakes were high, and there was so much to lose. I kept running after Coco down through the woods toward the edge of the creek. And when I turned around to look back, I tried to find my father but he was gone. I turned around, and everything was gone—just endless land like an empty field. And there was a woman walking toward me in the flat light. It was Lois, the neighborhood gossip, with her ferret perched on her shoulder. I stood in front of her, suspended forward to the present time, as her words pierced through me: "I'm so glad, honey. You're back."

I woke up the next morning wanting to go for a run, to shake off the trip. I ran out the front door and jogged left instead of right, up the hill instead of down. I'm not sure why I did that, because the previous mornings, I had never done this. I felt a rush of anger soar through me when I thought about all that I had learned: all of my faults, how terrified I am of real love, and if it would ever be possible—the willingness to be vulnerable because I've been so afraid of getting hurt again. And I thought about the dream and what it meant, and I knew that everything being gone meant that I was letting go.

I kept running, and when I got to the top of the street, I ran to the left and saw steps leading to a stone altar of some kind next to an abandoned building at the top of a hill with what looked like graffiti tags all over. The steps seemed like a good idea. I paced myself up to the very top and caught my breath. It was early and quiet. I heard a rustling noise and walked over to a shattered window. Shutters still hung inside the empty room. They blew against each other from the wind. I tried to look inside, but the glass was jagged, and it was hard to see through. I continued walking around the balcony. The building resembled the Kennedy Center, the same pillared square. When I turned the corner, I saw that someone had scrawled "Fuck Society!" in glittering black letters across the side facing the United States Capitol. What was this building?

Around the next corner, through tinted glass, I saw peeled wallpaper, and abandoned books and documents in glass cases. It looked like an old library—a law library, maybe, because a sticker placed on the other side of the glass panel said "No Trespassing." I tried to open the door, but it was locked. I kicked the wall, just because; because why would someone leave books like that to rot away. I kept running toward another building. A redbrick building that looked like a castle. *What is this place?* Finally, I looked up, and there was a giant white flag whipping in the wind: Howard University School of Law.

You have to be kidding me, I thought. *There is no way that I ran to the front lawn of Dad's law school. The universe is fucking with me.* I bent over laughing. I laughed so hard that I started to cry. I had never been there before. It occurred to me that my father had never taken me there. I kept running through the courtyard and around the building as class was being let out. I didn't want anyone to see me crying so I ran through the parking lot toward the edge of the cliff where the woods began.

Black and blue clouds floating above and toward me. Hurricane Arthur was rolling his way up the coast, but I didn't care. I ran along the grassy path next to towering oak trees, listening to the quiet rumbling of thunder in the distance. I slowed down to wipe my tears, and that's when I saw them: a buck and his fawn. How odd. Weren't fawns born in the spring? It was the middle of summer. The buck and his fawn walked toward me in the grass. I was waiting for them to leap back into the woods, but they didn't. *They didn't.* They stopped five feet from me, and that's when I locked eyes with the buck. His eyes were dark and steady, both of us frozen. He turned his head toward the woods and suddenly went galloping into the trees without a second thought. But the little fawn with her white spots and golden tale didn't follow right away. She stood there, staring at me. I looked at her fragile eyes, and I lost it. It was like she wanted to make sure I was okay. And I *was* okay, more than okay despite my uncontrollable sobbing—snot everywhere.

(It wasn't cute.) Then all of a sudden thunder roared, and the fawn took one last look at me and then hopped off into the woods to find her papa. This story was so much greater than me; so much greater than anything I could have ever anticipated. And I was powerless over it.

I sat down at the top of the grassy hill. I let the rain fall down and let the wind blow through me. I thought about the stories my father had told me as a young girl: about the Greek tragedies, about Zeus and Athena. I knew this was the end. It was so dramatic; it had to be this way. I could feel the wounds inside me were healing. I don't know what my father and I might have been to each other in a past life or if we'll meet each other in a future one. If this was supposed to be my lesson— our Greek tragedy—then so be it. Let the thunder roar and lightning strike! I wasn't afraid of him anymore. I felt so fucking free as I sat on top of that hill where his story began and where mine ended.

It was perfect.

-ACKNOWLEDGMENTS-

I would like to thank the army of women in my life who protected me and kept me steady as I trudged through deep waters. My deepest gratitude goes to Melissa Randall, whose guidance steered me through grief, where on the other side I found truth, whose ears and voice of support led me to reclaim my life. It would have been impossible without my mentor, Jill Schary Robinson, and her passion for writing, her wisdom and generosity, and for reminding me that writing is like magic. To Amalia Molina at the Center for Restorative Justice Works, for her brave and inspiring advocacy work for the children and families of the incarcerated, and for being a voice for the voiceless. To Jan Eliasberg, who has taught me a great deal about what it means to be a fearless, self-supporting woman, and who has held my hand every step of this journey. To Leslye Headland, for keeping me on track, and who suffered many of my phone calls filled with anger and tears, yet never failed to make me laugh. To the Palmer girls, Nancy, Molly, Carter, and Hope, for their lifetime of love and unwavering support; also for their kindness and acknowledgment during the most difficult years and for giving me a safe place to write, where I unexpectedly wrote the ending of my story. Thank you.

I am incredibly grateful to everyone at Gallery Books, beginning with my amazing editor, Alison Callahan, who, from our very first phone call, understood exactly how I wanted to tell my story. I am in awe of her work, always managing to pull more truth from me, propelling me to dig deeper and "go there," and for her support on the other side. Thank you to Louise Burke, Jennifer Bergstrom, Nina Cordes, Philip Bashe, Meagan Brown, Elisa Rivlin, Alexandre Su, and Susan Rella for their dedication and hard work.

I am forever indebted to Todd Rubenstein, who believed I could write this story on my own, and for his love and dedication to Inside-OUT Writers. A huge thank-you to the InsideOUT Writers's family: teachers and staff. To the alumni, who know more about resilience and courage than I ever will. And a special shout-out to my Girls D Unit at Central Juvenile Hall, for their extraordinary voices that keep me inspired and humble every week. A big thank-you to Scott Budnick, for introducing me to InsideOUT Writers and for his inspiring work at the Anti-Recidivism Coalition.

I would like to thank the wonderful team at Foundry Literary + Media: my agent, Peter McGuigan, who believed in *After Perfect* in its earliest stages four years ago when it was just a messy scrapbook of stories, and who showed up for me when I was finally ready to write it. Many thanks to Matt Wise and Kirsten Neuhaus. And a special thank-you to Aaron Karo, for guiding me through the proposal process, and Dan Farah, for stepping in when chaos ensued.

Thank you to Jill Schary Robinson's Wimpole Street Writers—my writer's group—for their camaraderie and fellowship, and whose stories and words inspire me to be a better writer. I owe a special thank-you to Hannah Sward, Tiffany Bushnell, Craig Robinson, and George Jordan.

There's nothing like having four brothers looking out for you with unconditional love and brutal honesty. David Petruzzi, Robert Krauss, Noah Gonzalez, and Max Crumm, words cannot express my love and thanks.

Thank you to Milana Rabkin, who was the first to say, "You should write a book." An enormous thank-you to Alice Fox, neighbor and friend, who spent hours listening to pages and making me fresh pots of coffee. France Demoulin, Samantha Colicchio, Claire Woolner, Blaire Borkowski, Kara Froula, and Melanie Thomas, for listening. Cole Williams, for keeping me fit and mindful. The Seidlitz family, Auntie Anne, Uncle Pete, Ashley and Elizabeth, and the McDowell family, Uncle Larry, Alex, and Brianne, for being there.

A very special thank-you to Sarah Fenske at *LA Weekly* for publishing my article "An Open Letter to the Makers of *The Wolf of Wall Street* and the Wolf Himself," and Hillel Aron, for passing it along. When my article went viral I received thousands of emails of love and support from across the globe. I read every single one. I'd like to thank all of those who wrote to me, and whose stories and words of kindness became my engine on the days I felt like giving up.

I'd like to thank my high school history teacher, Alex Haight, for being the first person to teach me how to construct an argument and write an essay.

To my little Havanese, Zelda Fitzgerald, who slept underneath my desk while I wrote most of these pages, and who always knew when I needed a good walk.

Lastly, I would like to thank my mom and my sisters, who are survivors of their own individual journeys. The pain on these pages belongs not only to me but also to them. I thank them for their bravery in encouraging me to "get it out, Christina, get it out," so that what was left inside of me could find its place to live. Thank you.

BOOK "MARKS"

If you wish to keep a record that you have read this book, you may use the spaces below to mark a private code. Please do not mark the book in any other way
